a century of
pop

A Century

# of Pop

Hugh Gregory

Bounty Books

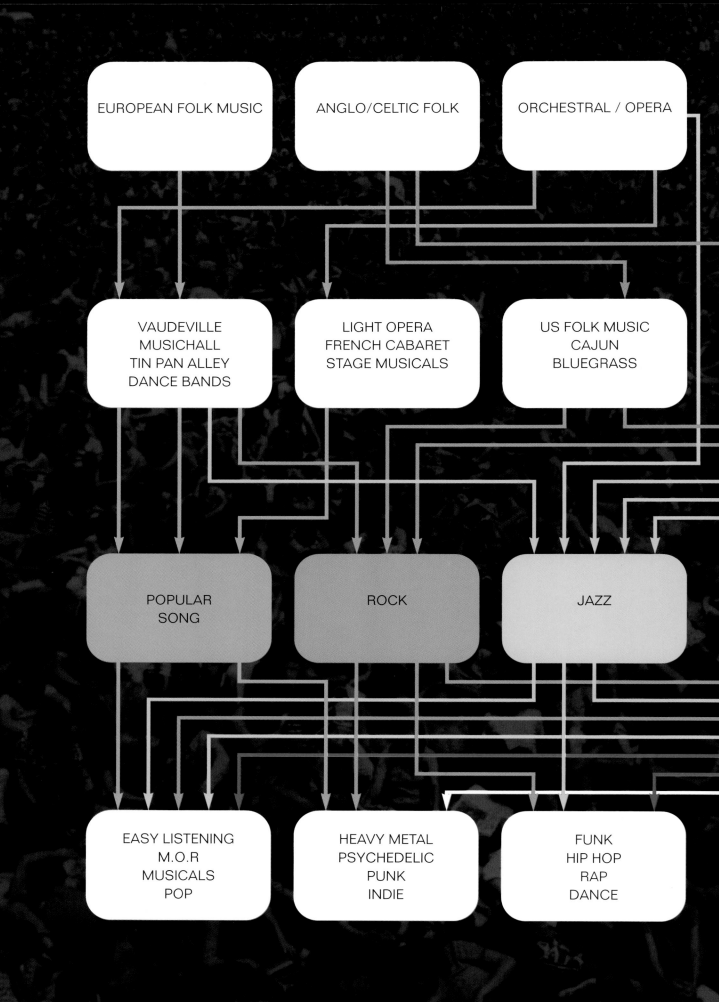

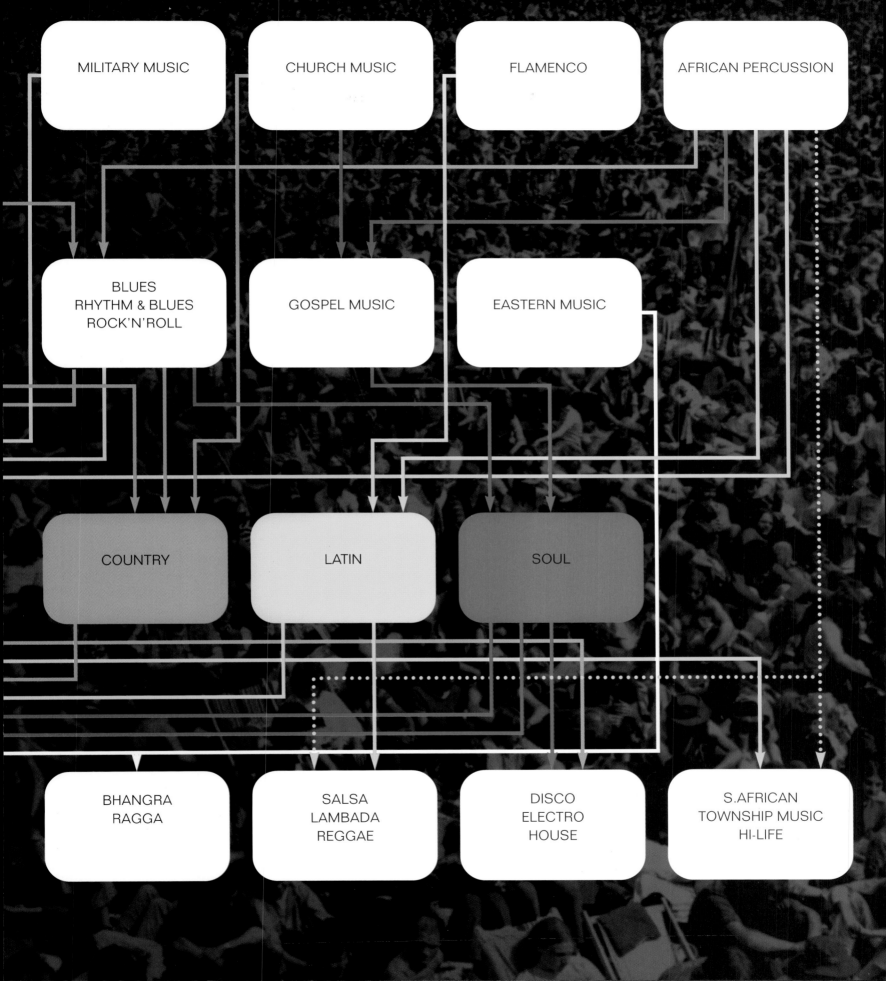

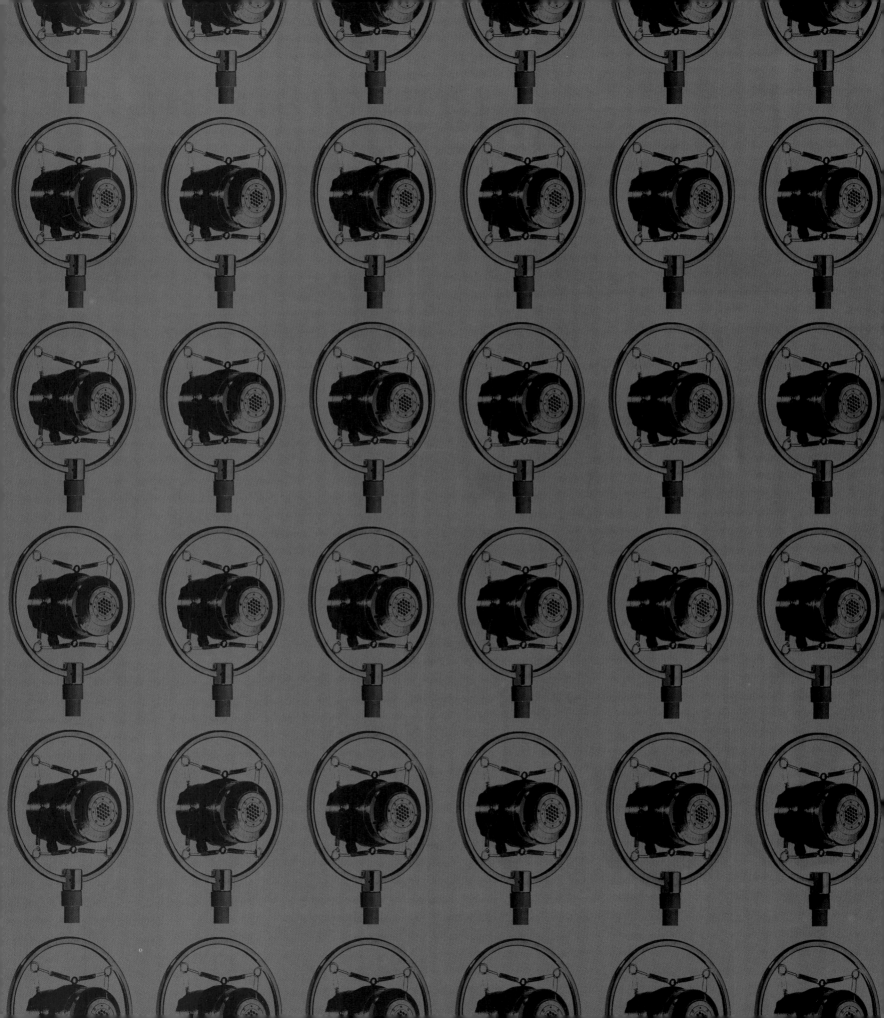

INTRODUCTION

There have been various definitions of pop music proffered over the years – immediate, disposable, of its time and so on – but the best definition seems to be that from whence the phrase came – quite simply, pop music is popular music.

With this in mind, any account of pop has to go back to when that mass popularity first occurred. Not with the advent of rock'n'roll, or the great song writers of the 30s. The defining moment for pop came right at the end of the last century with the invention of the gramophone or phonograph. Until then, in those pre-radio days, any musical experience was live, one-to-one between the performer and audience, albeit the former was often as musically amateur as the latter. The spread of the upright piano in domestic homes across Europe and America is evidence of that. Only when the proliferation of the gramophone occurred could the same piece of music be heard, theoretically at least, by millions of people at the same time.

The era of the hit tune had arrived.

Using the gramophone revolution as a chronological benchmark, this book looks at the relationships between influences and musical styles that have made up the mosaic of 20th century populist music. In doing so, though chronological markers take us from decade to decade, many of the styles, genres and individual artists described, defy such time based pigeon-holing, their influence and careers often spanning many decades.

Likewise, the choice of subjects can in no way be truly objective. Certainly the choice of individuals who were catalysts in one way or another is not definitive (why Patsy Cline and not Billie Holiday for instance?) but takes a sampling, impressionistic look at a culture which is itself based on selection from its own past and a less-than-empirical view of its reason for being.

Similarly the CD suggestions are just that – samples of an artist or genre which give an example of the music, not necessarily 'greatest hits' or even universally acclaimed 'finest works'. (The publishers would stress that the information regarding CD labels and availability is as accurate as possible at the time of going to press).

Pop music has provided something unique that simply could not have occured previously, a genuine soundtrack that has been common to all our lives.

And it has been reciprocal. Like the folk songs of troubadours in centuries gone by, passed on by word of mouth generation to generation, popular music has often reflected the real moods and circumstances of society itself – be it in patriotic songs in time of war, the American ballads of the Great Depression years, the protest pop during the Vietnam War or merely in lyrics that illuminate the social fabric of the time – in a far more direct way than 'art' music could ever hope to. However flawed, the two-way relationship between the people's music and the people themselves is a real one.

Popular music has always been driven by the mass technology, mass communication and the commercial dynamic of 20th century Western culture. At its best and at its worst, its very variety reflects the influences and complexities of that culture.

above: An early colour photo
of a musical group of Japanese
geishas in 1875; they would
entertain clients with self-
accompanied singing.

VOICE

A supreme vehicle of musical expression, the human voice was the first medium
through which music was created. While examples of this musical expression
undoubtedly took the form of chants, probably and more usually in tribute to one
deity or another, the Jewish faith offers a glimpse of that expression in its
undiluted form. For despite the fact that, say, the Zulus in South Africa have
retained ancient tribal customs, the influence of Christianity has had an affect. The
Jewish faith, by virtue of the persecution meted out to it over the centuries, has
been compelled to maintain an isolationist stance on matters of doctrine and ritual.
Furthermore, adherence to doctrine necessitated the preservation, in detail, of
customs and ritual. However, while examples of Jewish folk songs abound, the
liturgy of the Jewish faith has not been as bounteous as a catalyst for musical
expression as Christianity. Its influence has been more subliminal, providing
guidance on breath control and articulation. That the plainsong of the early
Christian church were adaptations of Jewish chants seems certain, although
the Celtic influence of 'sean nos' may have contributed as well.

While the classical tradition, through opera and European church music, has
exerted an influence upon vocal styles, the strongest impact has emanated from
Afro-Caribbean sources. Although these, too, have their non-secular roots, the
Afro-Caribbean influence permeates most strata of contemporary popular music:
jazz, Soul, R&B, gospel, blues, reggae, rock'n'roll and rock. Producer Sam Phillips
asserted that if he could find a white man that could sound like a black man, he
would make a fortune. He did and the person he found was Elvis Presley. Ever
since then, the vocal mannerisms of rock'n'roll have been overtly derivative of
Afro-Caribbean styles.

ROOTS

top right: Muslims in vocal prayer, in a photograph from 1885 taken in Egypt.

far left: The Muslim five-times-a-day 'calling to prayer' utilizes the human voice in a musical and practical fashion.

below: Gypsy musicans singing in the Camargue, France.

FOLK MUSIC

bottom: A cantor leads the singing in a Jewish Sabbath celebration in a synagogue in Krakow, Poland.

below: A 16th Century illustration of a travelling violin player from Poland.

right: The English folk song and dance collector Cecil Sharp (1859-1924).

WHILE THESE DAYS THE FOLK MUSIC OF EASTERN EUROPE IS A WIDELY PRIZED SOURCE OF ORIGIN FOR MANY EXTANT FORMS, for many years it ran the risk of sinking into obsolescence. That it avoided this fate was due in part to the gradual flow of immigrants towards the United States from the end of the 19th century and the nomadic life-style of the Gypsy. More significantly, though, it was composers such as Antonin Dvorak in Czechoslovakia and Bela Bartok and Zoltan Kodaly in Hungary, whose interest in the traditions of their homelands ensured that indigent styles were not allowed to die out. Dvorak delved deeply, publishing his first set of Slavonic Dances for piano duet in 1878; this was later orchestrated. This was followed by Slavonic Rhapsodies (1878), Symphony No. 6 (1880), more Slavonic Dances (1886) and Dumky Piano Trio (1891), all of which drew substantially from Czech folk idioms; the polka has proved the most durable, having established itself everywhere from ballrooms in Australia to bars in New Mexico. And interestingly, most of these forms shared the flattened 3rds and 7ths of the blues scale.

WHILE BELA BARTOK AND ZOLTAN KODALY'S OUTPUT FAILED TO MATCH THE OVERT POPULISM THAT DVORAK'S WORKS INSPIRED, the scholarship of their endeavours enabled styles to be preserved. In the long-term, this has enabled groups such as I Musicas and vocalist Marta Sebestyen to recreate arrangements of folk songs from the Carpathians in original form. The lack of documentation giving provenance for many styles has meant few Eastern European folk styles remain untainted, as it were, by the inexorable march of time and the greedy grasping fingers of commercialism. Be that as it may, some of the more arcane forms have cropped up in isolated pockets of the Appalachians. Furthermore, since the disintegration of the Soviet Union and the attendant collapse of Communism in Eastern Europe, old customs and traditions have gradually been revived.

ALTHOUGH IT HAS ONLY BEEN IN THE LAST TWO DECADES OR SO THAT THE CELTIC INFLUENCE HAS BEEN QUITE SO EMPHATIC AND OVERT, it has had more effect upon the development of the British folk song than any other single element. The reasons for this are manifold, but the principal factor is that the myths and legends of the Celts have been assimilated into the lives and experience of all Gaelic speakers without any let or hindrance. It is a part of the Gaelic heritage, which has evolved organically, absorbing the constraining influence of the Roman Church, as well as the imperialist repression of the English. While certain aspects of Celtic folklore espoused a non-doctrinal paganism, which were brutally suppressed when exposed, the continuity implicit in an organic evolutionary process ensured the survival of archaic instruments and forms such as 'sean nõs': an unaccompanied way of singing in literally the 'old style'.

By the end of World War II, many traditions in the British Isles – now radically depopulated through war – were in danger of dying out as those remaining moved from rural areas into cities. And it wasn't until the early 1950s that collectors such as Alan Lomax undertook a series of visits to the British Isles, recording in Ireland, Scotland, the Orkneys and the Shetland Isles. Although his trips didn't arrest the migration, they stimulated interest and record labels like Topic invested resources in documenting the traditions of the Anglo-Celtic folk song. Since the launch of the CD in the 1980s, that process of renewal has continued apace with staggering reissue programmes now in place that will ensure survival of ancient and archaic forms.

AS DISTINCT FROM FRETTED STRINGED INSTRUMENTS such as the guitar, banjo, mandolin and lute, the violin, viola, cello and double bass have underpinned the modern orchestra since the early part of the 18th century. That a string section is able to run the gamut of emotions from exuberance to pathos with negligible change in physical exertion suggests a profound versatility. Dating back to the 16th century when it was first manufactured in Italy, thereby supplanting the viol, the violin evolved from the fiddle, which, in turn, could trace its ancestry back through the rebec to the square-bodied morinchur from Mongolia and the sarangi from India.

From the moment it was introduced, composers of varying ability all took up their quills and started to reel off ream after ream of concerti for violin. Such was its impact and popularity that the violin was briefly one of the most popular instruments for the young to learn (after the piano). This popularity led to a disproportionately high ratio of precocious gifted soloists: Kreisler made his public debut at fourteen and Yehudi Menuhin made his debut at the age of eight.

The other factor in its enduring popularity lay in the abundance of folk songs that were passed down as fiddle tunes. For, especially, immigrants, the violin or fiddle was cherished as its portability enabled them to take it wherever they went, rekindling memories of their homelands with the tunes they brought with them. So it was, for example, that in the homesteads of the Appalachians, the folk songs of Eastern Europe or Ireland or Scotland entered American lore, creating genres such as Bluegrass. Indeed, its versatility made it popular with jazz musicians such as Stephane Grappelli and Joe Venuti, while rock musicians like Eddie Jobson and Jerry Goodman both used an amplified violin.

Strings sections were never confined to classical music – they were the prerequisite of pop records through the 30s and 40s, and re-emerged when groups like The Beatles memorably employed them and, in Nashville, Country producers such as Billy Sherrill used arrangements with what was quaintly known as the Nashville Strings to make his productions more appealing to a wider audience. Indeed, nowadays, strings sections seem to be used to touch upon the MOR nerve in all of us.

STRINGS

left: Medieval musicians playing at the court of the monarch.

left: 16th Century Japanese musicians in a print by the artist Okamura Masonobu.

PIPES

THE BASIC PRINCIPLE OF THE PIPE HAS REMAIN UNCHANGED SINCE ANCIENT TIMES. Indeed, in Upper Egypt, the rim-blown flute has been traced back to the epoch before the historic dynasties; these rim-blown flutes are still in use as, for example, the Arab nay and the Balkan kaval. Thereafter it became more widely known as the Shepherd's pipe, as it became popular in rural communities. From these humble origins, the woodwind sections of the orchestra gradually evolved. The pipe or whistle, though, has remained pivotal to the folk tradition. And it was in that context that its usage has always been most apparent: Anthony Baines in Musical Instruments Through The Ages quotes Julius Pollux from his work, Onomasticon, which was published in the 2nd century AD in Athens, saying that there were 'various peoples from Scythian tribes to the Celts and the islanders of the Ocean – presumably Britons – described as panpipers'.

The panpipes seem to have endured in their original form longer than most, as the Indians of the Andes in South America and the master tribesmen of Joujouka in Morocco still play these primitive instruments: Mozart used them for Papageno's signature tune in the opera, The Magic Flute. However, within the Celtic tradition, the pipe – whether they be bagpipes or Uileean pipes – has been responsible for imparting the flavour that has ensured survival of traditional forms. The bagpipes, especially, have become a key symbol in the iconography of the Scottish national identity, featuring prominently in military bands. In Ireland, the Uilleean pipes, as used by The Chieftains, among others, have become as much of a focus in the dissemination of Irish traditional music as the fiddle or the bodhran. If the growth of awareness in Celtic music has grown, so too has its English counterpart, with medievalists recreating the folk songs of the Middle Ages with pipe and tabor. Despite the primitiveness of the pipe, its popularity remains unchallenged.

right: Franz Schubert (1797-1828), in a short life the writer of symphonies, chamber music and over 600 songs.

below: With ballets like Swan Lake and The Nutcracker, certainly one of the most popular of orchestral composers, the Russian Pyotr Tchaikovsky (1840-1893).

EUROPEAN ORCHESTRAL

WHILE THE TERM ORCHESTRA WAS DERIVED FROM THE GREEK, MEANING THE AREA AT THE FRONT OF THE THEATRE WHERE THE CHORUS SANG OR DANCED, by the 18th century it had come to denote the instrumentalists who provided the accompaniment. However, during the 17th century, orchestras comprised strings sections supplemented by various wind instruments which were used for solos; harpsichords, organs or harps provided harmonic support. In the early part of the 18th century, the four-part string orchestra came into being. With the wind section comprising flutes, oboes, bassoons and horns, trumpets were later added, as was percussion or tympani.

Although orchestras – especially chamber orchestras, which were smaller – were regular fixtures in the royal courts, opera houses were the only institutions with a need for a large orchestra. It was with the symphonic form, which evolved through its inclusion as the overture (sinfonia) – often in three movements – to an opera, that the orchestra found its most persuasive medium. While J.C. Bach was an early exponent, Josef Haydn refined the form with 104 separate works to his credit. But it was the emotional depth and latent power of the symphonic works of Beethoven – who was influenced the most profoundly by Mozart – that defined the classical tradition.

By the 20th century, classical music had become a blanket appellation for all serious music, although many writers, especially those composing film scores, endeavoured to invoke the classical orchestral tradition to varying degrees of success. These included Alfred Newman, Bernard Herrmann, John Williams and the English composers William Walton and Michael Nyman.

right: One of the household
names of opera, Maria Callas
singing in a production of
Puccini's Tosca.

far right: World famous tenor
Placido Domingo during a
performance at London's Royal
Opera House in 1985.

below: A spectacular set for
Wagner's Götterämmerung at
the annual Bayreuth festival.

OPERA IS ONE OF ITALY'S GREATEST CONTRIBUTIONS TO WORLD CULTURE. It had its greatest flowering in the mid-19th century with the work of Rossini, Donizetti, Bellini, Verdi and Puccini.

Italy's operatic tradition began in Naples in the 18th century, and the early Neapolitan operas are still staged today. They had complex plots, usually with six characters and, often, with castrati playing the female parts. In its day, the Neapolitan style was performed everywhere across Europe.

Neapolitan opera was challenged for being artificial and decadent, and public taste turned more to comic opera, particularly in the French style. Gioacchino Rossini combined the two styles, beginning his career at La Scala and La Fenice. He moved on to Bologna and Naples, and also worked in Vienna and Paris. His best known works are The Barber Of Seville (1816), Cinderella (1817) and William Tell (1829). Gaetano Donizetti developed the operatic form with works such as Lucia di Lammermoor (1835). After early success in Paris, he returned to Italy to write operas for La Scala, where he dedicated operas to the Empress Maria Anna and became official composer to the Emperor Ferdinand I of Austria.

Vincenzo Bellini produced his first works while at the Naples Conservatory. He was commissioned to write Bianca e Fernado for the Naples opera. This led to commissions at La Scala.

THE GREATEST OF ALL THE ITALIAN OPERATIC COMPOSERS was Giuseppe Verdi (1813-1901). Although worldl acclaim lured him away, particularly to Paris, he always returned to Milan and Naples to stage his most famous works: La Traviatta, Macbeth, Rigoletto, Aida and Otello. Verdi's use of themes from Shakespeare culminated with Falstaff in 1893.

Giacomo Puccini brought Italian opera into the 20th century. After seeing a performance of Aida in Pisa in 1876, he decided that his future lay in opera. He went to Milan to study at the Conservatory. He was taken up by Verdi's librettist Arrigo Boito and had an early success with Le Villi at the Teatro dal Verme in Milan in 1884. Then he was taken up by La Scala, who put him on salary. Despite a turbulent personal life, he wrote a number of enormously popular works, notably La Bohème, Tosca and Madame Butterfly.

The Italian operatic tradition impacted on modern popular music from its earliest days, and as well as influencing the ballad-style of popular songwriting, Italian tenors from Enrico Caruso to Luciano Pavarotti have continued to thrill audiences worldwide.

OPERA

left: A bass clarinet built by
Nicola Papalin in the Paris
Conservatoire around 1815.

BRASS

THE ORIGINS OF BRASS INSTRUMENTS can be traced back to the Romans, who used tubas. During the Renaissance, as well, brass instruments such as the cornet, sackbut and slide and natural trumpet were used extensively. Although there were military associations, the introduction to the orchestra of the trumpet in the early years of the 18th century encouraged composers such as Handel and J.S. Bach to compose pieces utilising the trumpet. Despite this, and the fact that Monteverdi had in 1607 used five in his opera Orfeo, the practicality of the trumpet meant few could harness its restricted range until piston valves were introduced in the early 19th century. However it was the introduction of valves to the cornet, with its flexibility and versatility, that created a brass instrument capable of extended solos. This was to have a profound effect on the development of jazz, with the likes of Buddy Bolden and King Oliver establishing an improvisational framework within early jazz. The saxophone was the other instrument to have a significant effect upon the role of brass contemporary music.

Invented by Adolphe Sax in the mid-19th century, the saxophone (soprano, alto, tenor and baritone) attained its greatest popularity in the Swing bands of the 1930s and in the orchestras of Fletcher Henderson, Count Basie and Duke Ellington through such exponents as Coleman Hawkins, Lester Young and Johnny Hodges respectively. As the big bands slimmed down, it was the honking horn that defined the Jump Blues of Louis Jordan and the R&B of the post-war era. When rock'n'roll doffed its hat, the range and flexibility of the saxophone provided showmen like Rudi Pompanelli with the perfect prop. Although brass sections crop up in most strains of pop music these days, the saxophone has proved the most durable and versatile.

ALTHOUGH MILITARY BANDS CAN BE TRACED BACK TO THE ROMANS, IT SEEMS THAT WARFARE HAS ALWAYS HAD SOME KIND OF MUSICAL ACCOMPANIMENT. Whether the dissonances of wind instruments or the ominous rumble of the drums were deployed to strike terror to the hearts of the adversaries or merely to create aural signposting, it is not recorded. By the early 19th century, the provision of valves in the cornet inspired a number of virtuosi, including J. Forestier at the Theatre Italien and J.H. Maury at the Paris Opera. This, in turn, provided a focus for the military band. While its activities may have been confined to regimental or ceremonial events, the military band seemed to dovetail into the tradition of the marching bands.

Marching bands had their origins in Africa, where they accompanied funeral processions, warding off the evil spirits and shepherding the deceased from one world to the next. For despite the militaristic connotations of the march, it has not been used exclusively for military purposes – operas such as Mozart's The Magic Flute, Beethoven's Fidelio and Verdi's Aida feature marches. Perhaps the most celebrated of all, Elgar's Pomp and Circumstance – a perennial favourite at the last night of Henry Wood's Promenade Concerts at London's Royal Albert Hall – inspires national pride with more than a hint of jingoism.

above: New Orleans marching bands parade regularly at lodge meetings, funerals and, of course, annual Mardi Gras.

above: Father of modern military music, the American bandmaster and composer John Philip Sousa (1854-1932).

right: One of a series of sheet music c1920, of regimental marches of the British Army, arranged for solo piano.

BY THE MID-1800s, BRASS BANDS WERE NOT THE EXCLUSIVE PRESERVE OF THE MILITIA, for commercial concerns had founded brass bands, especially i n the North of England, to provide musical recreation for employees: The Grimethorpe Colliery Band and The Brighouse and Rastrick Brass Band being two notable examples. In the US, the brass band was given a fillip with the growth in popularity of the composer John Philip Sousa; among Sousa's compositions were 'The Stars and Stripes Forever'. Sousa's compositions proved especially popular with marching bands, particularly in New Orleans, which, with the ascendancy of the cornet, was one of the catalysts of Dixieland Jazz.

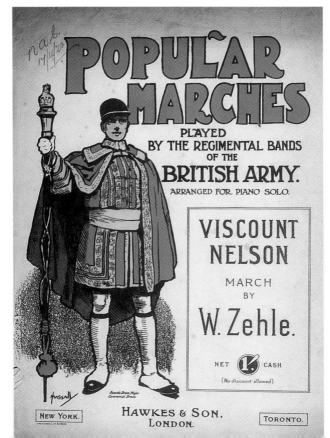

POPULAR MARCHES
PLAYED BY THE REGIMENTAL BANDS OF THE BRITISH ARMY.
ARRANGED FOR PIANO SOLO.

VISCOUNT NELSON
MARCH BY
W. Zehle.

NET CASH
(No discount allowed).

NEW YORK.   HAWKES & SON, LONDON.   TORONTO.

PIANO

left: An upright domestic
player-piano dating from 1919.

APPARENTLY, THE FIRST PIANO WAS MADE IN
FLORENCE BY BARTOLOMEO CRISTOFORI IN
THE EARLY PART OF THE 18TH CENTURY.
Named as an abbreviation of pianoforte, it comprised
strings that were struck by felt hammers, causing tones
that were both soft (piano) and loud (forte) to be
produced. This prototype was developed further by
the German organ-builder Gottfried Silbermann, who
designed the square or upright model where the strings
were parallel to the keyboard. However, in around 1770
in Vienna, Johann Andreas Stein refined the Silbermann
model, making its touch lighter and altogether more
shallow, almost matching the clavichord in its sensitivity
– Mozart, Beethoven and Haydn were all early
aficionados. The next refinement was the introduction
of the iron frame, which allowed thicker strings with
greater tension. This produced a more powerful and
sonorous tone. As its popularity expanded due to an
increasing domestic market, so firms such as Steinweg
(later Steinway), Bechstein, Blüthner, Bosendorfer and
Pleyel in France sprung up to develop its commercial
potential. This caused variants to be developed
according to usage: the concert grand and baby grand.
In 1829 the first upright model was developed by Robert
Wornum in London and it was this model that was to
become a vital item of furnishing in domestic settings.

THROUGHOUT THE 19TH CENTURY THE PIANO DOMINATED, encouraging composers such as Beethoven, Schubert, Chopin, Schumann, Brahms, Debussy, Grieg and Ravel to write concerti and sonatas exclusively for the piano. Furthermore, the piano was an ideal accompaniment for voice or small chamber ensembles, but could be used in counterpoint for orchestral pieces. While its use among the gifted and talented was natural, its presence in even the humblest of abodes brought music to a far wider audience. For the emergent middle-class, the piano was an essential item of furniture, guaranteed to confer a quasi-artistic leaning to even the dullest and least inspiring of households: music was becoming – in practical terms – available to more people than ever before. As the piano grew in popularity, so sales of sheet music – the one surefire way for composers to accrue wealth – increased accordingly.

left: An early keyboard instrument, the clavichord, in an engraving from 1661.

below: An ad for a 'piano player' or player-piano, which could be played conventionally, and also ran piano rolls that played the music automatically.

BY THE END OF THE 19TH CENTURY, not only was playing the piano a mark of social refinement, it was also the premier aid to composition: many tunesmiths and lyricists discovered their talent while taking the obligatory lessons. Although the piano flourished as great soloists, such as Daniel Barenboim, Murray Perahia, Vladimir Askenazy and Vladimir Horowitz, emerged during the 20th century, increasingly the boundaries of composition were tested by jazz musicians such as Thelonius Monk, Cecil Taylor, Keith Jarrett and Oscar Peterson; both of the premier bandleaders of the 20th century, Duke Ellington and Count Basie, chose to lead their orchestras from the piano. If the piano's influence on classical music waned during the 20th century, its impact upon popular music was profound, with Scott Joplin's piano rags and the emergent 'jass' style, exemplified by Jelly Roll Morton, heralding a popularity in black music that was to change attitudes towards rhythm, melody and harmony.

far left: Jelly Roll Morton pioneered piano-led jazz with a compositional talent that extended the music far wider than the usual 12-bar blues.

left: Pianist and composer Scott Joplin whose turn-of-the-century rags were the first hint of jazz style in popular music.

WHILE THE PIANO REMAINS ESSENTIALLY UNCHANGED, technology has played a part with the electric piano and electronic keyboard entering the armoury of gadgets currently at the disposal of most pop groups and rock bands. However, as an acoustic instrument, its power to encompass most moods of musical expression is unrivalled, capable of imbuing even the most banal sentiments with a pathos that would be unattainable in any other medium.

TIME FOR A SWEEPING STATEMENT: NO INSTRUMENT HAS EXERTED SUCH AN INFLUENCE ON THE DEVELOPMENT OF CONTEMPORARY MUSIC AS THE GUITAR. For even before it was amplified in the 1930s, the acoustic guitar had become the principal means of accompaniment for bluesmen and folk singers alike. Now at first that may appear to restrict the scope of its influence, but the fact is that the guitar was the favoured instrument of the immigrant and America was the land of the immigrant: few were going to toil across the Atlantic weighted down with pianos. In a nutshell, the guitar's portability has been at the root of its appeal as well its dual possibilities as a solo instrument or in ensembles.

GUITAR

THAT APPEAL WAS FIRST MANIFEST IN SPAIN DURING THE 15TH CENTURY, when as the vihuela (played with the bow) it was adapted as the de mano vihuela. In England, the gittern – another early form of guitar – along with the lute held sway until the 16th century when the five-stringed Spanish guitar started to gain in popularity in Italy, France and then England. Its emergent popularity was due in part to the simplicity of the notation of the chords, which could be represented by numbers or letters. This enabled the chords to be strummed, and it became the chosen instrument of the amateur, intent only upon providing a slight diversion. Those with grander musical aspirations turned to the violin or keyboard instruments. In France, during the reign of Louis XIV, it enjoyed its greatest popularity, as it was frequently used by the Italian comedians who were fixtures in the French theatre. That was followed by a period of decline in Europe when the mandoline from Italy achieved prominence, with Vivaldi composing a concerto for two mandolines and Beethoven writing several pieces for mandoline and piano.

below: Mandolins, lutes and such, precursors to the guitar, were often portrayed in popular mythology as the instruments of the gods.

HOWEVER, IN SPAIN THE GUITAR REMAINED THE 'NATIONAL' INSTRUMENT and, with the addition of a sixth string, the guitar was to undergo no further extensive modifications until amplification in the 1930s. It is interesting to note that while there was no great history of guitar-playing in Germany, as the lute continued to be popular, there were craftsmen in southern Germany building guitars and, in 1788, one such builder claimed to have built the first guitar with six strings. Tuned to E, A, D, G, B and E, with a range of three octaves and a fifth from E below middle C, this model was the one that came into common usage. In the early 19th century, the carol 'Silent Night' became the first composition to be written for performance in church with a guitar accompaniment; theoretically this departure should have encouraged more composers to write for the guitar. Despite this, its portability made it popular among troubadours and other peripatetics and this association with folksong continues to this day.

THE GUITAR'S NEXT BIG STEP FORWARD CAME IN THE 1930s, WHEN IT WAS ELECTRIFIED. Quickly it caught with blues singers and jazz musicians. Especially, within the context of a band, the guitar's soloing possibilities were greatly expanded, as it could now be heard above the honking horn sections. After World War II, a number of manufacturers, including Leo Fender, developed the solid body electric guitar. Marques such as Fender Stratocaster and Telecaster dramatically altered the way in which popular music would be performed: rock'n'roll. While the acoustic guitar remains popular with classical composers – many have written pieces specifically for Julian Bream – it is an essential tool in the iconography of folk music. And although some may hate to concede the point, the guitar made rock'n'roll.

above: A two-string instrument which adheres to the same principles as the guitar, from Northern Nigeria.

right: The modern electric guitar exemplified in a custom-built Les Paul model, made in ebony with nickel-plated 'hardware' machine parts.

PERCUSSION

above: Modern cymbals from the world famous American manufacturer Zildjan and Co.

left: A 16th Century engraving of a German military drummer on horseback.

THE NEW YORK TIMES ONCE SAID, and I quote: 'To call Max Roach a jazz drummer is like calling Shakespeare a strolling player.' That statement speaks volumes for the importance in contemporary music of the drummer/percussionist. When the rock era was at its peak in the late 1960s, there were so many shoddy drummers around that jokes about the competence of drummers abounded. Nowadays, technology has lent a helping hand with the introduction of the drum machine. This has meant that it is no longer necessary to use a sub-standard skin-basher if a machine can do the job more effectively. Consequently, one is less likely to be compelled to endure a lengthy, boring drum solo at a live concert unless the drummer actually can find his way around the kit with some degree of accomplishment. Similarly the the influence of Afro-Cuban rhythms on contemporary styles has elevated the role of percussion from that of rhythmic time keeper, in tandem with the bass, to that of a main contributor to the overall dynamics of any given unit.

While drums and percussion have always been on the cutting edge of indigent styles, they have been taken for granted. It was only with the evolution of Modern Jazz that the soloing possibilities of the drummer were properly recognised, causing stylists of the calibre of Gene Krupa and Buddy Rich to emerge. Although Krupa and Rich were fine time-keepers, their flamboyance as individuals inclined their solos towards the bombastic. However they did open the door for other great stylists such as Roach, Elvin Jones and Art Blakey, who understood that flamboyance was not synonymous with inventiveness. Indeed it is the influence of the great jazz drummers that informed session drummers such as Al Jackson of Booker T & The MGs, Earl Palmer and Roger Hawkins.

Furthermore, the profile of the percussionist has been elevated still further by the emergence of Evelyn Glennie, whose role as educator in the dynamics of rhythm transcends all contemporary styles.

THERE ARE RELIEFS DEPICTING ANCIENT ASSYRIANS STRIKING THEIR THROATS AS IF TO OBTAIN A SOUND. While the vocal chords are being used, there is no attempt to create speech or to sing a song: the purpose is solely instrumental. In most parts of Africa today, ululating is still practised. This serves to illustrate the extent to which the practice of rapping an object with the hand or banging two objects together to create a rhythmic effect has underpinned most notions of what is widely perceived as music. That most of these percussive effects were derived as part of tribal ritual predicates the assumption that the creation of music was a deeply spiritual experience designed to assist in worship. While missionaries from Europe brought Christianity to Africa and tribal customs and ritual were partly supplanted as tribes were converted, ancient beliefs continued to inform the way in which converts practised their new-found religion.

As the slave trade prospered, so African rhythms began to impinge upon indigenous styles, creating hybrids along the way. In New Orleans, for example, the brass and drums of the marching bands was an extension of the African tradition of honouring the deceased. In South America, the collision between Hispanic and African influences precipitated the highly rhythmic and percussive Latin American hybrids, with styles such as soca and salsa. While Afro-Cuban stars such as Machito and Tito Puente incorporated elements of jazz, becoming the toasts of New York in the process, it was the efforts of Nigerian Fela Ransome-Kuti, South African Hugh Masakela and Manu Dibango from the Cameroons, who did most to stimulate international interest in the traditions of African music. Consequently artists such as Malian Salif Keita and Senegalese Youssou N'Dour are now accorded international acclaim.

right: A drummer in the West African republic of Senegal, during the independence celebrations in 1958.

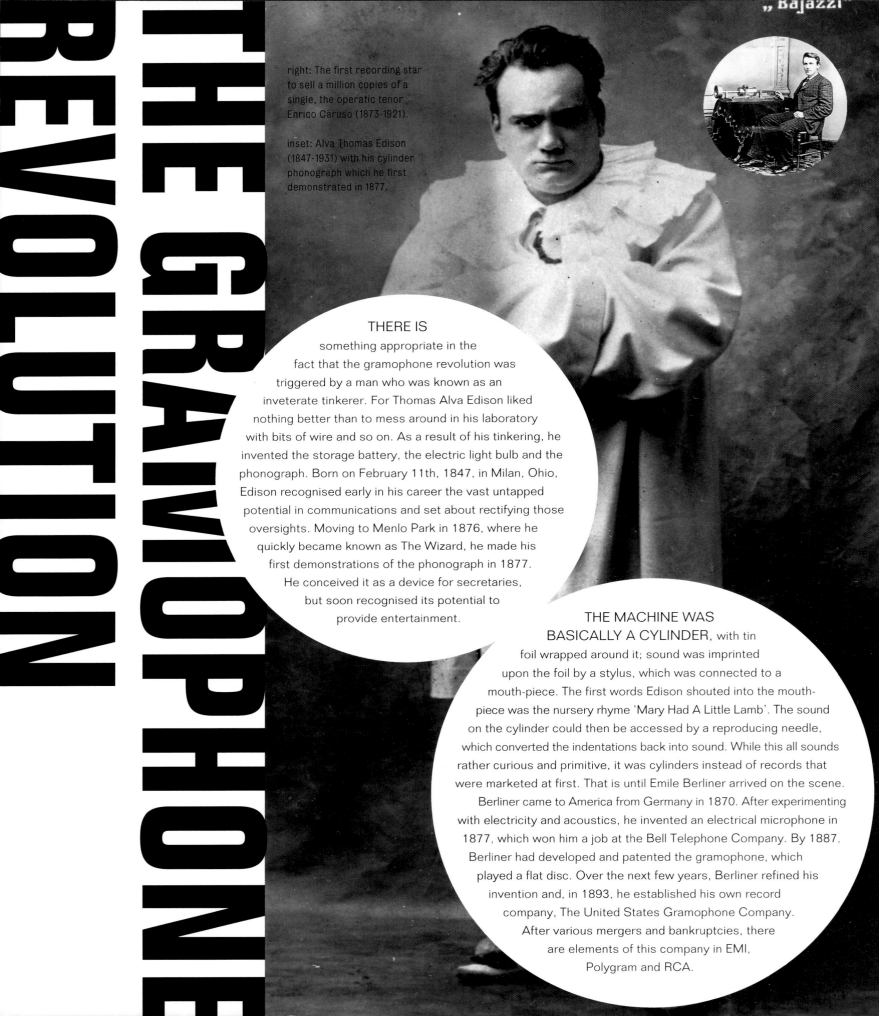

THE GRAMOPHONE REVOLUTION

„Bajazzi"

right: The first recording star to sell a million copies of a single, the operatic tenor Enrico Caruso (1873-1921).

inset: Alva Thomas Edison (1847-1931) with his cylinder phonograph which he first demonstrated in 1877.

THERE IS something appropriate in the fact that the gramophone revolution was triggered by a man who was known as an inveterate tinkerer. For Thomas Alva Edison liked nothing better than to mess around in his laboratory with bits of wire and so on. As a result of his tinkering, he invented the storage battery, the electric light bulb and the phonograph. Born on February 11th, 1847, in Milan, Ohio, Edison recognised early in his career the vast untapped potential in communications and set about rectifying those oversights. Moving to Menlo Park in 1876, where he quickly became known as The Wizard, he made his first demonstrations of the phonograph in 1877. He conceived it as a device for secretaries, but soon recognised its potential to provide entertainment.

THE MACHINE WAS BASICALLY A CYLINDER, with tin foil wrapped around it; sound was imprinted upon the foil by a stylus, which was connected to a mouth-piece. The first words Edison shouted into the mouth-piece was the nursery rhyme 'Mary Had A Little Lamb'. The sound on the cylinder could then be accessed by a reproducing needle, which converted the indentations back into sound. While this all sounds rather curious and primitive, it was cylinders instead of records that were marketed at first. That is until Emile Berliner arrived on the scene. Berliner came to America from Germany in 1870. After experimenting with electricity and acoustics, he invented an electrical microphone in 1877, which won him a job at the Bell Telephone Company. By 1887, Berliner had developed and patented the gramophone, which played a flat disc. Over the next few years, Berliner refined his invention and, in 1893, he established his own record company, The United States Gramophone Company. After various mergers and bankruptcies, there are elements of this company in EMI, Polygram and RCA.

THE FIRST ARTIST TO WIN LARGE PAYMENTS for his recordings was the great opera star, Caruso. By the 1920s, blues artists like Bessie Smith were selling thousands of records, but it was sales of Paul Whiteman's records that triggered the first real explosion, which reach its zenith in the Swing era. With the outbreak of war, recording bans were instituted. Part of this was due to the shortage of shellac (the raw material used to manufacture records), but also musicians went on strike to secure royalty payments from jukebox and radio plays.

"HIS MASTER'S VOICE"

THE GRAMOPHONE COMPAN
BY APPOINTME
SUPPLIERS OF GRAMOPHON
RADIO AND TELEVISION
TO HER MAJESTY QUEE

IN THE POST-WAR YEARS, the record industry consolidated until the birth of rock'n'roll. Although the 78 rpm disc was replaced by a smaller, less fragile 7" version, the 12" 'Long Player' was used primarily for serious (classical) music, jazz or movie soundtracks, with musicals like High Society, starring Frank Sinatra, Grace Kelly, Bing Crosby and Louis Armstrong featuring prominently. It was Sinatra again, who was responsible for illustrating the possibilities for the LP with Songs For Swinging Lovers. Conceived as a thematically linked series of songs, instead of the more common collection of singles, Songs For Swinging Lovers showed that buyers of popular music would purchase the LP. Still the rock'n'roll era remained the preserve of the single, until artists like Bob Dylan, and the rock bands of the late 60s established the LP – and its technological successor, the CD – as the ideal medium for the maturing rock audiences. That was only confirmed when groups such as Led Zeppelin and Iron Butterfly notched up formidable sales without even releasing singles.

The Hallma

Intr

FIRST

ONG

33⅓ R.P.M.

LAY

RECORDS

CTOBER 1952

PRICE SIXPENCE

above: A playbill outside the
Globe Theatre, Atlantic City,
announcing a Vauveville show
with Weber & Fields headlining.

right: Bert Williams, one of
many black performers who
nevertheless 'blacked up' in
minstrel-style. In 1901 he and
his stage partner George
Walker became the first black
Americans to record on disc.

VAUDEVILLE

In the same way that Music Hall was designed to amuse the British working classes, Vaudeville was the American equivalent. Evolving from the travelling Medicine Shows that toured the Mid-West throughout the 19th century, vaudeville provided entertainments that included knock-about comedy routines, acrobatics, juggling, songs and dances. After the abolition of slavery, many blacks found that one of the most immediate ways of capitalising upon their new-found liberty was to develop their musical skills. Although troupes of white entertainers had 'blacked-up', parodying black culture, after the Civil War all-black minstrel shows such as The Georgia Minstrels and the M.B. Curtis All-Star Afro-American Minstrels were formed; both forms of 'minstrelsy' continued touring into the early years of the 20th century.

However, the great importance of Vaudeville lay in the fact that it provided a platform for many genres of American music, and it was artists like Arthur Collins, Billy Murray and Nora Bayes who were the conduits from Vaudeville and the Broadway stage shows to the fledgling record industry.

Murray was raised in Denver, Colorado, and made his first recording 'Tessie (You Are the Only, Only One)' in 1903. This was followed by a string of other popular successes such as 'Meet Me In St. Louis', 'Yankee Doodle Dandy', and 'Give My Regards To Broadway'. Nora Bayes, a veteran of touring troupes, co-wrote 'Shine On Harvest Moon'. When this was featured in Follies of 1908, her future was assured temporarily, but after recording some patriotic songs during World War 1, her popularity waned. Vaudeville at its height threw up many more great names such as Weber & Fields and Jimmy Durante (whose career carried on in records and movies) but after the War, as the cinema became increasingly popular, it needed to respond to the market place, and through the 20s gradually gave way to stage shows or revues.

1899-1910

right: Bud Flanagan and Chesney Allen as Flanagan & Allen were Music Hall stars who crossed over into the recording world via huge hits like 'Run, Rabbit, Run' and 'Underneath The Arches'.

below: George Formby, with his ukelele-accompanied 'saucy' songs, was a household name in England, on the Music Hall and Variety stage, and in dozens of low-budget films through the 30s and 40s.

MUSIC HALL

WHILE THE BRITISH MUSIC HALL ATTAINED ITS GREATEST POPULARITY DURING THE LATTER HALF OF THE 19TH CENTURY AND ENDURED UNTIL THE OUTBREAK OF THE FIRST WORLD WAR, its antecedents could be traced back to the Elizabethan age. For the essence of Music Hall was to present varied entertainments that could appeal to the lowest common denominator: there was nothing inherently challenging about it. With that in mind, though, it should be remembered that this very requirement to appeal to the great majority was the ethos upon which most popular music was built, with Tin Pan Alley being its logical conclusion.

In the early years of the 19th century, song-and-supper rooms and tap-rooms began to appear, where the clientele could be regaled with slapstick comedy routines, acrobatics, juggling and songs. Taking the form of a primitive revue, a master of ceremonies would provide the links with jolly quips replete with bawdy innuendo. Despite the patronising and chauvinist attitude endemic in Music Hall, because of its very nature, it caused a bright array of talents to emerge, who in any other milieu might not have flourished to quite the same extent. Albert Chevalier (1861-1923) wrote and performed a number of songs and monologues that encapsulated facets of Cockney working-class life. Marie Lloyd, also London-born (1870-1922), with songs such as 'Oh! Mr Porter' and 'The Boy In The Gallery' epitomised the conniving sauciness of Music Hall – it was no mistake that the rise of the risque post-

card corresponded with Music Hall's ascendancy. While Music Hall was hardly profound, there was a kitsch sentiment that was often overstated but still rather sweet in its naiveté. Born in Scotland, Harry Lauder (1870-1950) with ballads such as 'I Love A Lassie', 'Roamin' In The Gloamin'' and 'Glasgow Belongs To Me' did much to establish the popular stereotype of the Scotsman – bedecked in kilt and sporran – as perhaps a figure of fun; neverhreless, he became a national institution, on both sides of the border.

NEWS

1899, OCTOBER: WAR BREAKS OUT BETWEEN THE BRITISH AND THE BOERS IN SOUTH AFRICA. THE CONFLICT LASTS FOR THREE YEARS

left: Music Hall superstar Charles Coburn, dressed in full character singing his hugely successful 'The Man Who Broke The Bank At Monte Carlo'.

below, left: Marie Lloyd was one of the biggest names on the Music Hall stage, with songs like 'Oh! Mr Porter'.

below: A national institution during the 30s and 40s, singer Gracie Fields was another performing and recording star who served an apprenticeship 'on the boards'.

If Music Hall was a uniquely British phenomenon – Vaudville being its American counterpart – it paved the way for the all-embracing Variety show, and, as with Vaudeville, is still the foundation upon which modern show-business is based.

However, Music Hall as such died out in 1914 when licensing restrictions were imposed with the outbreak of the First World War so as to ensure that the workers employed in the munitions factories were not too inebriated to do their job. Despite its demise figures such as George Formby, Gracie Fields and Flanagan & Allen all flourished, nurturing Variety and creating a template that would be replicated as television gripped the attention of the British public from the 1950s. Indeed, the BBC proved they had their finger on the pulse by starting a weekly show, The Good Old Days, that endeavoured to recreate the atmosphere and format of the Music Hall in its Victorian and Edwardian heyday; it ran well into the 1970s, with performers tapping into the seemingly insatiable British appetite for nostalgia.

AFTER THE
INTRODUCTION OF THE UPRIGHT
PIANO, demand for sheet music took off. While
church music had been notated in Hymnals and orchestral
composers had always scored their musical ideas, folk songs
were passed down by word of mouth from one generation to the
next. The reason for this lay in the musical literacy necessary to formal
composition or performance. But when the upright piano went into
mass production, it was the popular songs of the day that most
novices wanted to learn to play first – Beethoven's Sonatas or
Chopin's Nocturnes required a level of accomplishment
seldom available to those without any
formal musical training.

ONE OF THE
FIRST WRITERS to enjoy measurable
success as a songwriter was Stephen Foster.
Composing songs such as 'Oh Susanna' and 'The Old Folks
At Home', Foster produced instant classics of minstrelsy, which
combined elements of the folk song with a spare, melodic jauntiness.
Although there was something fundamentally objectionable in the way
he patronised black culture, he was one of the first to recognise its
inherent significance and value. So, in a sense, Foster was a
catalyst for later black writers, such as James A. Bland, whose
more than 700 songs included 'Carry Me Back To Old
Virginny' and 'Oh Dem Golden Slippers'.

ON A NIGHT LIKE THIS
Words by
Gus Kahn
Music by
Wm. Warvelle Nelson
ANSEL C. BEER & CO.
MUSIC DEALER

HOWEVER, WHILE THE GROWTH in popularity of Music Hall and Vaudeville had an undeniable impact – Charles Harris's 'After The Ball' sold over a million copies of sheet music – it was writers of light opera and early musicals such as Rudolph Friml, Gilbert & Sullivan, and George M.Cohan who enjoyed most success. Music Hall and Vaudeville lacked the gentility of the operetta and the raffish charm of the stage musical; most of the songs were fine for sing-alongs or barber shop quartets, but scarcely appropriate for middle class soirées. But it was Tin Pan Alley, which combined the salient elements of melody and gravitas, that ensured a continuing popularity for sheet music.

GRADUALLY, THE PIANO WAS SUPPLANTED BY THE GRAMOPHONE as the must-have piece of furniture, and records and radio were the boom items. Then the advent of sound in the cinema at the end of the 1920s was feared to be the final nail in the coffin of do-it-yourself domestic entertainment. Finally, as Swing became king, the masses flocked to the dance halls as never before. Nevertheless, sheet music continued to sell in significant quantities, helped by the 50s folk song revival which encouraged countless enthusiasts to pick up the acoustic guitar; indeed, the UK charts right up to the mid-50s were still calculated on sheet music rather than record sales.

right: Sigmund Romberg's Desert Song, a stunning cover for the vocal score (with lyrics by Oscar Hammerstein) which was published in 1927.

LIGHT OPERA

above: Agnes Baltsa and José Carreras in Bizet's Carmen, one of the popular works that bridged the gap between grand opera and light opera.

ALTHOUGH LIGHT OPERA SUPERFICIALLY MIGHT APPEAR TO BE THE EASY LISTENING OF THE TURN OF THE CENTURY – unchallenging with toothsome melodies and dainty lyrics – the clear signal it sent was that popular music need not be the preserve of the vulgarian. That polite society could embrace the waltz and the mazurka in a few easy steps suggested that the difference between the grand opera of Wagner and the operetta of Offenbach need not be insurmountable. Indeed, opera had only assumed grandeur through the aspirations of certain individual practitioners; its derivation – while never exactly humble – had always tended towards the readily accessible. Therefore, in a sense, light opera endeavoured to redress the imbalance engendered by the Teutonic intensity of Richard Wagner or the artful tragedies of Puccini. And with composers such as Sigmund Romberg, Rudolph Friml and Franz Lehar, light opera provided the foundation upon which the popularity of the stage and screen musical would be based.

Sigmund Romberg was born in Hungary, before moving to Vienna, thence to the United States in 1909. His first great success was Maytime (1917), which, when filmed, became a vehicle for Jeanette MacDonald and Nelson Eddy in 1937. It was followed by The Student Prince (1924) and The Desert Song (1926). While these were influenced by the great Viennese tradition of light, undemanding music as exemplified by Strauss, Romberg proved that he could transcend light opera and the immediacy of Tin Pan Alley with songs such as 'Lover Come Back To Me', which became a hit for Swing king Paul Whiteman and crooner Rudy Vallee. After moving to Hollywood, Romberg wrote film scores, before forming his own orchestra. Rudolph Friml, by contrast, studied piano and composition at the Prague Conservatoire before visiting the United States in 1901 with vioinist and composer Jan Kubelik. Initially, he persevered with classical music, composing piano concerti and chamber music, but in 1916 he composed the operetta Katinka, which was later followed by Rose

NEWS

1900, JUNE 20: BOXER REBELS ASSASSINATE THE GERMAN AMBASSADOR AND BESIEGE THE FOREIGN LEGATIONS IN PEKING IN PROTEST AGAINST FOREIGN INTERVENTIONS IN CHINA

above: The souvenir booklet for the 1925 London production of the Romberg operetta Rose Marie starring Edith Day.

above, right: A poster for a George Edwardes production of The Merry Widow.

Marie (1923) and The Vagabond King (1925). Friml endeavoured to make the grade as a composer of film scores, but failed to establish himself despite the popularity of the filmed version of Rose Marie, with Jeanette MacDonald and Nelson Eddy. Franz Lehar was another student of the Prague Conservatoire, but it was in London in 1907 that his biggest success, The Merry Widow, caught the mood of Edwardian England, sparking a fashion for 'Merry Widow' style hats and dresses; it proved to be his biggest success with only The Land Of Smiles coming close. And that was due more to the popularity of the great tenor Richard Tauber, who recorded 'Yours Is My Heart Alone' from The Land Of Smiles.

However, it was the partnership of librettist Sir William Gilbert and composer Sir Arthur Sullivan that had shown the way. Staging their shows at Richard D'Oyly Carte's Opera-Comique in London, their first hit was Trial By Jury (1875), which was followed by HMS Pinafore (1878) and The Pirates Of Penzance (1879).

From 1881, they were based at the newly-built Savoy Theatre on the Strand, where they triumphed with Iolanthe (1881), The Mikado (1885), The Gondoliers (1889) and The Grand Duke (1896), among others. It is testimony to the enduring appeal of Gilbert and Sullivan that while light opera has not endured well – sounding particularly dated – The D'Oyly Carte Company remained operational until 1982. Five years after it was closed down, it was revived on a smaller scale to perform Gilbert and Sullivan's works. Furthermore, it is worth noting that Sullivan also contributed to the cannon of religious music with the internationally-familiar anthem 'Onward Christian Soldiers'.

U.S. FOLK

BACK IN THE LATE 1940S AND EARLY 1950S, THE WEAVERS BLAZED A TRAIL, SCORING ONE HIT AFTER ANOTHER. While there was nothing especially surprising about this, the manner and scale of their success astonished everyone. Although hearing these records today, one is struck by how over-produced they are, they vindicated the accessibility of the folk song. Furthermore their capacity for choosing songs that literally embraced all facets of the genre by writers such as Woody Guthrie ('So Long, It's Been Good To Know Ya'), Leadbelly ('Goodnight Irene') and Stephen Foster ('Oh Susanna') demonstrated an acute awareness of the historical significance of the American folk song within the context of 20th century society.

By drawing from Foster's repertoire they confounded the notion that US folk song was just a synthesis – or reworking – of external stimuli from other cultures. For Foster had that rare capacity of tapping into indigent American culture and transposing it into a populist hybrid. Nowhere was this more apparent than in his mining of the deep seam of black American culture that – while enslaved and disenfranchised – was beginning to make its presence felt through the rapid spread of work songs and the medicine shows. Although Foster's perception of black culture was patronising in the extreme, it was certainly no more so than that of James A. Bland – the best-known black American songwriter of the 19th century and writer of songs such as 'Carry Me Back To Old Virginny'.

Foster's beginnings could not have been more different though. Born in Pennsylvania on July 4, 1826, Foster's upbringing was comfortable and was advantaged enough for him to learn the piano. In 1844, he composed and published his first song, 'Open Thy Lattice Love'. Later during a stay in Cincinnati, he sold the rights to a pile of songs to the publisher W.C. Peters. These included 'Oh Susanna' and 'Old Uncle Ned'; the former was to become the anthem of the Gold Rush of '49. However it was songs such as 'The Old Folks At Home', 'Camptown Races' and 'My Old Kentucky Home' that became staples of the minstrel's – or troubadour's – style. While Stephen Foster by and large adhered to steotyped popular imagery and the minstrelsy style, the far more romantic 'Jeanie With The Light Brown Hair' possessed a hint of Irish balladry in its makeup. Foster died in 1864.

VARIOUS ARTISTS
THE ANTHOLOGY OF AMERICAN FOLK MUSIC
Smithsonian Folkways

CD CHECKLIST

american folk music

Likewise Anglo-Celtic folk songs constituted a principal inspiration in the make up of the US folk tradition, but it was always localised. Different elements were manifest from the foothills of the Appalachians in the South to the mining communities of the North-east. And it is this characteristic that dominates American folk song: it was an amalgam of different influences that drew from its inherent peripateia. Constantly mutating every time a song was sung, it took on the flavour of the particular region. Therefore, while regional styles such as Cajun inferred the bayous of Louisiana, Bluegrass denoted a style of musical arrangement and instrumentation more than an actual geographical area.

With the spread of communication and the emergence of radio, so the practical applications of folk song became blurred as a wide-ranging commercialism began to take hold. Throughout the late 1930s and 1940s, folk songs were still sung, but they became marginalised by the growing commercialism of the music industry. When the folk song revival came about in the early 1950s, it was as much a consequence of 'witch hunt' Senator Joe McCarthy deeming all protest singers Communists – so making them potential martyrs – as it was the recognition that the reason folk songs had endured was because they were good songs. While The Weavers introduced an anodyne quality to the performance of folk music, they literally galvanised interest among a college-educated middle-class. So it was from these classes that the next generation of practitioners emerged.

Although some like The Kingston Trio and The New Christy Minstrels followed the populist sing-along style of The Weavers, others like Ramblin' Jack Elliott and Bob Dylan followed Guthrie's template, using their songs as a chronicle or critique of contemporary society. To this day, folk song in the US still exercises an influence, but the form has altered radically.

below, left: 'Big Daddy' Burl Ives' speciality was children's songs from the American folk repetoire, like 'Jimmy Crack Corn', 'On Top Of Old Smokey' and 'There Was An Old Lady'.

below: The Weavers, with Lee Hayes second right, on an English TV show in the early 60s. Their biggest hit, Leadbelly's 'Goodnight Irene', was a surprise US No 1 in 1950.

G DADDY (Burl Ives)

Brunswick

APPALACHIAN MUSIC

UP UNTIL THE 1920S, SOUTHERN FOLK MUSIC WAS LARGELY UNKNOWN BEYOND ITS IMMEDIATE ENVIRONMENT. Then through the collections of songs gathered together by folklorist and collector John Lomax and the Englishman Cecil Sharp, Southern folk music began to assume an altogether broader profile. For Sharp's collection, Folk Songs From The Southern Appalachians, isolated the origin of songs and many of them were found to be English, Highland Scottish, Scots-Irish, Catholic Irish or Welsh. Into this melting pot was thrown contributions from Germany, Spain and France, as well as Native American Indian, but all of this was overlayed by the influence of the blues and gospel.

However, during the 1920s, the pioneering Ralph Peer started to make field trips into isolated rural communities throughout the South. What he emerged with were recordings that began to illustrate a hybrid that was uniquely American. For not only were the songs themselves indicative of an unprecedented inter-racial and inter-cultural cross-pollination, the instruments and the arrangements reflected an aspect of rural community life that, while not unknown, had been little considered. With the banjo and fiddle, these were instruments that had been handed down from generation to generation, forming the cornerstone of family life, used for family entertainment or on sombre occasions such as funerals.

Out of these humble origins both Peer and Lomax started to assemble a picture of rural American life that had started to evolve when the first settlers landed. From these origins, old time music – later described as Hillbilly – started its long and gradual evolution into country music.

Despite the influence of academics like Lomax, it was the influence of The Carter Family that gave a popular voice to these songs. Alvin Pleasant Carter was born on April 15, 1891, at Mace Springs in Virginia. One of nine children, A.P. Carter started his career singing in church alongside his elder sister and two uncles. On June 18, 1915, he married Sara Dougherty, a vocalist who also played the autoharp, guitar and banjo; Maybelle Addington joined the group in 1926 after marrying A.P.'s brother, Ezra. In 1927, Ralph Peer produced their first sides for RCA; this relationship lasted for seven years, during which time they recorded titles like 'Keep On The Sunny Side',

above: The Carter Family in the early 1930s with (l-r) Maybelle Addington, A.P. Carter and his wife Sarah Dougherty.

left and below: The great Jimmie Rodgers, billed as 'America's Blue Yodeler' and 'The Singing Brakeman'. In songs like 'Blue Yodel' and 'Muleskinner Blues' his delivery owed as much to the blues as to cowboy songs.

bottom: Genuine 'hillbillys' dancing to the tune of banjos and fiddle in front of a primitive farmhouse in West Virginia, photographed in the 1920s.

'Bury Me Under The Weeping Willow', 'Wildwood Flower', 'I'm Thinking Tonight Of My Blue Eyes', 'Single Girl' and 'Will The Circle Be Unbroken'. The rise of The Carter Family corresponded with that of fellow RCA recording artist Jimmie Rodgers, but while Rodgers' songs espoused the hedonistic doctrine of 'the flesh', The Carter Family remained models of clean living and sobriety, and advocates of family life (although they did record the occasional risqué number, like 'There'll Be A Hot Time In The Old Town Tonight').

While Carter claimed authorship of many of these songs, there is little doubt that a lot of them had been in existence in some form or another for literally centuries. The Carters' arrangements, however, were traditional to a fault, with archaic instruments such as the autoharp and jew's harp supplementing the now popular guitar alongside the banjo and fiddle.

These days they are ponderously referred to as The First Family Of Country; that would seem to be an over-simplification, signifying more their connection to Johnny Cash, who is now married to June Carter, one of Maybelle's daughters. For they brought a familial approach to music-making into the studio: there was little or no artifice commonly associated with that practice these days. They made no effort to bury the regional cadences of their speech in their singing; in the late 1960s The Band echoed that naturalism, allowing each vocalist's regional characteristics to shine through, imbuing their work with a gravitas and authenticity that was at odds with the very concept of rock music.

As communications have improved out of all proportion, the isolated pockets of rural communities have become less attenuated, but even so, the family – along with the church – remains the bedrock of music-making, and these Southern Folk songs are still being handed down from one generation to the next.

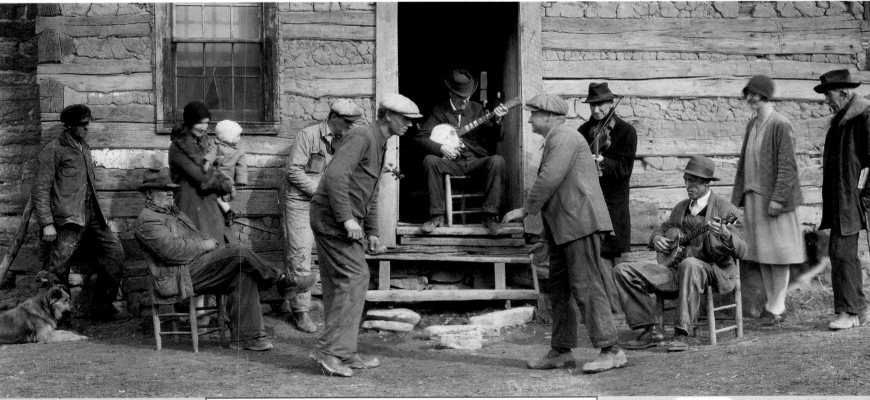

EARLY BLUES

top: Bumble Bee Slim (1905-1968) was an itinerant singer and guitarist before settling in Indianapolis and later Chicago, from where he made dozens of records during the 1930s.

above: Like so many bluesmen, Peetie Wheatstraw's career only took off after moving north, in his case to St Louis, after which he recorded 161 titles between 1930 and 1941.

IT IS SAID THAT GERTRUDE 'MA' RAINEY FIRST ENCOUNTERED THE BLUES WHILE TRAVELLING IN MISSOURI AS PART OF A VAUDEVILLE TROUPE IN 1902. Perhaps that was her first knowing recognition of an extant form, as opposed to the articulation of sound or feeling that all black people knew and understood only too well, but had never thought to describe it as anything other than the wail of the human spirit in extremis. Whatever. For the blues evolved through the chants, hollers and work songs that in turn had been acquired through a combination of African rhythms, hymns and ballads. After the abolition of slavery, many blacks headed away from the rural South towards the growing urban heartlands of the industrial North, often settling briefly in towns such as Kansas City or St Louis. While these staging posts attracted a variety of often shady characters, even they needed to be entertained.

As the minstrel and medicine shows flourished, so itinerant troubadours started to appear; even the barrelhouse, boogie woogie of pianists such as Meade-Luxe Lewis, and Albert Ammons, though associated strongly with Chicago, had some of its roots in the raffish ebullience of these half-way houses. However, it was songwriters such as W.C. Handy, who first used the term 'blues' generically, describing the song's style in its very title: it didn't matter whether it was a lachrymose ballad or an uptempo boogie, if it was called a 'blues' it was unequivocally of Afro-American origin.

In 1920 a vaudeville singer from Cincinnati called Mamie Smith was encouraged by songwriter Perry Bradford to go to Chicago to record some tracks for the OKeh label. Although Smith had been plying her trade on the Harlem music hall stage, Bradford was aware of the number of other black female songstresses like Sippie Wallace, Victoria Spivey and Sara Martin who had made the transition from the music hall stage to the recording studio. Of the songs Mamie cut 'Crazy Blues' was the one that had the effect of galvanising other record companies into signing female blues singers: Ma 'Mother Of The Blues' Rainey and Alberta Hunter signed to Paramount, and The Empress Of The Blues Bessie Smith went to Columbia. The other significant factors in the emergence of the female blues singers were the arrangements: usually their male counterparts accompanied themselves singly on the piano or the guitar, the guitar

left: Many of the major record companies marketed their music to black audiences as 'race records', a term first coined by OKeh in 1920.

right: By the time he made his first records in 1929, Charley Patton was the foremost blues singer in Mississippi, with a repetoire he had begun before 1910 when he was in his teens.

far right: Like the Charley Patton portrait, Blind Lemon Jefferson pictured from a series of trading cards by the artist Robert Crumb, issued by Yazoo Records in 1980.

CHARLEY PATTON

BLIND LEMON JEFFERSON

above: While not the complete original that some enthusiasts claim – his technique devloped the styles of Charley Patton, Son House and others – in a short career the great Robert Johnson created the template for post-war Chicago blues.

CHARLEY PATTON
FOUNDER OF THE DELTA BLUES
Yazoo

having become widely available through mail-order outlets. The women responded to the demand for blues records by recording with five- or six-piece jazz combos or pianists like James P. Johnson and Fletcher Henderson; and Sara Martin is best remembered for the sides she recorded with King Oliver's band.

Early bluesmen such as Charley Patton and Blind Lemon Jefferson, while not brilliant guitarists, evolved distinctive styles that enabled them to reflect the travails of a rural background. Blind Lemon Jefferson was one of the major Texan stylists to emerge before the Depression bit. His high-pitched expressive vocals on self-penned items like 'Black Snake Blues', 'Pneumonia Blues' and 'See That My Grave Is Kept Clean' were given greater emphasis by his guitar style, which was spare and elliptical. Although he died early (from exposure, in Chicago), he influenced Texan musicians such as Leadbelly, Lightnin' Hopkins and T-Bone Walker, as well as the Mississippi-based B.B. King.

Patton's vocal style on titles such as 'Frankie & Albert', 'Pony Blues', 'Screamin' & Hollerin' The Blues' and 'Some Of These Days I'll Be Gone' caused many to adopt his mannerisms with the result that his barking, hectoring inflexions became a template for successive generations such as Son House, Robert Johnson and Howlin' Wolf. But while these early bluesmen developed solid reputations in their own right, it wasn't until the late 1920s and 1930s with the proliferation of recorded material that the blues had acquired widespread currency.

1906, APRIL 18: HUNDREDS ARE KILLED AND $400-MILLION WORTH OF DAMAGE IS CAUSED AS SAN FRANCISCO IS DEVASTATED BY EARTHQUAKE

left: Considered the 'father of the blues', WC Handy was certainly the first composer to publish blues-based songs in the form of Tin Pan Alley sheet music in any quantity.

WINDS OF CHANGE

The second decade of the 20th century was dominated by war, yet despite the horror that engulfed all the major nations of the world, popular music continued to thrive. Most central to the war spirit of course was the spread in popularity of patriotic songs. Music hall stars and vaudeville artists sang the songs the 'lads' took to the front – 'A Long Way To Tipperary' and such.

But it was also the era of Tin Pan Alley, when the songwriting industry boomed as never before. The piano in every home had fuelled the demand for sheet music over the previous twenty years, and – remembering that America never actually joined the war in France until 1917 – Tin Pan Alley, centred on New York's Broadway and to a lesser extent London's Denmark Street, fulfilled the need with a burgeoning production line of sentimental ballads, novelty numbers and the new Ragtime specialities.

It was the latter that signalled even greater changes to come. Ragtime had come into people's homes via the player-piano with the piano rolls of composers like Scott Joplin, cross-fertilised with the rural blues that was still only heard in the cotton fields of Mississippi, and fed the music-rich melting pot of New Orleans where was evolving a sound more radical that any before or since this century – jass, or as it was soon to be known, jazz.

1910-1920

right: The British Music Hall star Vesta Tilley who made patriotic songs – in full male uniform – the main part of her act during the dark years of the First World War.

above: The Times Square
district on New York's
Broadway, the hub of the Tin
Pan Alley songwriting world.

right and far right: Before the
advent of the great Broadway
songwriters who produced
classics via hit shows, the main
pop fodder to come out of Tin
Pan Alley consisted of grossly
sentimental or novelty items.

TIN PAN ALLEY

MUSIC PUBLISHER AND SONGWRITER HARRY VON TILZER ALWAYS CLAIMED THAT THE PHRASE TIN PAN ALLEY WAS COINED IN HIS OFFICE IN NEW YORK. Even so, Tin Pan Alley has come to be associated with not so much a place – although associations still exist with Denmark Street on the north side of Charing Cross Road in the heart of London's Theatreland – but more with a style or, indeed, attitude towards songwriting. For the essence of the good Tin Pan Alley writer was the ability to sell songs. That this required the talent to craft a song was one thing, that it necessitated the powers of a clairvoyant in predicting the mood swings of the general public was an entirely separate issue.

And there is little doubt that Von Tilzer had all these gifts in abundance. He started his career as a tumbler in the circus before entering burlesque and then vaudeville. While in vaudeville, he started writing songs. In 1898 he scored his first big hit with 'My Old New Hampshire Home', which was recorded by Frank Stanley; this was followed by 'I'd Leave My Happy Home For You', which became a hit for Arthur Collins. Settling in New York, despite having sold the copyrights of his songs, he became a partner in the prestigious music publishing firm, Shapiro and Bernstein. In this new set-up, he penned 'A Bird In A Gilded Cage'. The royalties from this enabled him to establish his own publishing firm in 1902. Among his other hits were 'Down Where The Warzburger Flows', 'On A Sunday Afternoon', 'Please Go 'Way And Let Me Sleep', 'Wait Till The Sun Shines Nellie' and 'Just Around The Corner'. By the mid-1920s, Von Tilzer had abandoned writing in favour of administering his publishing assets, which had been greatly enhanced by material from writers such as George Gershwin and Irving Berlin.

Whatever the merits of his claims to having invented the phrase, Von Tilzer certainly showed a knack for combining the popular appeal of vaudeville within the sentiment and whimsy of light opera. He wasn't the only one though. Charles Harris, the author of 'After The Ball', was probably the first writer to pen a song to a style or brief. And it was Harris's earlier example that caused Von Tilzer to set up his own publishing firm. George M. Cohan managed to combine these elements as well, demonstrating an affinity with the stage musical.

Although Tin Pan Alley never lost its glitter, styles changed, and once that had happened, the furniture needed changing as well. However, the modus operandi differed little, and writers like Irving Berlin and Rodgers & Hart all showed they could write to a brief. The modern corollaries would probably be writers such as Elton John, Tim Rice and Dianne Warren, among others. In Nashville, country music is based almost exclusively upon the ability to pen radio-friendly material. Writers such as Kostas, Harlan Howard and Bob McDill, among others, pride themselves on their ability to write to order. Therefore the traditions of Tin Pan Alley have changed very little over the last century – perhaps, though, now the rewards are greater.

1911, NOVEMBER 14: NORWEGIAN EXPLORER ROALD AMUNDSEN BEATS BRITISH CAPTAIN SCOTT IN THEIR RACE TO BE THE FIRST PERSON TO REACH THE SOUTH POLE

PATRIOTIC SONGS

ALTHOUGH THE PATRIOTIC SONG SEEMS TO HAVE BECOME EXTINCT AS A PHENOMENON, THE ECHOES STILL REVERBERATE. For the modern corollary would, perhaps, be the football anthems that appear in the UK with every World Cup or FA Cup final. Similarly, the death of Princess Diana in a car crash was commemorated by the recording of a rewritten version of Elton John's 'Candle In The Wind'. What these songs have in common – though in very different ways, admittedly – is their attempt to reflect a nation's feelings or hopes: in other words, they are morale boosters. A more specific military-associated example appeared in the American charts over thirty years ago, when, in the midst of the Vietnam War in 1966, 'The Ballad Of The Green Berets' topped the US singles chart, sung by an actual member of the US Army Special Forces (Green Berets) Staff Sgt Barry Sadler.

Originally, though, the patriotic song was the preserve of music hall or vaudeville in World War I, as writers such as George M. Cohan sought to express the sentiments of the public with songs like 'Over There', which became one of Nora Bayes' biggest hits; Bayes had other hits with 'The Man Who Put The Germ In Germany' and 'Someday They're Coming Home' (1918). The American Quartet, featuring Billy Murray, tapped into the nationalist fervour with 'It's A Long Way To Tipperary' and 'Goodbye Broadway, Hello France'. For English audiences 'It's A Long Way To Tipperary' and 'Pack Up Your Troubles' were popularised by Australian Florrie Forde. What many of these songs had

left: Many names on the British Music Hall stage, like singer Ella Shields, took on a patriotic persona during the Great War.

1912, APRIL 15: TITANIC SINKS ON HER MAIDEN VOYAGE AFTER COLLIDING WITH AN ICEBERG OFF THE COAST OF NEWFOUNDLAND. OVER 1,500 PASSENGERS DROWN

right: Another female Music
Hall star, Jean Aylwin dressed
up in full military uniform.

far right: Certainly the most
famous of all First World War
anthems, 'It's A Long Way To
Tipperary' is here advertised
as being sung by The Soldiers
Of The King.

MISS JEAN AYLWIN   T 1146

THE MARCHING ANTHEM ON THE BATTLEFIELDS OF EUROPE.
THE
IMMORTAL
IT'S A LONG, LONG
WAY TO TIPPERARY.

Written and Composed
BY
JACK JUDGE
AND HARRY
WILLIAMS.

Sung by THE
SOLDIERS
OF THE KING

Copyright.   LONDON, ENGLAND.   Price 6ᵈ net
B. FELDMAN & Cᴼ 125, 127, 129, Shaftesbury Avenue, W.C.2.

in common, though, apart from sentiment, was that they all seemed to resonate with the influence of Sousa's military marches.

By the Second World War, the effect of radio and the popularity of records and films had turned the entertainment industry into the growth business of the decade. Therefore, its potential as a propaganda machine was vast. In 1941 USO (United Service Overseas) was launched, which organised tours by artists such as The Andrews Sisters, Bob Hope and Bing Crosby to entertain the troops. War bonds were issued, with film stars and musicians alike going on promotional tours to sell them. Victory discs, featuring jazz artists like Lionel Hampton and Count Basie, were released, despite the recording ban instituted by the American Federation of Musicians. Indeed the combined might of the American entertainment industry appeared to suspend work for the duration of hostilities, with many such as Glenn Miller losing their lives in the process.

In the United Kingdom, ENSA (Entertainments National Service Association) concerts were instituted to provide light relief from the hostilities for Commonwealth servicemen. While one of the great patriotic songs of the war years was Flanagan and Allen's 'Run, Rabbit, Run', patriotism was no laughing matter, which was emphasised by the unabashed sentiment of Vera Lynn's 'White Cliffs Of Dover'. This attitude was amplified by the reaction to Noel Coward's sardonic 'Don't Let's Be Beastly To The Germans', which was promptly banned. Even so, the entertainment industry in the UK did its part, with ENSA staging over two and a half million performances up until 1946 when it was disbanded.

If the overt patriotic song might appear to have had its day, the sentiments remain undimmed. The USO, after being disbanded briefly, was re-established when the Korean War broke out. Now the brief of the USO has but one objective: to entertain wherever US service men go.

right: The legendary and tragic Edith Piaff who went from street singer to cabaret star with emotional songs about the gritty side of life including sex, drugs and death.

below left: The Harlem club singer who ended up as the biggest name on the French revue stage, the sensational black star Josephine Baker.

FRENCH CABARET

FROM THE 1880s UNTIL THE 1930s, CABARET FLOURISHED IN MOST EUROPEAN CITIES – NOT LONDON, THOUGH. The pace was set in the early years in Paris, where night clubs such as Le Chat Noir – pianist and composer Erik Satie was a regular performer – were a logical extension of the café society that had always formed such a strong part of Parisienne life.

By 1925, jazz had emerged as the principal attraction when clarinettist Sidney Bechet appeared with Josephine Baker in La Revue Negre. To claim that its success was completely due to Baker's lack of clothes would be unfair in the extreme, but it certainly didn't harm it. For Baker, it marked the start of a love-affair with France that would continue until her death in 1975; indeed, during the Second World War, she was a member of the Resistance, winning the Croix de Guerre and the Legion D'Honneur. After La Revue Negre, Baker carved out her own territory at Les Folies Bergere, where she appeared in a girdle made out of bananas. Meanwhile, she cut sides such as 'J'ai Deux Amours', which became her theme tune, appeared in films such as La Sirene Des Tropiques (1927), Zou-Zou (1930) and Princesse Tam-Tam (1935), and starred in the opera by Offenbach, La Creole (1934).

Meanwhile at The Hot Club Of France, The Quintet, with guitarists Django Reinhardt, Joseph Reinhardt and Roger Chaput, violinist Stéphane Grappelli and bassist Louis Vola, contributed in no small part to the intellectual probity of jazz in French café society

between the wars. Elsewhere in Europe, Germany especially, the ascendancy of the Nazi party was reflected in the decadent atmospheres of the night clubs where the songs of Kurt Weill and Bertolt Brecht mirrored a society in free-fall; the Hollywood musical Cabaret, directed by Bob Fosse and starring Liza Minnelli, provides an interesting overview of the period.

After the war, as Parisienne chic, through designers such as Coco Chanel and Christian Dior, caught the imagination of the beau monde, songstresses such as Edith Piaf, with songs such as 'La Vie En Rose' and 'Les Trois Cloches', suggested a world-weariness. While Piaf's world-weariness may have been prompted by her war experiences, when nothing was as it seemed, French intellectuals such as Jean-Paul Sartre espoused a philosophical nihilism, euphemistically dubbed existentialism. Piaf, known as The Little Sparrow, became the catalyst for a generation of writers and singers such as Gilbert Becaud, Juliette Greco, Charles Aznavour and Charles Trenet. If they weren't all gripped by a comparable ennui, they certainly implied a quiet desperation.

Of all the writers to emerge, Jacques Brel, with songs like 'If You Go Away' and 'The Dove', made the transition to become a performer of repute and intensity, almost matching the impassioned soulfulness of Piaf with Music For The Millions (1964). It is testimony to Brel's far-reaching impact that his songs have been covered, with translations by Mort Shuman (of the songwriting partnership fame Pomus and Shuman) and Canadian

left: An archetype for a later model, the existentialist image suited the angst-driven French chanteuse of Julette Greco.

poet Rod McKuen, by Frank Sinatra, David Bowie, Tom Jones, Marc Almond and Scott Walker.

Despite the keenly held contention that France has contributed little to the state of popular music, it is interesting to observe the number of performers who have found eager audiences in France when their popularity has declined in their country of origin. These have included Argentinian diva Mercedes Sosa, Nigerian high-life bandleader Fela Anikulapo Kuti and Spanish guitarist Pacio Ibanez. In Germany, chanteuse

Ute Lemper has, with All That Jazz (1996), kept the spirit of the cabaret alive, while English actress and vocalist Marianne Faithful has unwittingly staked out a comparable territory; Lemper appeared in the London production of the musical Chicago.

JAZZ

THE TERM JAZZ HAD ITS ORIGINS IN NEW ORLEANS, WHERE 'JASS' MEANT SEXUAL INTERCOURSE. With those salacious origins, jass came to be a catch-all denoting anything that was exciting. It would seem that it was in Chicago in 1916 when Johnny Stein was leading a band that a member of the audience yelled out, 'Jass it up, boys!' Probably apocryphal, but Stein eventually renamed his band Stein's Dixie Jass Band, which eventually became The Original Dixieland Jazz Band. Whatever its semantic derivations may be, jazz drew from the Ragtime of Scott Joplin and the Dixieland of New Orleans. Dixieland grew out of the New Orleans marching bands, but it was the appropriation of the cornet that enabled the Dixieland style to evolve its familiar pattern where extended solos could be improvised. While the instrumental arrangements were critical, it was the blues and the work songs of the Afro-American culture that informed the subtext of jazz, giving it a robust emotional depth and strength.

While songwriters such as W.C. Handy provided detail to this subtext, cornetists such as Buddy Bolden, Freddie Keppard, Bunk Johnson, King Oliver and Louis Armstrong were the early stars of jazz, with much of their popularity stemming from their exploits. Bolden, in particular, never cut a record, and the only wax cylinder went missing aeons ago. Bolden was to die in 1931, having been incarcerated in a mental hospital since 1907. Bunk Johnson never recorded until 1942, but he recalled Bolden playing titles like 'Make Me A Pallet On The Floor'. As for Johnson, he disappeared from sight until 1939, when he, along with George Russell, spearheaded a Dixieland revival. In 1947, Johnson was on hand to appear in the film, New Orleans, with Billie Holiday and Meade Luxe Lewis. Keppard, too, didn't record until 1923, by which time much of his fire and originality had been snuffed out. So it was left to Armstrong and Oliver to fly the flag.

Oliver joined trombonist Kid Ory's band in 1912, before leading his own band, which was to include a

NEWS

1918, JULY 16: THE RUSSIAN ROYAL FAMILY ARE MURDERED AS THE BOLSHEVIKS TAKE CONTROL IN RUSSIA

above: Jelly Roll Morton's Red Hot Peppers made, along with Louis Armstrong's Hot Five, the very best recorded examples of New Orleans jazz.

above left: Rediscovered and achieving fame as part of the 1940s Dixieland revival, Bunk Johnson was a big New Orleans name early in the century.

youthful Armstrong. His own band was short-lived and he soon rejoined Ory where he acquired the sobriquet 'King', which marked his accession to the title of New Orleans' best cornetist. In 1919, he went to Chicago where he worked with Bill Johnson of The Creole Jazz Band. Pretty soon, Oliver had taken over the band's leadership and had sent for Armstrong to become the second cornetist, supplementing a lineup that already featured pianist Lil Hardin and clarinettist Johnny Dodds. From 1923, Oliver made some of the most important recordings in the history of jazz, where his melodic style provided inspiration for his protégé Louis Armstrong.

Although jazz was an indelible expression of the black man's experience, white bands such as The Original Dixieland Jazz Band were quick to seize upon its potential as a vehicle for entertainment: little more than an extension of the minstrel shows that had long been a popular aspect of vaudeville. The emergence of blues singers such as Bessie Smith and Ma Rainey,

themselves experienced vaudevillians, ensured that the profile of jazz was little more than light entertainment. Even clubs such as The Cotton Club in New York's Harlem presented two distinct faces: the jovial, smiling version for the club's affluent white patrons, and the laidback, lowdown blues for the after-hours sessions. Therefore, while Paul Whiteman was able to dilute the Dixieland style and come up with Swing, it was hardly surprising that the more robust corollary should, through bandleaders such as Duke Ellington and Count Basie, be more readily identifiable as products of the Afro-American experience. Louis Armstrong showed the way forward by presenting identical personas to the general public; the perception of that persona and music was a matter of opinion. For as much as Armstrong elevated the profile of jazz, so performers like pianist Jelly Roll Morton forged the links between the undiluted New Orleans style and the mainstream jazz of the 1930s, when Ellington and Basie redefined the parameters of jazz.

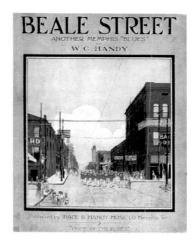

W.C. HANDY

THE AUTHOR OF 'ST LOUIS BLUES' STILL SEEMS TO EXERT A CURIOUS POWER OVER THE JAZZ FRATERNITY. And it isn't because that title has been recorded more than any other single title, nor is it because he is widely regarded as the founding father of Afro-American music. More it is a question of style: the triumph over adversity and the way in which the victories were dealt with. For Handy had more style than a high-class couturier could muster over an entire career – let alone season. Handy understood that you can't cut corners until you know what the pattern is. So he made it his business to find out. In so doing he recognised the historical significance of the performing arts within black culture.

Born in Florence, Alabama, on November 16, 1873, the son of a preacher man, William Christopher Handy played cornet in local brass bands and studied composition at Huntsville College. While touring vaudeville as a member, and musical director, of Mahara's Minstrels, Handy first encountered the blues in the rural backwaters of Mississippi in the mid-1890s. In 1903, he gave up touring with the minstrels to concentrate upon touring the South with the nine-piece band he had formed.

For the band, he began to compose. While the process was hesitant at first, he published his first tune, 'Memphis Blues' – formerly known as 'Mr Crumb' – in 1912. That was followed by a string of titles such as 'Beale Street Blues', 'St Louis Blues', 'Joe Turner Blues', 'Yellow Dog Blues', 'Loveless Love' and

'Aunt Hagar's Blues', among others. The success of 'St Louis Blues' was immediate as everyone from jazz and blues musicians to dance and military bands came to perform or record it. Soon, his writing had supplanted his performing career as his principal source of income. In 1918, having moved to New York, Handy established his own music publishing firm with partner Harry Pace. By 1921, Pace had set up the first black-owned record label, Black Swan, and scored significant hits with Ethel Waters' version of 'St Louis Blues'; Fletcher Henderson was the label's recording director. It didn't last long, though, for the label was absorbed by Paramount in 1924.

In 1926, Handy published Blues: An Anthology, which had the effect of causing many to look upon the blues in an entirely new light. Although his eyesight deteriorated during the 1930s, causing him to go completely blind in the early 1940s, his Book Of Negro Spirituals (1939) provided a welcome context for producer John Hammond's Carnegie Hall concerts, Spirituals To Swing. In 1941, Handy published his autobiography, Father Of The Blues, which later became the basis of a Hollywood biopic entitled St Louis Blues (1957), starring Nat King Cole. Handy died on March 28, 1958, in New York City.

Today his influence still reverberates through the works of gifted musicians such as trumpeter Wynton Marsalis and in producers such as Quincy Jones, both of whom have endeavoured to continue investigating the context of the evolution of Afro-American styles.

left: The great W.C. Handy, hit composer of such classics as 'Beale Street Blues' and his undoubtedly most famous work 'St Louis Blues'.

1920, JANUARY 16: PROHIBITION BECOMES LAW THROUGHOUT THE UNITED STATES AS THE 18TH AMENDMENT TO THE CONSTITUTION GOES INTO EFFECT

RADIO

THE ASCENDANCY OF RADIO in the 1920s and 1930s stimulated the popularity of the dance bands, kicking the Swing era into gear. In the US, most of the big bands broadcast from the country's leading hotels and radio stations. In 1932, in the UK, Henry Hall succeeded Jack Payne as the leader of the BBC Dance Orchestra, becoming at a stroke one of the most powerful figures in the British entertainment industry.

Meanwhile, in the US, the greatest threat to the omnipotence of radio was the emergence of the jukebox. However jukebox manufacturers were not to escape the exigencies of war. For on May 1, 1942, the War Production Board commandeered the plants of many jukebox manufacturers to help the war effort. This was at a time when the demand for jukeboxes was spiralling out of all proportion. No army base or youth club was complete without a jukebox. By August 1944 record companies were finding it increasingly hard to service jukeboxes, which were assimilating up to 75 per cent of their output, while the retail market absorbed the balance. Such was the influence of the jukebox that some record labels expressed fears that playing records over the air would damage sales, with some like Decca actively prohibiting the practice. By the end of the Second World War, as the number of independent record labels and radio stations proliferated, so opinion gave way and radio and later television became the premier promotional tools.

THE POST-WAR YEARS SAW THE EMERGENCE OF HIGH-PROFILE DJs such as Alan Freed. While working as an announcer at WJW, Cleveland, he convinced local record store owner Leo Mintz to sponsor an R&B show, Record Rendezvous. His rasping delivery went down a storm with young audiences, who had never heard anything quite like the unadulterated rawness of groups like The Orioles and vocalists like Ruth Brown. After changing the name of his show to The Moondog Rock'n'Roll Party, he promoted a number of concerts. Such was the success of these ventures that he was lured to WINS in New York. As his influence grew, he appeared in three films – Rock Around The Clock and Rock, Rock, Rock (1956) and Don't Knock The Rock (1957) – and hosted his own TV show, Rock'n'Roll Dance Party. The bubble was soon to burst as Freed became implicated in the payola scandal: the music publishers association – ASCAP – contended that Freed was given perks to play records. He pleaded guilty to bribery at the Congressional hearings and was eventually indicted for tax evasion. He died on January 20, 1965, before the case came to trial.

DESPITE THE POPULARITY OF ROCK'N'ROLL IN THE US, it didn't significantly affect the programming for those with specialist tastes: The Grand Ole Opry for country fans, for example, had thrown open its doors as early as the 1920s, followed by its biggest rival the Louisiana Hayride. In the UK, by contrast, the BBC had never got to grips with what the young wanted to hear. By the mid-1960s, 'pirate' stations were broadcasting non-stop pop music from ships anchored off the coast in the North Sea. The Marine Broadcasting Act in 1967 rendered these operations illegal, and the BBC responded by introducing Radio 1, staffed by DJs from the pirate stations. Radio 1 has managed to reflect accurately the changing tides in popular taste, even in the face of stiff opposition from independent commercial stations such as Capital.

But after over 70 years, radio remains the best promotional device for popular music. In the US with its proliferation of literally thousands of local stations, commercially and community funded, in the UK with a now-deregularised network of commercial and local BBC channels, and across the globe wherever signals are received music stations will be found crowding the airwaves. Despite TV being the major medium in people's lives, sound-only radio is still perfect for any kind of music.

THE RECORD BOOM

By the mid-20s, most American homes had a phonograph. Wax 78 rpm discs were selling by the million, and every taste and community was catered for. Hillbilly songs, blues numbers, jazz novelties, all competed for a slice of the market, much of it catered for by small independent record labels specialising in one or another segment. Even the big major companies, like Victor and Columbia, had their specialist labels. In the case of the blues and gospel of Black America, this resulted in the now notorious 'race records' catalogues. The phonograph (or gramophone) record also made available to every home the first great era of the Broadway musical, which heralded a golden age in songwriting of what are now 'standards', that carried on through the next three decades.

1920-1930

above: An ad from Paramount records, one of the US labels that initiated a 'race' catalogue to serve black record buyers with gospel, folk, novelty and classic blues releases.

right: The 'Ol' Man River' scene from Showboat; the Jerome Kern/Oscar Hammerstein II show which opened in 1927 represented a turning point in the stage musical.

STAGE MUSICALS

above: A poster for the original Broadway production of Rogers and Hart's Pal Joey in 1940, with Vivienne Segal and George Tapps in the lead roles.

UNTIL THE EMERGENCE OF ANDREW LLOYD WEBBER AND TIM RICE AND PRODUCER CAMERON MACKINTOSH, THE STAGE MUSICAL HAD BEEN A VERY AMERICAN PHENOMENON. Their combined success with modern musicals, such as Evita, Phantom Of The Opera and Les Miserables returned the stage musical to its roots. For its antecedents could be traced back to William Shakespeare who, as with Feste, the jester in Twelfth Night, would use a song as a light, diversionary tactic, but also as an oblique comment on the play's main theme. Similarly, Louis XIV at Versailles would be entertained by players who incorporated words and music. Superficially light-hearted, these entertainments may have possessed an extra dimension that sought to comment upon the affairs of the court, but that was due more to the demands of topicality than to challenging protocol. The notion of drama and music remained unassailably high-brow as opera, with its production values and sometimes complex storylines, dominated until the late 19th century, when the light opera of Franz Lehar and Sigmund Romberg started to attract audiences beyond the cultured elite.

Despite the arrival of light opera, impresarios such as George Edwardes developed thematic shows of song and dance as early as 1892 when In Town and Gaiety Girl (1893) attracted substantial audiences. However it was Lehar's The Merry Widow that kick-started the genre into action, inspiring a spate of musicals such as Watch Your Step (1914), Chu Chin Chow (1916), No, No Nanette and Rose Marie (1924) and The Desert Song (1926). Writers like Irving Berlin, Rodgers & Hart, Jerome Kern and Otto Harbach, Rodgers & Hammerstein, George & Ira Gershwin and, even, Noel Coward, who was not above casting aspersions over the legitimacy of the form, used the theatre almost as a vehicle for some of the definitive popular songs of the 20th century.

Although individual songs often over-shadowed the opus whence they came, many shows such as Berlin's Annie Get Your Gun (1946), Rodgers & Hart's Pal Joey (1940), Kern & Hammerstein's Showboat (1927), Rodgers & Hammerstein's Oklahoma (1943), George & Ira Gershwin's Lady Be Good (1924), Frederick Loewe's My Fair Lady (1956) and Coward's Cavalcade (1931) succeeded in becoming popular by virtue of

their narrative strengths. As a result, many of these shows were filmed, marking Hollywood's Golden Age between the late 1930s and early 1950s when the the musical provided distraction – allegedly – from the rigours of the Depression and World War II. This was hardly a surprising development in itself, for many had predicted that with the coming of sound to the movies in The Jazz Singer, the stage musical would become obsolete. For Busby Berkeley in The Gold Diggers Of 1933, with its visual tricks and elaborate production values, indicated the way forward, but still Hollywood depended on the stage musical as a vital sounding board.

During the late 1940s the stage musical was challenged by television more than cinema and its decline was precipitate. But in the late 1950s that decline was arrested by a series of musicals that revelled in the starkness of the sets: it was almost as if the theatre had come to terms with the limitations of the genre and decided to make those a virtue rather than a hindrance. Leonard Bernstein's West Side Story (1957) paved the way for the expressionist naturalism of shows such as A Chorus Line and Cabaret. While Hollywood filmed these shows, it proved the resilience of the genre and now as the stage musical booms once again, the circle is complete as Andrew Lloyd Webber's biggest success, Sunset Boulevard (1994), confirms: a stage musical based on a film. Furthermore Pete Townsend's rock opera, Tommy, finally made it to the stage after it had been filmed and recorded as a show. As Al Jolson prophetically opined in The Jazz Singer, 'you ain't seen nothing yet!' He could be right.

above: In 1943 Oklahoma! marked a radical breakthough in the stage musical, with a dynamic integration of book, song and dance on a scale never seen previously. As with many shows that followed, its narrative strength enabled it to transfer to the Hollywood screen virtually unchanged.

1922, NOVEMBER 26: BRITISH ARCHAEOLOGIST HOWARD CARTER OPENS THE SEALED TOMB OF THE ANCIENT EGYPTIAN PHARAOH TUTANKHAMEN IN LUXOR TO REVEAL SOME OF THE GREATEST TREASURES OF ALL TIME

right: The original poster for Porgy and Bess, the Gershwin masterpiece with lyrics by Ira Gershwin and DuBose Heyward.

below: George Gershwin composing at the piano

GEORGE & IRA GERSHWIN

THE PARTNERSHIP OF GEORGE & IRA GERSHWIN WAS THE TRANSCENDENT INFLUENCE ON THE DEVELOPMENT OF POPULAR SONGWRITING IN THE FIRST HALF OF THIS CENTURY. Both separately or individually they impacted on just about all facets of contemporary music. George was born Jacob Gershvin on September 26, 1898, and his older brother Israel (Ira) was born on December 6, 1896. Both were born in New York to an itinerant businessman, who actively encouraged his sons' artistic leanings by providing them with a piano. Initially, Ira took lessons, but his interests were more literary than musical; as a student he would write pieces for his college magazine. George, on the other hand, took up the piano with some enthusiasm and studied under the tutelage of Charles Hambitzer, who gave him a solid grounding in classical music and in mastering the finer points of playing the piano. This mastery enabled him, after a stint as a song plugger, to become accompanist to the vaudeville entertainer Nora Bayes. By this time, Ira had started to compose lyrics under the pseudonym of Arthur Francis and, in 1918, Bayes performed the first song the two brothers wrote together, 'The Real American Folk Song'. That, however, was not George's first composition; that honour belonged to 'When You Want 'Em, You Can't Have 'Em, When You Have 'Em, You Don't Want 'Em', which he wrote with Murray Roth and which became a hit for Sophie Tucker.

In 1919, George scored his first big hit, 'Swanee'. Later to be popularised by Al Jolson and to become the clarion call of sound in the movies, it featured a lyric by Irving Caesar. By 1924, Ira – whose first big success was the stage musical Two Little Girls In Blue (1921) – had become George's regular lyricist. Together they wrote a plethora of tunes and shows that included Lady Be Good (1924), Oh Kay! (1926), which featured 'Someone To Watch Over Me', and Funny Face (1927). Apart from these stage musicals, songs such as 'Nice Work If You Can Get It', 'Let's Call The Whole Thing Off' and 'They Can't Take That Away From Me' have become popular standards with everyone from Frank Sinatra and Ella Fitzgerald to jazz musicians such as Miles Davis and Gerry Mulligan offering up their readings. In 1924, Swing bandleader Paul Whiteman performed George's symphonic work, Rhapsody In Blue, at the concert An Experiment In Modern Music at New York's Aeolian Hall; other pieces

right: One of the most memorable instrumental readings of the music from Porgy and Bess was the 1958 collaboration between Miles Davis and arranger Gil Evans.

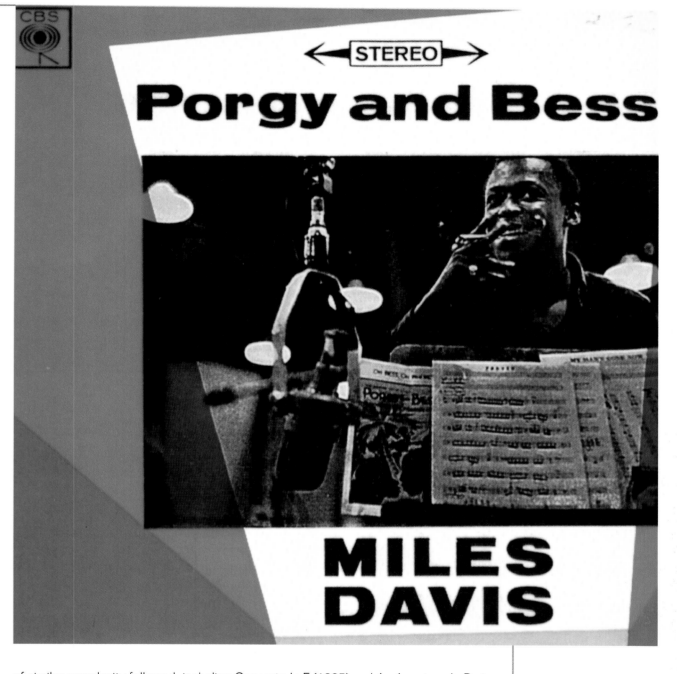

of similar complexity followed, including Concerto In F (1925) and An American In Paris (1927). But his best was yet to come, for in 1935 he presented the opera Porgy And Bess. Delving deep into the cultural heritage of Black America, it encapsulated elements of blues, folk and jazz without ever losing its dramatic coherence. If its reception was initially muted, it certainly made up for it in later years, when its broad-based themes proved adaptable to virtually any medium – TV, stage or film.

George died of a brain tumour on July 11, 1937. Ira continued to work, collaborating with Vernon Duke (Goldwyn Follies, 1938), Kurt Weill (Lady In The Dark, 1941), Jerome Kern (Cover Girl, 1944), Harry Warren (The Berkleys Of Broadway, 1949) and Harold Arlen (A Star Is Born, 1954), until his retirement in the early 1960s. Ira died on August 17, 1983.

right: In Jazz On A Summer's Day, the film record of the 1958 Newport Jazz Festival.

centre right: Louis mugging it with Bing Crosby – who he influenced immensely in the crooner's early days – on the movie set of High Society.

far right : 'Satch' at his height as a real pop star in the late 20s, after his recordings with the Hot Five and Hot Seven catapulted him to solo fame.

LOUIS ARMSTRONG

below: Louis Armstrong's recording career began with the legendary Hot Five sides in the mid 20s, and continued for forty years with hit singles, live albums, movie soundtracks and a host of collaborations which included (bottom) his critically acclaimed 1957 album sessions with Ella Fitzgerald.

THE LARGER THAN LIFE FIGURE OF TRUMPETER AND CORNETIST LOUIS ARMSTRONG SEEMED TO BESTRIDE THE JAZZ AGE LIKE A COLOSSUS. For Armstrong's technical virtuosity as a musician was beyond reproach, while his ability to draw from his roots in vaudeville and minstrelsy showed him to be at ease in any milieu: on stage, on a Hollywood sound-stage, in a club – anywhere. And wherever he played, whatever he did, he did it with style and grace, ensuring that everyone he worked with was keen to repeat the experience.

Born on July 4, 1898, in New Orleans, Louisiana, his early life was spent in the red-light district of Storyville, where he learnt to play the cornet in the Coloured Waif's Home. As a teenager, he delivered coal, but started to sit in with the Kid Ory band, among others, replacing King Oliver, who had moved to Chicago, on one occasion. In 1919 he got his break as a professional musician working alongside drummer Baby Dodds on the Mississippi riverboats in Fate Marable's band. By 1922, Armstrong had gravitated to Chicago to play in King Oliver's Creole Jazz Band, which led to recording sessions for Columbia, Gennett and OKeh. With Oliver and Armstrong developing a novel dual cornet style, titles such as 'Chimes Blues' and 'Riverside Blues' showed his potential. In 1924, Armstrong met his future second wife, Lil Hardin, who encouraged him to go to New York to join Fletcher Henderson's band. Despite the constraints imposed by the tight arrangements in Henderson's band, Armstrong's improvisational style

won him admirers and, with his star in the ascendant, Henderson got him to sing 'Everybody Loves My Baby'. This adaptability encouraged classic blues singers like Bessie Smith and Ma Rainey to use Armstrong as an accompanist on titles such as W.C. Handy's 'St Louis Blues' and 'See See Rider Blues' respectively.

On his return to Chicago in 1925, Armstrong appeared in Erskine Tate and Carroll Dickerson's bands, as well as leading his own outfit, but more important were his recordings with the Hot Five or, occasionally, Hot Seven. Cutting around sixty sides for the OKeh label, Armstrong confirmed that he had mastered the New Orleans ensemble style of playing and had, in fact, moved way beyond it, establishing full improvisation as the way forward in jazz. With line-ups that included Lil Armstrong and Earl 'Fatha' Hines (piano), Johnny Dodds (clarinet) and Kid Ory (trombone), Armstrong shifted from cornet to trumpet.

While his stature as a highly individual jazz musician developed, he took on a parallel career as a popular

NEWS

1926, JANUARY 27: SCOTTISH INVENTOR JOHN LOGIE BAIRD MAKES THE WORLD'S FIRST TELEVISION TRANSMISSIONS

vocalist, performing scat vocals on 'Heeby Jeebies' (1926) and then appearing in the Broadway revue, Hot Chocolates, where he sang Fats Waller's 'Ain't Misbehavin'' (1930). Throughout the 1930s, Armstrong's career as a vocalist flourished as he recorded ballads such as 'You're Drivin' Me Crazy' and 'I'm Confessin'' and pop songs like 'You Rascal You'. Furthermore, he recorded with a host of stars, such as The Mills Brothers, Tommy Dorsey, Louis Jordan and Ella Fitzgerald. In 1936, his film career started with an appearance in the musical Pennies From Heaven, co-starring Bing Crosby, and that was followed by appearances in Arthur Freed's Cabin In The Sky (1943) and New Orleans (1947).

In the meantime, he continued leading a series of big bands that succeeded in harnessing the contemporaneous enthusiasm for Swing, while retaining the flavour of the New Orleans style. Touring the US constantly combined with occasional visits to Europe, Armstrong did much to elevate the profile of jazz and this achieved its apotheosis with the formation of the Louis Armstrong All-Stars in 1947. Featuring the likes of trombonist Jack Teagarden, clarinettist Barney Bigard and Earl 'Fatha' Hines, the All-Stars were the highest-paid jazz group on the circuit and, despite frequent changes in personnel, managed to combine showmanship with musical excellence. Indeed, in 1960, they were sponsored by the US government and Pepsi-Cola to undertake a 45-date tour of Africa. While that might have appeared adventurous, Armstrong's

appearance alongside Frank Sinatra, Bing Crosby and Grace Kelly in the musical High Society had predicated the aura of invincibility that surrounded him.

During the 1960s he co-starred with Barbra Streisand in the musical Hello Dolly (1964) – Armstrong's record 'Hello Dolly' dislodged The Beatles, who had notched up 14 consecutive weeks at the top of the US charts. But this wasn't a flash in the pan, for other hits included Edith Piaf's 'La Vie En Rose', Fats Domino's 'Blueberry Hill', Kurt Weill's 'Mack The Knife' and 'What A Wonderful World'. He also recorded several jazz albums, cutting selections from George Gershwin's Porgy & Bess (1960), with Ella Fitzgerald, as well as collaborations with Duke Ellington and Dave Brubeck.

Although in the post-war years he was regarded as something of an 'Uncle Tom' by many young Blacks, Armstrong was raised at a time when the riposte to militancy was a beating, at best, so he had learnt how to use the system to his own advantage. He died of kidney and liver failure on July 6, 1971, in New York.

CLASSIC BLUES

AFTER MAMIE SMITH RECORDED 'CRAZY BLUES' IN 1920, RECORD LABELS INDULGED IN A FEEDING FRENZY. These were the early days of the record industry and any method that might generate sales was considered fair game. The blues, too, was in its infancy as an indigent style. W.C. Handy had already established some parameters with a body of influential songs such as 'St Louis Blues', but it was female singers such as Alberta Hunter, Ma Rainey, Bessie Smith, Clara Smith, Victoria Spivey and Ethel Waters who assembled a canon of recorded material that has come to be regarded as Classic Blues. For these Classic Blues sides were distinct from their male counterparts in that most of these female vocalists used small jazz groups or pianists such as Clarence Williams or Fletcher Henderson.

While Bessie Smith was the most influential in the long-term, Ma Rainey's output has only been overshadowed due to the inferior quality of the recording facilities she had at her disposal. When she first started recording the blues in the 1920s, she had already led an accomplished career in vaudeville. In 1923, she recorded titles like 'See See Rider Blues', with Henderson and Louis Armstrong, 'Oh My Baby Blues', with Coleman Hawkins, and 'Deep Moanin' Blues', with future gospel writer Thomas A. Dorsey and guitarist Tampa Red. Once the Depression cut in, Ma Rainey's career was over and she retired in 1933. Victoria Spivey's career lasted longer, but the circumstances were little different from those of Rainey. Recording 'Black Snake Blues' in 1926 to her own piano accompaniment, she went on to cut 'Toothache Blues' (1928), with guitarist Lonnie Johnson, 'Funny Feathers' (1929), with Armstrong, and 'Moanin' The Blues' (1929), with Henry 'Red' Allen's New York Orchestra. For the remainder of her career, she toured constantly, playing the clubs and even starting her own label in the 1960s to reissue her old material.

Ethel Waters, though, was the doyenne of the black entertainer. Known initially as 'Sweet Mama Stringbean', she performed in vaudeville until 1921 when she hooked up with Fletcher Henderson. This led to sessions for W.C. Handy's Black Swan label, where she cut titles like 'St Louis Blues', 'Tiger Rag' and 'Georgia Blues'. Sessions with pianists James P. Johnson and Clarence Williams followed. In 1925, she replaced Florence Mills in Plantation Revue. Gradually, she moved more towards the theatre for

MA RAINEY
MA RAINEY'S BLACK BOTTOM
Milestone

BESSIE SMITH
THE COMPLETE RECORDINGS, VOL.1-4
Columbia

left: The great Ida Cox, from a newspaper advertisement which described her as 'The Uncrowned Queen of the Blues'.

below left: The label for Ma Rainey's 'Dream Blues', during her recording career which lasted through the 1920s.

sources of material, appearing in and recording Harold Arlen's Stormy Weather in 1933. However, she continued to work with jazz musicians such as Duke Ellington or the Swing bandleaders Tommy and Jimmy Dorsey and Benny Goodman. As her career progressed, she was brought to Hollywood with greater frequency for roles in films such as Cabin In The Sky (1942), Pinky (1949) and The Sound And The Fury (1959).

Alberta Hunter's career as a vocalist commenced in a Chicago brothel before gravitating to the more salubrious company of musicians such as Armstrong, Henderson, Sidney Bechet, Eubie Blake and Fats Waller. While her records were excellent, it was in the London production of Showboat, opposite Paul Robeson, that her career temporarily ignited. In 1954 she retired from showbusiness and took up nursing; then, after her retirement from nursing, she resumed her showbusiness career, providing the soundtrack for the movie Remember My Name, in 1978.

Although these blues performers were at their peak in the years before the Depression, they provided the link between the rural blues and the big band jazz vocalists of the 1930s, such as Billie Holiday and Mildred Bailey.

right: The Empress of the Blues, Bessie Smith, in a series of albums of her greatest recordings that was released during the 1950s.

the BESSIE SMITH story VOL.2

Blues to Barrelhouse

WEEPING WILLOW BLUES
JAZZBO BROWN FROM MEMPHIS TOWN
THE GIN HOUSE BLUES
POOR MAN'S BLUES
ME AND MY GIN
NOBODY KNOWS YOU WHEN YOU'RE DOWN AND OUT
GIMME A PIGFOOT
TAKE ME FOR A BUGGY RIDE
DO YOUR DUTY
I'M DOWN IN THE DUMPS
BLACK MOUNTAIN BLUES
NEW ORLEANS HOP SCOP BLUES

PHILIPS Minigroove 33⅓

1927, MAY 21: AMERICAN CHARLES LINDBERGH COMPLETES THE FIRST SOLO, NON-STOP ATLANTIC FLIGHT FROM NEW YORK TO PARIS

BESSIE SMITH

IN ALL PROBABILITY IF BESSIE SMITH HADN'T EMERGED WHEN SHE
DID, THE HISTORY OF BLACK AMERICAN MUSIC WOULD HAVE BEEN
SUBSTANTIALLY DIFFERENT. For Smith, dubbed The Empress Of The Blues,
took blues and jazz and imparted her own style to the phrasing, which ultimately
rendered it accessible and appealing to countless others. As a consequence, Smith's
influence is discernible in the work of Dinah Washington, Diana Krall, Mahalia Jackson,
Billie Holiday and Janis Joplin.

Born in Chattanooga, Tennessee, on April 15th, 1894, Smith developed her skills
on the vaudeville circuit, alongside Ma Rainey, among others. After starting to work
with jazz bands, she was signed to the Columbia label by Frank Walker in 1923.
Accompanied by Fletcher Henderson or Clarence Williams, her early sides included
'Down Hearted Blues' and 'Gulf Coast Blues', which became immediate hits,
selling in excess of 750,000 copies, and even covers of Ma Rainey's 'Backwater
Blues' and 'Moonshine Blues'. The following year, Columbia launched a specialist
label for the 'race' market with 'Chicago Bound Blues'; this was followed by a
collaboration with Louis Armstrong on 'St Louis Blues'. Although many others have
recorded 'St Louis Blues', the Smith-Armstrong version comes pretty close to being
definitive. Furthermore, she didn't restrict herself to Armstrong either, for she often
worked with cornetists Joe Smith and Tommy Ladnier, clarinettist Don Redman and
pianist James P. Johnson.

Despite her mastery of the blues, she also recorded songs like Irving Berlin's
'Alexander's Ragtime Band', 'I Want Every Bit Of It', 'On Revival Day' and 'A Good
Man Is Hard To Find'. However, with the coming of the Depression and with it a
change in tastes, Smith slipped out of vogue. Throughout her heyday, though, she had
toured in shows such as Harlem Frolics, Steamboat Days and Happy Times. These
kept her in touch with her roots in the theatre. In 1929, she starred in a short
dramatised film, St Louis Blues, but as her popularity waned her contract with
Columbia was not renewed; producer John Hammond did, however, cut some sides
for the Columbia subsidiary OKeh in 1933, with Jack Teagarden, Chu Berry and Benny
Goodman. Although only four sides were cut, Smith showed her versatility by

classic blues

below and opposite: Bessie Smith, true to the Vaudeville tradition from which she emerged, was a flamboyant, stylish dresser, wearing spectacular outfits that confirmed the commercial 'show biz' – indeed, 'pop' music – nature of the blues market, in which she was without doubt the most successful participant.

matching the vitality of what was later to be described as Swing. Even so these remained her final sessions.

While her popularity was unassailable at its peak and she was earning large amounts of money, her husband, Jack Gee – a former policeman – was totally unscrupulous in the handling of her finances, even using her money to set up the career in showbusiness of mistress Gertrude Saunders. When she died (September 26, 1937) in Clarksdale, Mississippi, as the result of injuries received in a car crash, she was interred in an unmarked grave on the outskirts of Philadelphia. Despite various benefits, her grave remained unmarked until 1970 when singer Janis Joplin, among others, provided the cash for a gravestone.

1928, SEPTEMBER 15: BRITISH SCIENTIST SIR ALEXANDER FLEMING REPORTS HIS DISCOVERY OF PENICILLIN, ONE OF THE MOST IMPORTANT ADVANCES IN THE HISTORY OF MEDICINE

below and right: Bill Monroe, the founding father of what later came to be known as Bluegrass, seen also (centre of picture) with his group The Blue Grass Boys performing on the Grand Ole' Opry.

BLUEGRASS

ACOUSTIC IN ORIGIN, BLUEGRASS HAS ALWAYS BEEN ASSOCIATED WITH THE RURAL MOUNTAIN REGION OF KENTUCKY, NORTH CAROLINA AND NORTH-EAST TENNESSEE. It became popularised in the 1930s by Bill Monroe and his group, The Blue Grass Boys, who gave Bluegrass its status as one of the premier indigenous folk styles of the US. However, its history was rather more blurred, springing from a vast number of string-bands in the 20s and early 30s, who in turn were influenced by gospel, old-time traditional music and the blues. As often the case, Bluegrass was a hybrid that owed its existence to a floating population of immigrants from the UK and Eastern Europe. Scrutiny of the folk songs collected by Hungarian composer Bela Bartok suggests a stronger link with Bluegrass than might be immediately apparent.

As Bluegrass evolved, it took on different regional flavours: the Bluegrass from Northern California has a stronger folk bias than its Los Angeles counterpart, which seems to draw as much inspiration from The Hot Club Of France of Django Reinhardt and Stephane Grapelli as from the hill regions of Tennessee. Similarly the Bluegrass scene of Washington D.C. was at variance to that of the Carolinas: for example Earl Scruggs's three-finger banjo picking style – a trademark of Monroe's sound during Scruggs's tenure with The Blue Grass Boys – was a characteristic of the region in North Carolina where Scruggs was born.

Bluegrass hit a commercial peak after the war, when Monroe along with Flatt & Scruggs and The Carter

NEWS

1929, OCTOBER 28: PLUMMETING SHARE PRICES ON THE NEW YORK STOCK EXCHANGE – THE WALL STREET CRASH – HERALD THE BEGINNING OF THE GREAT DEPRESSION OF THE THIRTIES

left: As Lonzo & Oscar the Sullivan brothers were a country-comedy act with their roots in Bluegrass, popular in the 1940s and 50s via regular appearances on the 'Opry.

below: One of the so-called 'newgrass' singers, Emmylou Harris' music helps keep the Bluegrass tradition alive.

Brothers helped give it wider acceptance through their broadcasts from Nashville's Grand Ole Opry. What was even more striking was that Bluegrass, with its close harmony vocals, proved itself to be ideally suited to radio, for the use of open mics gave the unamplified acoustic instruments an immediacy that was not half as effective in a concert hall or club environment. As the influence of radio grew, so broadcasters became less keen on allowing any specific regional style to dominate. Consequently by the time Elvis Presley and rock'n'roll emerged, regional styles of folk music had been supplanted in the affections of the listening public. It is worth mentioning, however, that one of Elvis's earliest sides was none other than 'Blue Moon Of Kentucky', which was composed by a certain William Monroe.

For much of the 1950s, Bluegrass languished as a regional style, beloved by its followers, but marginalised nevertheless. In the early 1960s, it was revitalised by the development and growth of a festival circuit. Initially, this circuit had its roots in religious camp meetings, where the tone was pious and the mood was zealous. Gradually, however, as they grew in popularity, professional musicians of a religious bent were booked to play these events. Taking place throughout the summer months, the quality of musicianship quickly attracted young musicians keen to demonstrate their chops alongside their putative heroes. Into this atmosphere, a new generation of Bluegrass players emerged and many of them, such as Vassar Clements, Peter Rowan and Buddy Spicher, ended up playing in

Monroe's group, as well as Ricky Skaggs in Ralph Stanley's Clinch Mountain Boys. From this point it was but a small step to the folk festival circuit: Monroe set the precedent in 1963 with his appearance at the University of Chicago Folk Festival.

By the early 1970s, younger players were using amplified instruments (acoustic instruments with pick-ups) and another variant came into circulation. Dubbed 'newgrass', it used Bluegrass as the template, but allowed more room for improvisation and experimentation. Although Bluegrass remains traditional in flavour, performers such as Emmylou Harris, Steve Earle and Alison Krauss have consistently demonstrated that far from being an obsolete form, Bluegrass is as penetrative as ever and illustrative of one of America's most purist of folk styles.

POP ESCAPISM

The 1930s saw popular music, as both an industry and as part of the social fabric, flourish as never before. It was the time of the great songwriters, their work now appearing on the cinema screen (after the birth of sound 'talkies' in 1927) as well as the Broadway and West End stage. Jazz-influenced music proliferated too, in the form of the big Swing bands that met an unprecedented demand from dancers in the dance halls and ballrooms that were the main social activity of the decade along with the cinema – especially among the single young. By the end of the decade, bandleaders like Harry James and Benny Goodman were truly the pop stars of their day.

Ironically, the escapism the music and movies represented was set against the worst ravages of the Depression, and in America particularly this impacted on the popular folk music of the day, in the Dust Bowl ballads of Woody Guthrie, and Black blues and gospel music across the rural South. But whatever the realities in the open spaces where much of later US popular music was being born, back in the big cities the Wild West was still represented by Hollywood's singing cowboys with clean fringed shirts and pearly white teeth, household names across the English-speaking world.

1930-1940

right: Bandleader Ray Anthony
wields his trumpet among a
crowd of chorus-girl fans.

left: The great Irving Berlin
(wearing glasses) at a
Broadway rehearsal in 1962.

THE POPULAR SONG

WHILE THE CONCEPT OF 'THE POPULAR SONG' WAS VERY MUCH THE RAISON D'ETRE OF TIN PAN ALLEY, where writers such as Harry Von Tilzer and George M. Cohan endeavoured to prophesy or cajole the mood swings of the general public, both vaudeville and music hall had contributed to its genesis. It was generally accepted that there were certain chord progressions that could trigger specific responses in the listener – diminished fifths and minor keys could elicit nostalgia, for example – and patriotic songs such as Cohan's 'Over There' used this method successfully to produce the desired effect. Songwriters were also endeavouring to win larger audiences by adapting indigent American styles to address broader themes, and, with the coming of sound to the film industry and the emergence of radio as the principal means of popular entertainment, there was suddenly a vast market for new songs.

Through this need for songs, bandleaders were obliged to pull in every trick in the book to make their band different from the rest. Vocalists were one way to do this; the other was by employing an arranger who had such a distinctive style that his handwriting in the arrangement was instantly recognisable. Against this backdrop, popular hits from the shows could be transformed to highlight the individual strengths of each performer or soloist. Furthermore, arrangers could make adjustments to the songs so that they would fit snugly into the band's repertoire. Often this meant making significant changes: for example, in Pal Joey (1940), there is a spoken coda, which effectively introduces 'My Funny Valentine'. These codas were theatrical devices used to mark a smooth transition from spoken dialogue to song. If a band was going to play 'My Funny Valentine', some arrangers adapted the coda to the requirements of the band. Of course, some bands just dispensed entirely with the coda.

Consequently, the popular hits of the 1930s and 1940s possessed structures that were strong enough to withstand any amount of rearranging. Hence the term 'a standard' was coined. Although novelty songs also enjoyed popularity, these were designed to reflect contemporaneous moods, attitudes or trends. Therefore, their shelf-life was proscribed. Above all, though, the popular songs were governed by the dictates of the 78 rpm record, which meant that no song could exceed three minutes in duration. This

below right: Magazines that were devoted purely to song lyrics were popular, as well as the actual sheet music.

below: A typical piece of sheet music on the cover of which, as well as the songwriting credits, there was usually featured a photo of the main artist to have recorded the song.

was deemed as the optimum timespan for playlisting by radio stations. That situation continued until the rock era.

With the decline in popularity of the big band and the growth of independent record labels after the Second World War, more and more songwriters began to emerge, causing a greater choice of material on offer for singers to record. Still, however, periodically a song was penned that stirred imaginations: 'My Way' was Frank Sinatra's theme song for a spell. Such was its impact that it has been recorded by everyone from Sid Vicious of the Punk band, The Sex Pistols, to Elvis Presley. The Beatles' 'Yesterday', penned by Paul McCartney, has been covered by around 1500 different artists at one time or another. Even 'I Don't Know How To Love Him' by Andrew Lloyd Webber and Tim Rice from the musical Jesus Christ Superstar has been covered by artists such as opera star Kiri Te Kanawa.

In the 1990s, few writers seem inclined to come up with songs that can endure in quite the same way as their counterparts in the 1930s and 1940s were able to do on a regular basis.

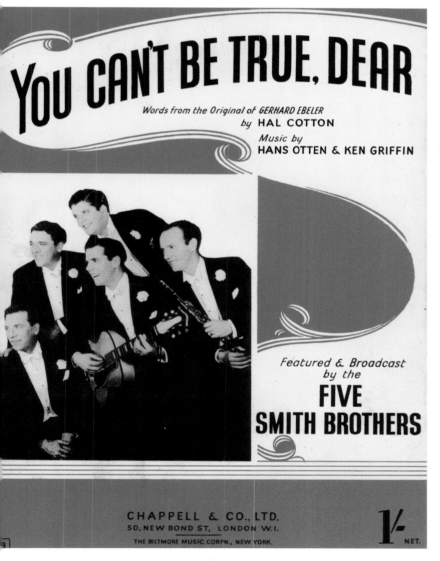

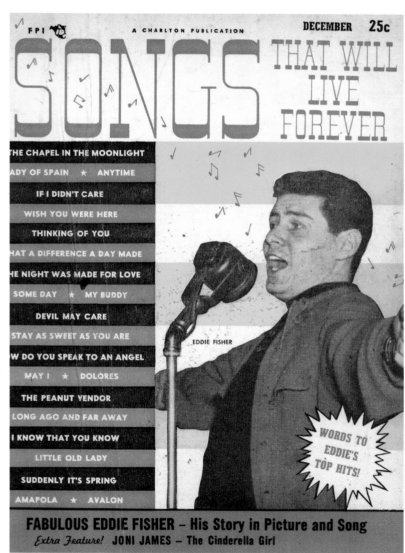

1930: MAHATMA GANDHI LAUNCHES HIS CAMPAIGN OF PEACEFUL CIVIL DISOBEDIENCE IN OPPOSITION TO BRITISH LEGISLATION IN INDIA

GREAT WRITERS

above: Sheet music for Rogers and Hammerstein's 'It Might As Well Be Spring' which carries details of the motion picture in which it was featured.

IF ANY EPOCH COULD BE DESCRIBED AS A GOLDEN AGE FOR THE SONGWRITER OR COMPOSER, it would be the era from the end of the First World War until the beginning of the Second World War. For during those 20-odd years, the entertainment industry underwent a series of drastic alterations that changed Western society irrevocably. Naturally, most of those changes were brought about by the creeping sophistication of technology, but political and economic factors also contributed in no small way.

In the first instance, and most significantly, was the inexorable rise in popularity of the gramophone record and the emergence of radio as the principal means of entertainment. These elements stimulated the market-place, creating an almost insatiable appetite for entertainments that could appeal to a broad cross-section of society. Therefore, while there was still a place for the comparatively highbrow classical music, it was the record industry that had the ability to reflect what was going on at the grass-roots. The Grand Ole Opry, broadcasting from Nashville radio station WSM from December 1927, endeavoured to satisfy the disparate agricultural communities. While the shows broadcast a mix of Hillbilly music, popular song and cornball humour, this early form of country music was very parochial and simplistic, but it assisted awareness of writers such as Jimmie Rodgers, Vernon Dalhart and Carson Robison. If country music received a fillip, the Swing era positively boomed as broadcasts from the nation's top dance halls were transmitted, coast to coast. While Tin Pan Alley writers such as Harry Von Tilzer and George M. Cohan and composers of light opera such as Rudolph Friml and Sigmund Romberg created a backdrop, it was the new younger writers, such as Irving Berlin, George and Ira Gershwin, Rodgers and Hart, Rodgers and Hammerstein and Jerome Kern, who could respond to and reflect the economic privations and social uncertainties of the period. Furthermore, despite the popularity of the stage musical, writers were responding to the challenge of composing tunes that would satisfy radio's needs: tunes required versatility now.

None answered the challenge better than Buddy DeSylva, Lew Brown and Ray Henderson, who managed to capture the spirit of the jazz age with titles such as 'Black Bottom', 'The Birth Of The Blues', 'Varsity Drag', 'The Best Things In Life Are Free',

the popular song

left: An Irving Berlin song sheet from 1914 of 'Along Came Ruth', which Berlin claims on the blurb to be 'the best song I ever wrote' – though in retrospect, certainly not one of the most memorable.

below: A semi-invalid, Cole Porter was perhaps the greatest songwriter of the century, with masterpieces that included 'Love For Sale', 'I Get A Kick Out Of You', 'Anything Goes', 'Everytime We Say Goodbye' and many more.

'You're The Cream In My Coffee', 'Button Up Your Overcoat' and 'If I Had A Talking Picture Of You'.

When sound came to the movies, a new range of possibilities opened up for the songwriter. For now the most obvious avenue to exploit with sound films was the musical. Without the physical limits imposed by the theatre stage, writers could now use vast subjects as the canvas for their shows. Oscar Hammerstein and Jerome Kern's Showboat was one of the first shows to be filmed; its suitability as a vehicle was predicated by the fact that it was filmed three times (1929, 1936 and 1951). Additionally, Kern's score depended heavily upon the influence of Black culture for its impact; the song 'Ol' Man River' was written for Paul Robeson after Kern had witnessed one of Robeson's gospel concerts. This suggested that writers would increasingly look beyond their own backyard for inspiration and that musical styles would cross-pollinate and mutate.

1931: THE NUMBER OF PEOPLE OUT OF WORK GROWS DRAMATICALLY IN MOST COUNTRIES, WITH UNEMPLOYMENT FIGURES DOUBLING IN MANY CASES BY THE FOLLOWING YEAR

THE SINGERS

THE FIRST GREAT RECORDING STAR OF THE 20TH CENTURY WAS OPERA STAR ENRICO CARUSO. Now, nearing the end of the century, the opera singer Luciano Pavarotti possesses almost as much commercial clout as his distinguished antecedent. Between these twin peaks of vocal excellence, a wide plain of varying styles have unfolded in the interim. While opera and stage musicals have afforded countless singers such as Kathleen Ferrier, Janet Baker, Joan Sutherland, Kiri Te Kanawa, Lesley Garrett, Richard Tauber, Robert Tear, Placido Domingo, Jose Carreras, Judy Garland and Ethel Merman the opportunity to shine, it has been in jazz or gospel that some of the century's great vocal stylists have emerged.

Of them all, Dinah Washington was one of the most important, providing a stylistic conduit between the gospel purity of Mahalia Jackson to the earthy ribaldry of R&B vocalist Big Mama Thornton. And in so doing, she provided the inspiration for generations of female vocalists to come, from Ruth Brown to Nancy Wilson, from Diana Ross to Millie Jackson, from Peggy Lee to Celine Dion, and from Cassandra Wilson to Whitney Houston. From 1943, when she first started working with Lionel Hampton, until her death in 1963, she cut titles like 'Baby Get Lost', 'I Wanna Be Loved', 'Cold Cold Heart', 'Trouble In Mind', 'Teach Me Tonight', 'What A Difference A Day Makes' and 'This Bitter Earth'. Dinah excelled with the steamy R&B of tunes like 'Baby Get Lost', but could also give a perfectly good account of herself on pop tunes such as 'I Wanna Be Loved', which was also covered by The Andrews Sisters. However, the high points occurred when she dug back into her gospel background and cut tunes like 'This Bitter Earth', which – as Ray Charles had done – fused elements of the secular and non-secular, resulting in a transcendent performance with virtually universal appeal. That was not all. For although Dinah records were targeted initially at black audiences, it soon became clear that she could cross over to white audiences. And this became manifestly clear by the national success of 'What A Difference A Day Makes' and 'September In The Rain'. To this day, Dinah remains under-rated.

Both Ella Fitzgerald and Billie Holiday, through their work with the bands of Chick Webb and Count Basie, possessed immaculate phrasing and timing. Where Ella excelled was in her ability to stamp her own indelible signature upon any tune she handled,

above: Two of the great interpreters of the popular song who teamed up together on a number of occasions, Billy Eckstine and Sarah Vaughan.

above right: Billie Holiday injected a unique jazz/blues style into her performance of standards and in doing so changed pop singing forever.

above: Ella Fitzgerald was certainly the best-known jazz-based singer to cross over into the popular mainstream.

centre: Dubbed 'The Misty Miss Christy', June Christy brought the cool approach of modern jazz to her delivery of a song.

right: From songs like 'The Folks Who Live On The Hill' to her big single hit 'Fever', Peggy Lee brought a smokey but perfectly pitched style to bear on a wide variety of material.

which was a feat in itself, as much of her material was culled from the great writers of the era, such as Cole Porter, Irving Berlin and George and Ira Gershwin. Billie Holiday was more in the mould of Classic Blues performers like Bessie Smith in that she could take a tune like 'What A Little Moonlight Can Do' or 'I Cried For You' and imbue it with such a depth of feeling and emotion that these hackneyed sentiments assumed a potency out of all proportion. This, consequently, made her rapport with soloists such as Lester Young and Johnny Hodges seem telepathic.

But while the Swing era yielded great individual stylists like Frank Sinatra, Dick Haymes and blues shouters such as Count Basie vocalist Jimmy Rushing, the most influential and pioneering singer to come out of the golden era of the popular song was Bing Crosby. With a background that included a stint in the Paul Whiteman Orchestra in the 1920s, he became the biggest-selling record artist of the whole period from the late 1890s to the early 1950s, with over 300 hits that ranged from 1931's 'I Surrender Dear' to his last Top Ten entry (in his lifetime) 'True Love', with Grace Kelly in 1956. His 'White Christmas' long held the accolade as the biggest-selling single of all time, making the charts again and again, both before and after his death in 1977.

Influenced by both the vaudeville approach of Al Jolson and the jazz styling of Louis Armstrong, Crosby almost single-handedly invented modern pop singing, with a casual, slightly husky voice that utilized the new-fangled microphone to supreme effect, singing to it as if it was the sole listener rather than warbling into it like it was some electronic megaphone, which was the approach adopted by most of his contemporaries in the early 30s. Nicknamed 'The Groaner', Bing Crosby laid the stylistic basis for all the crooners that would follow in his wake.

The crooners and big band singers through the 1940s developed this to a finely-honed art form, so much so that they are the yardstick by which so-called 'quality' singers have been judged ever since. And following the rock'n'roll era, individual stylists such as Barbra Streisand have managed to transcend genre to create their own distinctive styles. However, nowadays, at the end of the century, sophisticated production techniques have rendered instinctive talents like phrasing less important. Except, of course, in opera, where phrasing and timing remain the premier assets.

1932: CHARLES LINDBERGH'S SON IS KIDNAPPED FROM THE FAMILY HOME IN NEW JERSEY. THE CHILD IS FOUND DEAD TWO MONTHS LATER

FATS WALLER

IN COMMON WITH MANY FORMER STARS OF VAUDEVILLE, SUCH AS BESSIE SMITH, FATS WALLER'S INFLUENCE WAS TRANSCENDENT. His innate exuberance allied with an infectious geniality brought to life songs like 'Honeysuckle Rose', 'Ain't Misbehavin'' and 'Your Feet's Too Big'. Born on May 21, 1904, the son a Harlem Baptist minister, Waller started to play the piano at the age of six. When he was 14 he won a talent contest playing James P. Johnson's 'Carolina Shout'. While he showed an affinity with the stride piano, his phrasing brought in elements of Ragtime and Boogie-woogie: his style in other words had a swaggering gusto that fully expressed his robust nature. In 1920 he was signed by Ralph Peer to the OKeh label, where he recorded Mamie Smith's 'You Can't Keep A Good Man Down' and 'Muscle Shoals Blues'. During the 1920s, he developed his repertoire by working as a pianist accompanying silent films, while recording with Johnson, Fletcher Henderson, Adelaide Hall, Bessie Smith and the great baritone Gene Austin.

In 1925, he published his first composition, 'Squeeze', featuring lyrics by Clarence Williams. This led to a songwriting partnership with Andy Razoff, which resulted in compositions such as 'My Very Good Friend The Milkman' and 'Blue Turning Gray Over You'. As a consequence, he became sought after as a collaborator on revues such as Keep On Shufflin' (1928), with Johnson, and Hot Chocolates (1929), with Razoff; the latter featured 'Ain't Misbehavin''. While 'Ain't Misbehavin'' could reasonably be described as Waller's theme song, it crossed over to become a massive popular hit for a number of performers, including Louis Armstrong and Ruth Etting. This ability to pen a tune that had crossover potential was further illustrated with 'Honeysuckle Rose', which became a hit for The Dorsey Brothers and Fletcher Henderson, and 'I've Got A Feeling For You', which struck gold for Gene Austin. Other hits followed, including 'I'm Crazy 'Bout My Baby', 'Keepin' Out Of Mischief Now' and 'The Joint Is Jumpin''. Although his songs were delivered with a beaming lasciviousness, there was a tenderness and, even, innocence to tunes like 'Keepin' Out Of Mischief Now' or 'Ain't Misbehavin'' that, innuendo notwithstanding, were difficult to take exception to.

Throughout the 1930s Waller's career flourished, as he starred in several long-running radio shows, appeared in 'soundies' – designed for the visual jukeboxes –

the popular song

that were the precursors of videos, and made appearances in movies such as Hooray For Love (1936) and Stormy Weather (1943). As if anticipating the demise of the big band and the ascendancy of Jump band combos like Louis Jordan's Tympani 5, in 1934, Waller recorded with a five-piece backing band known as The Rhythm. The fact that he chose to record novelties such as 'Your Feet's Too Big' alongside 'I'm Gonna Sit Right Down And Write Myself A Letter' also proved just how far Waller was in touch with the mood of the time, when R&B would supplant Swing as the principal source of entertainment. Indeed when Waller ran a big band himself, it was one of his least successful ventures; interestingly, Louis Jordan failed to make the big band work for him either. After the outbreak of war, Waller continued touring, dying of pneumonia whilst travelling to New York from Los Angeles in 1943. During the 1970s, the stage musical Ain't Misbehavin' enjoyed a Broadway run.

Even after all these years, Waller remains an entertainer of the highest pedigree, who seemingly never needed to compromise: you got what you saw.

left: A typical publicity shot of the wide-eyed Fats Waller, taken in London in 1948.

right: A more candid shot of Waller which shows the wilder, earthier side to his delivery which became apparent when he got into full swing.

1933, JANUARY 30: ADOLF HITLER BECOMES GERMAN CHANCELLOR. IN A YEAR'S TIME HE WOULD BECOME FÜHRER OF THE THIRD REICH, LEADING GERMANY INEXORABLY TOWARDS WAR

left: The universally acclaimed 'King of Swing' Benny Goodman, whose band was one of the first to have teenage bobby soxers jitterbugging in the aisles during their concert appearances across America.

SWING

below: Trumpet giant Harry James, one of the main players in the Swing boom, whose highly commercial band featured star vocalists that included Dick Haymes and the young Frank Sinatra.

TIME FOR ANOTHER SWEEPING STATEMENT: JAZZ HAS EXERTED THE BIGGEST INFLUENCE OF ALL MUSICAL GENRES ON CONTEMPORARY MUSIC IN THE 20TH CENTURY. For evidence of such a bold assertion, one only needs to go back to the 1930s when Swing was King. Although Ragtime, Dixieland, the blues and gospel had all impacted upon contemporary music to some extent, Swing crossed over, adapting to the demands of the market-place without becoming diluted. The point was that Swing reflected a fundamental aspect of music making: either you could Swing or you couldn't. There was no middle ground. Another point was that Swing – like R&B – evolved through the demands of audiences to be entertained. As the US sank deeper into the mire of Depression during the 1920s, entertainment became more essential: something had to deflect attention from the economic grimness and the climate of social deprivation.

The turning point came one evening in February, 1924, when Paul Whiteman presented a concert at New York's Aeolian Hall, entitled An Experiment In Modern Music. One minute Whiteman was just another leader, fronting a big band with the gallumphing grace and elegance of an elephant in tights, the next he was 'The King Of Jazz' – it should have been 'King Of The Jazz Age'. That evening, playing light opera standards and Gershwin's 'Rhapsody In Blue', he showed the possibilities for a big band when playing what could best be described as a form of Symphonic Jazz. Fletcher Henderson took note and, with arranger Don Redman, put together a big band that luxuriated in its power. With Redman's arrangements and musicians such as Louis Armstrong and Coleman Hawkins, Henderson's band was the standard by which others were judged. Naturally, as Duke Ellington and Count Basie started to develop their big band style, white musicians like Benny Goodman, Tommy Dorsey and Glenn Miller started to adapt Henderson's arrangements.

However, each band needed its own figure-head – Goodman and Artie Shaw were fine clarinettists, Dorsey's trombone was his trademark and later drummer Gene Krupa, vibraphonist Lionel Hampton and trumpeter Harry James formed their own outfits. While many of these bands boasted high quality musicianship and star names, they drew crowds that just wanted to dance. As the dance bands dominated, so vocalists

BEST OF BIG BANDS
DORIS DAY
WITH LES BROWN

I LET A SONG GO OUT OF MY HEART

Words by IRVING MILLS and HENRY NEMO   Music by DUKE ELLINGTON

AS FEATURED WITH GREAT SUCCESS BY *Benny Goodman* AND HIS ORCHEST[...]

MILLS MU[...]
Music Publi[...]
1619 Broadway, N[...]

were added and crooners such as Frank Sinatra, Bing Crosby and Dick Haymes were able to perform their own versions of popular hits from stage shows or the great writers of the day, but with the added lustre of sparkling new arrangements. Therefore, while the Swing era possessed formidable popular appeal, some of the bands, such as Chick Webb's with Ella Fitzgerald and Count Basie with Lester Young, were able to break genuinely new ground. Because of its widespread use as the prime dance music of the day, Swing created almost single-handedly the mass popularity of the gramophone record as the premier entertainment medium.

It was with the vocal accompaniments, however, that the Swing era brokered a new phase in the development of popular music, for styles varied so wildly. Vocal groups such The Ink Spots and The Mills Brothers provided the template for later R&B groups such as The Orioles and The Ravens; solo performers such as Sinatra inspired a range of singers from the uptown crooning of Tony Bennett, through the easy accessibility of MOR performers like Andy Williams, to the relative purism of jazz stylists like Mel Tormé. Female vocalists like Ella Fitzgerald, Sarah Vaughan and Dinah Washington were – through their phrasing – able to encompass elements of the blues and gospel in their interpretations.

By the outbreak of war big bands had become uneconomic to run and a slimmed-down ensemble supplanted them, with musicians like Louis Jordan playing a style of Jump Blues that provided the basis for rhythm & blues.

above: Sheet music for a Duke Ellington tune, 'I Let A Song Go Out Of My Heart', which was recorded by (among others) Benny Goodman.

left: The youthful Doris Day with Les Brown ('and his band of renown') when she was a Swing band singer before her days of Hollywood stardom.

1934, MAY 23: OUTLAWS BONNIE AND CLYDE ARE KILLED IN A POLICE AMBUSH IN LOUISIANA. BOTH THEY AND BANK ROBBER JOHN DILLINGER HAD BECOME POPULAR HEROES IN DEPRESSION-TORN AMERICA

GLENN MILLER

above: Glenn Miller in a familiar pose, actually taken as a publicity shot for the 1942 movie featuring him and his band, Orchestra Wives.

DESPITE HIS PREMATURE DEATH OVER THE ENGLISH CHANNEL DURING THE SECOND WORLD WAR, the music of Glenn Miller continues to evoke the Swing era in the minds of most people. For not only did he write or arrange memorable tunes such as 'Moonlight Serenade' and 'Little Brown Jug', he was also portrayed by the ever phlegmatic James Stewart in the movie about his life, The Glenn Miller Story (1954).

Born in Clarinda, Iowa, on March 1, 1904, Miller grew up in the rural backwoods of Nebraska. In 1917, he was given his first trombone, which led to appearances with local dance bands. After studying at the University of Colorado, he performed with Boyd Senter's band in Denver, before packing up and heading out west to Los Angeles in 1926. Joining Ben Pollack's dance band, he turned his hand to arrangement, working on ''Deed I Do'. This was followed by another move, this time to the East coast, where he played with and arranged for Victor Young – who was himself soon to move out to Hollywood to work on soundtrack scores – cornetist Red Nichols, Ozzie Nelson – the father of rock'n'roll teen idol Rick Nelson – and, more significantly, the Dorsey Brothers' Orchestra. Miller's work with the Dorseys was to prove decisive with his arrangement of 'Stop, Look And Listen', which anticipated the call-and-response style of Swing. Furthermore Miller composed 'Dese Dem Dose', which led to greater productivity as a writer. Although Miller was not above harnessing phrases from other sources, he displayed an uncanny knack for stitching all the pieces together, making the whole infinitely superior to the sum of the individual parts.

Moving on once again, he joined English bandleader Ray Noble and put together an orchestra for him, which featured four saxophones and a clarinet. With every job he undertook, it seemed that another piece in the puzzle slotted into place for him, but the 'Glenn Miller Sound' would not be fully developed until the third incarnation of his orchestra. In 1935, he formed his first orchestra, which duly cut some sides for Columbia. In 1938, the third lineup of the orchestra came into being and its success was immediate, as hoards of young dancers went ape, jitterbugging all over the place.

Over the next three or four years, with vocalists like Kay Starr and crooner Ray Eberle, Miller's repertoire expanded to include titles like 'In The Mood', written by saxophonist Joe Garland and Fats Waller's lyricist Andy Razoff, and adopted by the British dance bandleader Joe Loss; 'Moonlight Serenade'; 'Little Brown Jug'; 'Pennsylvania 6-5000'; 'Tuxedo Junction'; 'When You Wish Upon A Star' from Walt Disney's Pinocchio; Harold Arlen's 'Over The Rainbow' from the Judy Garland musical The Wizard Of Oz (1940); Harry Warren's 'Chattanooga Choo Choo' from the movie Sun Valley Serenade (1941); 'Blueberry Hill', later a hit for rhythm and blues pianist Fats Domino; and 'American Patrol'. As it transpired, 'American Patrol' turned out to be his final hit, because he was drafted into the US Army Airforce, leading a service band for the USO.

Since his disappearance, the name of the Glenn Miller Orchestra has been kept alive, as officially authorised bands, initially under the leadership of clarinettist Buddy DeFranco, have toured the world constantly. Indeed, in the UK, the Syd Lawrence Orchestra built their career upon imitating the 'Miller Sound'. Above all, though, Miller's style of arrangement made a significant impact on bandleaders such as Nelson Riddle and Henry Mancini.

below: A moodily lit publicity photograph, typical of the period, featuring the Miller brass section, although an emphasis on the reeds on many numbers was what characterised the band's unique sound.

1935, APRIL: DUST STORMS SWEEP ACROSS THE AMERICAN MIDWEST, DESTROYING MUCH OF THE WORLD'S CORN CROP AND FORCING OVER 70,000 PEOPLE TO FLEE THE 'DUST BOWL' STATES

above: A publicity picture of Leadbelly, dressed as the rural working man in keeping with the wholesome image of the humble rural folk singer.

right: An altogether more atmospheric picture of Leadbelly in action, by the photographer William Gottlieb.

LEADBELLY

ALTHOUGH HIS PERSONAL LIFE WAS A DISASTER AREA, LEADBELLY DID MORE THAN ANY OTHER COUNTRY BLUES GUITARIST AND COMPOSER TO ELEVATE THE PUBLIC PERCEPTION OF THE BLUES AND FOLK SONG. While Woody Guthrie spoke eloquently on the plight of the agrarian class and their marginalisation by the growth of industrialised society, Leadbelly cut to the heart of the predominantly ill-educated and disenfranchised Black working class. Leadbelly's eye for

detail and ability to harness a simple melody with work-a-day images enabled him to address audiences beyond the immediate ambit of the blues singer.

Born Huddie William Ledbetter on January 29, 1889, in Mooringsport, Louisiana, Leadbelly spent his early years in Leigh in Texas. Here he learned to play the accordion, acquiring the nickname of Leadbelly in the process, as a result of his imposing physical presence and his supposed implacable demeanour. In the run-up to World War I, Leadbelly worked the bars, picking up

NEWS

1935, OCTOBER 2: ITALY INVADES ETHIOPIA. DESPITE EMPEROR HAILE SELASSIE'S APPEAL TO THE LEAGUE OF NATIONS AND AN INTERNATIONAL OUTCRY, MUSSOLINI'S FORCES ARE ALLOWED TO REMAIN IN POWER

left: Pete Seeger, a major player in the American folk music revival, who helped promote the work of Huddie Ledbetter, and worked with him on radio and in live dates.

the guitar and harmonica and, later, the piano as he went. In the course of his travels, he linked up with the great Texas bluesman, Blind Lemon Jefferson. Although Leadbelly never developed the wide-ranging stylistic variations of Jefferson, he adopted the spare style that would later become synonymous with Texan bluesmen such as Lightnin' Sam Hopkins.

Despite his popularity, Leadbelly's physical presence made him a target for local hard-men keen to prove their mettle. As a consequence, he served a term in Huntsville Penitentiary for murder between 1918 and 1925 and again for attempted murder in Angola, Louisiana, from 1930 until 1934. It is not beyond the realms of possibility that these two stints in prison did much to inform Leadbelly's subsequent preoccupation with humanitarian concerns. Indeed such was his eloquence that he was paroled into the care of folk-song collector and archivist John Lomax.

Under Lomax's eagle-eye, Leadbelly was launched into a series of lucrative, but perhaps slightly patronising, tours of concert halls up and down the East coast. Apart from the touring, Lomax initiated recording sessions for the Library Of Congress. Over the next eight years, Leadbelly cut around 200 sides for the Library Of Congress and the American Record Company (ARC). Accompanying himself on his trusty 12-string in a roistering barrelhouse style more frequently associated with the piano, he cut songs such as 'Alberta', 'The Boll Weevil', 'Cotton Fields', 'Midnight Special', 'Rock Island Line', 'Goodnight Irene', 'Pick A

Bale Of Cotton', 'Good Mornin' Blues' and 'Black Betty', among others. Meanwhile Leadbelly remained a magnet for trouble and, in 1939, he was incarcerated once again for assault. When he was released he linked up with other notables such as Pete Seeger, Woody Guthrie, Sonny Terry and Brownie McGhee and Josh White, which resulted in a ground-breaking radio series, Folk Songs Of America, for New York's WNYC.

Through the 1940s, Leadbelly recorded for a string of labels, including RCA Victor (1940), on which he was teamed with the Golden Gate Quartet. Other labels included Asch, Disc, Stinson and Capitol, before he moved out to the West coast in 1946.

While the civil rights movement had not yet achieved the momentum it would acquire in the 1960s, the contribution from Blacks to the war effort had galvanised many into believing that their basic human rights were being ignored. And Leadbelly proved to be one of the most eloquent spokesmen through his association with People's Songs Inc. Politically motivated, People's Songs sought to expand their influence through a series of tours, championing not just causes, but also – indirectly – the concept of folk song as a tool to highlight the inherent shortcomings of the extant social structure.

In 1947 Leadbelly returned to New York, where he remained until his death on December 6, 1949. In the years since his death, Leadbelly's role as an innovator has spiralled with titles such as 'Rock Island Line' and 'Goodnight Irene' acquiring genre-crunching popularity.

CAJUN

FORMERLY COLONISED BY THE FRENCH, LOUISIANA IS STILL A CULTURAL HODGE-PODGE, with the south being predominantly Latin and therefore Catholic, and the north substantially Protestant. Added to this combination are substantial pockets of French-speaking Creoles, who were brought in by immigrants as slaves to work the cotton fields. On top of this is the influence of New Orleans, but New Orleans has always been a law unto itself, operating a completely separate agenda from not only the rest of the US, but also the rest of the state. Even so, New Orleans has provided a regional catalyst that has ensured that Cajun – unlike most of its counterparts – has been more susceptible to external stimuli than say the folk music of the Appalachians.

Initially Cajun was generically an accordion-led style that combined elements of the blues and gospel with the traditional songs of the region's French-speaking population, descendants of Acadian (of which Cajun is a corruption) French Canadians who settled there. More

recently Cajun has come to be regarded as a sub-genre of country music, while its urban black counterpart is known as Zydeco, a form of R&B that is accordion-led, rather than guitar or piano-based.

Although the accordion is central to the rhythmic core of Cajun, the fiddle is no less significant, if only because it was through the fiddle that fresh songs and ideas entered the culture. This tended to occur as lone fiddlers travelled throughout the Southwest, entering fiddle contests. These fiddle contests have exerted as much influence on the cross-pollination of ideas and styles as the medicine shows or the migration northwards by aspiring blues musicians from the cotton fields of the Mississippi Delta.

However, as Cajun has existed as a genre adumbrating a regional style, it has reflected the trends and fads nationwide. Therefore the emergence of rock'n'roll galvanised a number of young performers such as Jimmy C. Newman and Bobby Charles into recording songs that were aimed at rock'n'roll

NEWS

1936, JULY 17: CIVIL WAR ERUPTS IN SPAIN, WITH GENERAL FRANCO LEADING THE NATIONALIST INSURRECTION AGAINST THE REPUBLICAN GOVERNMENT. THE BLOODY WAR LASTS FOR THREE YEARS

left: Multi-instrumentalist Doug Kershaw is best known for his Cajun fiddle playing and songwriting. His 1961 hit 'Louisiana Man' helped to introduce the Cajun sound to mainstream record fans.

centre: One of the newer faces on the Cajun music scene, Boo Zoo Chavis.

right: The great Clifton Chenier who almost single-handedly put Zydeco music on the map.

audiences while retaining the rhythmic characteristics of Cajun. Similarly, Zydeco has spawned a number of performers that have used rap and hip hop to interface the basic rhythmic structure of Cajun, giving it a zing of contemporaneity.

Despite all this, there is a latent conservatism that has enabled the traditional form of Cajun to survive intact. Therefore exponents such as Nathan Abshire and The Balfa Brothers, featuring fiddler Dewey Balfa with his brothers Burkeman, Harry, Rodney and Will, were not required to adapt to changing fashions. For they were – if you like – the keepers of the flame that necessarily ensured that the traditions of Cajun music remained alive. Indeed, when Dewey died in 1992, his daughter Christine stepped in and formed her own band, Balfa Toujours.

At the other end of spectrum, accordionist Clifton Chenier provided a starting-point for inheritors of the tradition such as Rockin' Dopsie, Buckwheat Zydeco and his son C.J. Chenier. Chenier honed his distinctive

style playing the clubs of Port Arthur, Texas, and southern Louisiana in the late 1940s. Initially his audience were oil workers or the French-speaking Black communities, but as his reputation grew so his sphere of influence expanded. By 1955 he was recording for Specialty in California and for the Chess subsidiaries Checker and Argo. But it was a bunch of albums for the Arhoolie label, including Bon Ton Roulet (1966) and Bogalusa Boogie (1975), that brought Cajun out of the bayous and into the mainstream of the American and European folk/blues festival circuit. In 1984 he won a Grammy for I'm Here. In a sense, this was the record industry offering an acknowledgement of the influence of Cajun. While that influence is on the increase, at its core there remain a nucleus of players who still play the way their grandfathers did.

VARIOUS ARTISTS
LOUISIANA CAJUN CLASSICS
Arhoolie

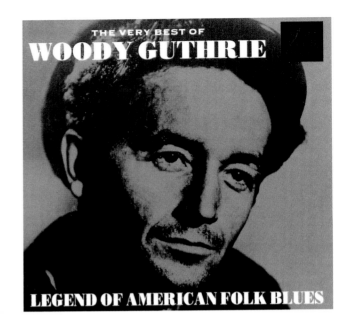

right: Woody Guthrie seemed to be rarely photographed without his trademark cap, a detail that didn't go unnoticed with the youthful Bob Dylan.

THE VERY BEST OF
WOODY GUTHRIE
LEGEND OF AMERICAN FOLK BLUES

WOODY GUTHRIE

THE MUSIC OF WOODY GUTHRIE OCCUPIES A SPECIAL PLACE IN THE HISTORY OF THE US. He became the voice of the Depression of the 1930s, when his songs spoke graphically of the plight of the many migrant workers. He was born Woodrow Wilson Guthrie on July 14, 1912, in Okemah, Oklahoma; after his mother's death from Huntington's Chorea (a chronic nerve disorder) and his father's financial problems, he moved to Pampa, Texas, to live with an uncle. His uncle taught him how to play the guitar and introduced him to the old traditional tunes, which Woody adapted with his own lyrics. His first composition, 'Dusty Old Dust' (1935), was written to the tune of Carson Robison's 'The Ballad Of Billy The Kid'. For the next two years, he travelled the country drawing inspiration from hymns, ballads, the blues and dance tunes.

In 1937, having based himself in Los Angeles, he started to work with his cousin, Jack Guthrie, and broadcast over KFVD. His developing repertoire included 'Pretty Boy Floyd', 'Dust Bowl Refugees', 'I Ain't Got No Home', 'Gypsy Davy', 'Oklahoma Hills', 'This Land Is Your Land' and 'John Henry'.

As his profile grew, so did his commitment to political reform and socialist principles. The significance of his work was quickly grasped by official bodies like the Library Of Congress, for whom he recorded many hours of material under the guidance of Alan Lomax in 1940. Consequently, radio broadcasts with Leadbelly and Pete Seeger became more frequent, leading to the formation of The Almanac Singers with Seeger and Lee

Hays. The following year, Guthrie was commissioned to write a song-cycle celebrating the building of hydro-electric dams in the Pacific Northwest, which included 'Grand Coulee Dam' and 'Pastures Of Plenty'.

By 1943, his overt Communist sympathies had started to land him in serious trouble, culminating in a ban from all the US radio networks. This had little real effect on him, and his autobiography, Bound For Glory, was published to considerable acclaim. The following year, he was signed up by Moe Asch to cut a number of albums for Folkways, which included songs such as 'Plane Wreck At Los Gatos (Deportees)', which was based around a newspaper article about a plane full of migrant workers that crashed with no survivors; like many of Woody's other songs, it showed his compassion for, and anger at, the suffering of others.

By 1950, he had started his fight against the Huntington's Chorea that was to claim his life. While he physically declined, his reputation increased, with his songs being covered by Ramblin' Jack Elliott, The Carter Family, The Weavers, Pete Seeger, Ewan MacColl and Bob Dylan. On October 3, 1967, Guthrie died; his songs have continued to be covered by artists too numerous to mention, and the sphere of his influence shows no sign of letting up.

His song 'This Land Is Your Land', in particular, has become a more potent American national anthem than 'The Star-Spangled Banner' will ever be. In 1976 his autobiography Bound For Glory was turned into a movie starring David Carradine as Woody Guthrie.

DUST BOWL BALLADS
Rounder

CD CHECKLIST

NEWS

1937, JUNE 3: EDWARD, DUKE OF WINDSOR, MARRIES AMERICAN DIVORCEE WALLIS SIMPSON, A MARRIAGE NOW POSSIBLE AFTER HIS ABDICATION FROM THE BRITISH THRONE THE PREVIOUS YEAR

Robin Ca[...]

right: Eddie James 'Son' House survived into his 80s, and even managed a tour of the UK during the early 1970s.

below: While the virtuoso B.B. King took the Country Blues onto the concert stage in a much more sophisticated form, Lightnin' Hopkins stayed true to its roots, making over 100 albums during his career.

SON HOUSE

COUNTRY BLUES

THERE IS A SCHOOL OF THOUGHT THAT MAINTAINS THAT THE ORIGINS OF COUNTRY BLUES CAN BE FOUND IN THE MISSISSIPPI DELTA. Some of the region's favourite sons have included Charlie Patton, Robert Johnson, Son House, John Lee Hooker, Howlin' Wolf, and Muddy Waters. However, while John Lee Hooker, Howlin' Wolf and Muddy Waters found fame in Chicago Blues and B.B. King found that the independent labels of Los Angeles like Modern were the best route to success, it was Robert Johnson and Son House who seemed to define the Delta style of Country Blues.

Robert Johnson was born on May 8, 1911, in Hazlehurst, Mississippi. Inspired by Lonnie Johnson and Leroy Carr, Johnson honed a guitar style that was visceral and intense while songs like 'Love In Vain', 'Crossroads', 'Hellhound On My Trail', 'Ramblin' On My Mind' and 'Come On In My Kitchen' possessed an unyielding emotional commitment. That his limited output has become staples in the repertoires of

countless players like Eric Clapton, Stevie Ray Vaughan, Taj Mahal and Keith Richards confirms his immense impact. Although his death in Greenwood, Mississippi, on August 16, 1938, remains shrouded in mystery, with most opinion suggesting that he was poisoned by a jealous husband, the mystery has only intensified the legend.

Son House, though, survived well into his eighties, long enough to give historians a worm's eye view of the early years of the Country Blues. Eddie James House was born on March 21, 1902, in Riverton, Mississippi. Spending his early years as a preacher, he started playing the blues in the 1920s, recording sides such as 'Preachin' the Blues' in 1930. As a consequence, he was known to Charley Patton, and a young Robert Johnson was rumoured to have been influenced by House. After being recorded by archivist Alan Lomax in the early 1940s, House spent many years in obscurity until he was rediscovered in the mid-1960s when he recorded The Legendary Son House: Father Of Folk Blues (1965).

Everybody Should Hear
KoKomo Arnold Sing
'Milk Cow Blues'
It's The Greatest Record
Ever Made
Order Number 7026

above: 'Milk Cow Blues' was Kokomo Arnold's biggest hit, and went on to be recorded as a rock'n'roll number by both Elvis Presley and Eddie Cochran in the 1950s.

One of the finest blues albums to appear in the 1960s, it made no concessions to changes in fashion, but concentrated on interpreting Classic Blues with spare accompaniment; it ranks alongside Johnson's King Of The Delta Blues Singers as one of the greatest-ever records of the blues.

For inasmuch as the blues reflected the tribulations of rural life, House was not the only bluesman to approach it with something approximating a religious experience. Blind Willie Johnson from Marlin, Texas, belongs to that almost obsolete tradition of the singing preacher. His powerful attestations were, like Reverend Gary Davis, never didactic, but delivered with utter conviction. Although he rarely recorded, his sides speak volumes for the role of religion in the development of Black music.

Lightnin' Hopkins was never a preacher, but he was one of the blues' most gifted natural poets with the ability to compose songs in much the same ad hoc way that a gifted raconteur might tell a story. This approach

to songwriting gave his work an inspired vitality that was powerful, lucid and fluent. His guitar-playing, echoing his earliest influence Blind Lemon Jefferson, was economical, underscoring his cryptic observations on the mundane realities of life. While a master of the 12-bar blues, he cut many Boogies with pianist Wilson 'Thunder' Smith, among others, and was never governed by constraints of style or form, improvising or extemporising with a verve and aplomb that only John Lee Hooker has been able to match. Whether as a soloist or backed by a band, Hopkins was prolific by any standards, recording over a hundred albums.

The importance of the basic 12-bar blues as a form in modern popular music cannot be overestimated; it formed a fundamental building block for jazz, Tin Pan Alley, rock'n'roll and all that followed.

And although the Country Blues remains grounded in the agrarian communities of the 1930s, performers such as Taj Mahal, Eric Bibb and Jessie Mae Hemphill have perpetuated the tradition in the 1980s and 1990s.

ROBERT JOHNSON
KING OF THE DELTA BLUES SINGERS
Columbia

CD CHECKLIST

1938, JULY 14: HOWARD HUGHES LANDS HIS PLANE IN NEW YORK AFTER FLYING AROUND THE WORLD IN THREE DAYS, 19 HOURS AND 17 MINUTES

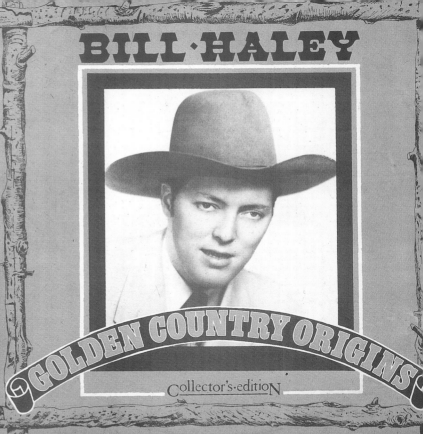

BILL·HALEY

GOLDEN COUNTRY ORIGINS

Collector's·edition

TEX Ritter
COWBOY SONG
FOLIO

Songs of the
trail and camp-
fire as sung by
Tex Ritter in
Grand National
pictures . . .

RICE 50 CENTS
CEPT CANADA & FOREIGN

SAM FOX PUB. CO.
CLEVELAND   NEW YORK

1930-1940

far left: Tex Ritter was the first country singer to sign with Capitol Records, in 1942, after already launching a screen career which saw him in over 50 movies as a singing cowboy.

far left, below: Ritter had his biggest hit with the theme from the 1952 Gary Cooper/Grace Kelly drama High Noon, and set a trend for Western films to feature a theme song.

left: Rock'n'roll pioneer Bill Haley recorded as a cowboy artist with the Four Aces of Western Swing, Down Homers and Saddlemen, the latter becoming The Comets in 1953.

below left: After many hits with The Golden West Cowboys, Cowboy Copas' solo career was brought to an end in the same 1963 plane crash that killed Patsy Cline.

COWBOY SONGS

COWBOY SONGS WERE EXTENSIONS OF THE ANGLO-CELTIC BALLADS THAT HAD DEVELOPED FRESH ROOTS IN THE APPALACHIANS. As frontiersmen moved out towards the West coast, tales of their exploits were recounted through song. From the South, Hispanic influences filtered through from Mexico into Texas and southern California. Moreover, Hispanic ballads freely utilised the waltz and, later on, the tango, while the saga song, as it came to be described, tended to adopt a more lugubrious, downbeat style.

By the end of the 19th century, cowboy songs had become staples in vaudeville and music hall, as the travelling medicine shows gathered up songs about Western heroes such as Jesse James and Buffalo Bill and the trails to towns such as Santa Fe and El Paso. In 1910 folklorist John A. Lomax published the collection Cowboy Songs And Other Frontier Ballads, but it was not until the 1920s that performers such as Carl Sprague, Goebel Reeves and Otto Gray began to make their mark as 'singing cowboys'. However, Jimmie Rodgers, whose sobriquet was The Singing Brakeman, seemed to encapsulate the spirit of the pioneering frontiersman although lacking the razzle-dazzle glamour that Hollywood bestowed upon the genre.

The advent of sound in the movies enabled Hollywood to capitalise still further on this fascination with the myth of the Old West, and the actors and singers Roy Rogers and Gene Autry were able to sustain dual careers and groups such as The Sons Of

Pioneers were frequently cast in Westerns. In 1935, Patsy Montana scored the first big country hit for a woman when 'I Want To Be A Cowboy's Sweetheart' rocketed up the charts; it also consolidated yodelling as a perfectly plausible characteristic of country music. Although the Western-styled image of country music became more entrenched with performers such as Hank Snow and Tex Ritter building their careers around the paraphernalia of the Old West, singers and writers such as Hank Williams, Lefty Frizzell and Buck Owens recorded songs that had contemporary relevance. With the coming of the rock'n'roll era, cowboy songs began to slip out of vogue – that is, until Marty Robbins cut the influential Gunfighter Ballads And Trail Songs (1959). With this album, which featured titles such as 'The Hanging Tree', 'El Paso', 'Big Iron', 'The Fastest Gun Around' and 'Battle Of The Alamo', Robbins extended interest in cowboy songs, updating the genre and making it acceptable to a new and younger audience. Robbins was not the only one to plough this particular furrow, as Johnny Cash recorded albums such Bitter Tears (Ballads Of The American Indian) (1964) and The Last Gunfighter Ballad (1977), and performed on the soundtrack for the film The Sons Of Katie Elder (1965).

In the 1980s and 1990s, Western imagery has been perpetuated by the use of cowboy hats and boots, which are now virtually inseparable from the media perception of country music, and the basic structure of the cowboy song has become one of the staple forms in modern country music.

1938, NOVEMBER 8: VIOLENT ANTI-SEMITISM FLOURISHES IN GERMANY, CULMINATING IN THE 'NIGHT OF BROKEN GLASS', WHEN THOUSANDS OF JEWS ARE KILLED OR ARRESTED AND THEIR PROPERTY DESTROYED

right: The Staple Singers could be considered the Carter Family of gospel, a musical dynasty that helped popularise the music beyond the parameters of its social origins in the church.

far right: Aretha Franklin made the 1987 album One Lord, One Faith, One Baptism live at her father's church in Detroit, featuring Mavis Staples and the Rev. Jesse Jackson preaching an anti-drugs sermon.

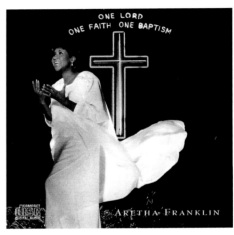

GOSPEL

DURING THE 1930S IN THE US, GOSPEL BECAME THE DOMINANT CHURCH MUSIC.

Spirituals, or the songs of deliverance, were a lifeline for enslaved Africans being transported across the Atlantic to the New World. For if the white man gave anything of positive value to the Africans, it was the faith upon which their culture in the United States would be based. As they were put to work on plantations and malcontents were gathered into chain gangs, so the work songs began to emerge. Drawing from the rhythms of their African homeland, the work songs reflected the horrendous quality of their lot, while offering hope that salvation and deliverance would be conferred upon those who believed.

After the emancipation of the slaves, the songs of deliverance assumed wider significance in the daily life of black people: faith remained pivotal. For although they had been delivered, they remained marginalised and impoverished. At the beginning of Reconstruction, many of those tasting freedom for the first time organised themselves into minstrel shows or four-part harmony vocal groups. One of the earliest references to the quartet tradition occurred in 1851 in Virginia when Fredericka Bremer reported: 'I first heard the slaves, about a hundred in number, singing at their work … they sang in quartettes … in such perfect harmony, and with such exquisite feeling that it was difficult to believe them self-taught.'

By the dawn of the 20th century, four-part harmony singing was well established in black communities across the United States and appeared to be dominated by males. Apparently any four young black males who chanced to meet could immediately harmonise a song, hence the popularity of the barbershop quartets. Formal and informal quartets worked in churches, at singing parties in private homes, in schoolyards and even on street corners. Some groups evolved specifically to sing each week in church. As the four-part harmony group established itself, with groups such as The Silver Leaf Quartette Of Norfolk forming, writers such as Thomas A. Dorsey, formerly a bluesman, known as Georgia Tom, began writing songs such as 'Precious Lord, Take My Hand' and 'Peace In The Valley'. Then, in 1938 and 1939, producer John Hammond organised Spirituals To Swing concerts at the Carnegie Hall with appearances from jazz musicians such as Count Basie and Charlie Christian, bluesman Big Bill Broonzy and the gospel group The Golden Gate Quartet. The success of these concerts generated immense interest, for not only did it present the opportunity of financial security, it was also something that was second nature to most Black people.

In 1937, the great Mahalia Jackson made her recording debut, and despite the risqué nature of her performances – she was often banned in the rather more staid churches – she came to embody the inherent artistry of gospel. After World War II, 'Move On Up A Little Higher' became the first gospel record to sell over a million copies. Her success encouraged a whole host of other female performers, most notably Clara Ward,

NEWS

1939, SEPTEMBER 1: GERMANY INVADES POLAND. TWO DAYS LATER FRANCE AND BRITAIN DECLARE WAR ON GERMANY AND THE SECOND WORLD WAR BEGINS

Sallie Martin and Dinah Washington. While Washington moved over to singing the blues, R&B and jazz, her roots in gospel imbued her performances with emotional depth and intensity. Aretha Franklin, too, grew up with the church as her backdrop as her father, the Reverend C.L. Franklin, was one of the most prominent Black American pastors. And it was Aretha along with Ray Charles and James Brown who brought the intensity of gospel to secular audiences with Soul.

To this day, gospel remains pivotal to the Black American experience. Significantly, it has also featured as an element in the music of white singers as diverse as Ry Cooder, Bob Dylan and Lyle Lovett. And it is ample evidence of its potency and popularity across the cultural board that Bluegrass musicians such as Doyle Lawson and Quicksilver have kept the God-fearing image of country music very much alive as well.

above: Washington Phillips was a street-corner preacher and musican who was recorded in the 1920s singing gospel hymns and accompanying himself on the autoharp.

left: Sunday morning church has long been central to the religious practice of Black American communities.

WARTIME POP

The entry of the United States into World War II reflected basic differences in how both Britain and the US went about the business of boosting morale. In Britain, there were sentimental ballads like Vera Lynn's 'White Cliffs Of Dover', designed to inspire a stiff upper-lip determination. In the US, with bandleaders like Glenn Miller touring constantly, performing up-tempo tunes such as 'In The Mood' and 'Little Brown Jug', and the up-and-at'em bravado of The Andrews Sisters with hits such as 'Boogie Woogie Bugle Boy', Cole Porter's 'Don't Fence Me In', 'Rum And Coca Cola' and 'Jingle Bells', the implications were clear: Don't mess with us. For the war effort became an integral part of the US entertainment industry. The pursuit of freedom may have been a subtext, but flag-waving was an occupation in its own right. That was what the country wished to do. And the entertainment industry was not about to flout the collective will of the people.

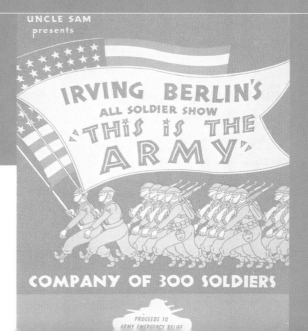

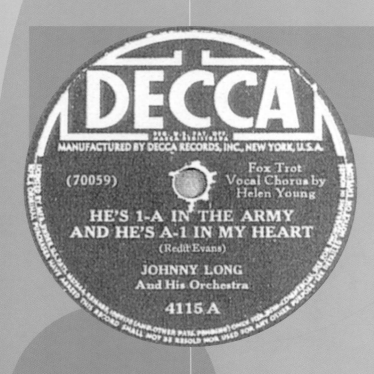

1940-1950

PRODUCERS
ARRANGERS

THE ROLE OF THE PRODUCER AND ARRANGER

was originally that of a shadowy figure who patrolled the murky, subterranean depths of record company offices. The change in perception was gradual at first but, as it picked up momentum, it metamorphosed into a full-scale overhaul of the way in which record companies went about their business. The first significant factor was the recognition by freelancers that it was quite possible for an individual to undertake a field trip, for example, to the Southern States, record a local performer, pay him for his performance and song, take the recording back to a record label such as Paramount, OKeh or Vocalion and lease it to them. Or, perhaps, sell the whole performance as a package. Considerations such as payment for radio airplay were not an issue. Against this backdrop, individuals such as Ralph Sylvester Peer was one of the first talent scouts to recognise the potential value of acquiring copyrights of Hillbilly songs and jazz compositions. From 1920 Peer became one of the first to make trips to the South, where he recorded blues singer Mamie Smith and Fiddling John Carson; the latter's sides were the first genuine country sides. Thereafter, he signed artists like The Carter Family and Jimmie Rodgers to the Victor record label.

IT WASN'T
UNTIL AFTER THE WAR that
the producer began to exert a real influence
upon the growth of the music industry with the
consolidation of the independent record label. For the
independent label allowed individuals such as bassist/
songwriter Willie Dixon at Chess, arranger/songwriter Jesse
Stone at Atlantic and engineer/arranger Joe Scott at Duke to
flourish. Gradually, producers such as easy listening expert Mitch
Miller or arranger Nelson Riddle began to exert a more high profile
influence. By the early 1960s, producers such as Leiber & Stoller, Phil
Spector and Allen Toussaint were signing artists to their own
production companies and leasing out records to the major labels.
However, major labels such as EMI still employed producers.
George Martin, with The Beatles, was such a significant part of
their recording process that he was known as the 'Fifth
Beatle'. Martin's high profile, as well as that of some of
his contemporaries, contributed to the producer
becoming almost as glamorous a figure
as his performing charges.

THE ROCK
ARENA CREATED A NEW
MARKET-PLACE for producers such as
Glyn Johns, Jimmy Miller, Chris Thomas and Steve
Lillywhite. This fostered a greater degree of independence
right across the board, encouraging Soul producers such as
Kenny Gamble and Leon Huff to set up their own record labels, a
practice that has continued with production teams like LA and
Babyface and Jimmy Jam and Terry Lewis. As producers have grown
more influential, artists have in turn become more demanding, with the
likes of Madonna and Prince extracting such high premiums from
record companies that they are virtually autonomous. Additionally the
growth of sampling has made the producer once more a technician,
but there are still those, like Steve Albini and Brian Eno, who have
instinctive flair rather than just control of the technology. The
bottom line is the Tin Pan Alley side of pop music, whereby
commercially-minded production teams geared to the
singles market will emerge periodically, often
only to fall out of fashion almost as
quickly as they appeared.

far left: Songs For Swingin' Lovers! was the 1956 album that marked Sinatra's artistic high point at Capitol Records, which lasted through to the end of the decade.

left: Billy May was the arranger on the equally memorable Come Fly With Me from 1958.

right: Sinatra, no stranger to the movie screen, with Bing Crosby in the 'Did Ya' Ever' sequence from High Society.

far right: Into middle age, and Ol' Blue Eyes kept recording and touring, becoming one of the richest men in showbiz – here with Luciano Pavarotti.

FRANK SINATRA

FRANK SINATRA WAS BORN FRANCIS ALBERT SINATRA ON DECEMBER 12, 1915, IN HOBOKEN, NEW JERSEY. HE WON AN AMATEUR TALENT CONTEST IN 1935. By 1939, he had joined the orchestra of Harry James. After a spell with James, Sinatra joined Tommy Dorsey's Orchestra, where he remained for the next three years. During that time, he cut over 90 sides for Victor. While these sides kept the spirit of Swing rocking and teenage bobbysoxers dancing, they suggested that Sinatra's range and shadings far exceeded most of his contemporaries. For Sinatra was able to take songs by great writers such as Irving Berlin and Cole Porter and make them sound as if they were being heard for the first time. Over the next ten years, Sinatra recorded around 250 sides for Columbia and in the process became a national institution.

In 1950, when producer Mitch Miller joined Columbia, Sinatra's popularity took a dive, for Miller made the cardinal error of trying to encourage Sinatra to cover R&B and country hits. For any other performer the results could have been catastrophic; for Sinatra though, as his film career kicked into gear with musicals like Anchors Aweigh (1945) and On The Town (1950), it only emphasised his strengths. Moving to Capitol in 1953, he was teamed with Nelson Riddle. Within a year Sinatra had scored a massive hit with 'Young At Heart' and nabbed an Oscar for his performance in From Here To Eternity, which he followed three years later, co-starring with Bing Crosby and Grace Kelly, with the

musical High Society. That wasn't all though, for as the LP began to challenge the 78 rpm disc as the state-of-the-art, Sinatra was on top of the game, recording albums like Songs For Young Lovers (1954), Swing Easy (1955) and Songs For Swinging Lovers (1956). Despite the emergence of rock'n'roll – for which he had nothing but disdain – Sinatra continued to expand his audience by maintaining his appeal for those who had grown up with him, so to speak. Therefore songs like 'You Make Me Feel So Young' had a special resonance, but also this same audience was becoming more affluent as they matured. And it was they who bought LPs rather than singles.

In 1961, Sinatra formed his own record label, Reprise, and started cutting albums that were overtly jazzy in their arrangements. Although albums such as Ring A-Ding-Ding with arranger Johnny Mandel, a Basie alumnus, Sinatra Swings with Billy May, and Sinatra Basie and It Might As Well Be Swing with Count Basie, the latter featuring arrangements by Quincy Jones, attested his strong allegiance to jazz, Sinatra's overall style had spawned so many imitators that it had become a template in itself. Among those to model their vocal style upon Sinatra were Matt Monro, Andy Williams, Vic Damone and Jack Jones. Furthermore Sinatra proved more than willing to react to fresh stimulus where appropriate. To that end, in 1967, he collaborated with Antonio Carlos Jobim, cutting a bossa nova album, which had become the latest Latin American dance craze to sweep the US. Although rock'n'roll had been

NEWS

1941, DECEMBER 7: JAPANESE AIRCRAFT BOMB THE US NAVAL FLEET AT PEARL HARBOR IN HAWAII – AMERICA JOINS THE SECOND WORLD WAR

anathema, where good songs were concerned the rule book was torn up and thrown away. Consequently, Sinatra cut versions of The Beatles' 'Yesterday', Simon & Garfunkel's 'Mrs Robinson' and Stevie Wonder's 'You Are The Sunshine Of My Life', among others.

Then, in 1969, he recorded what was to become his signature tune – 'My Way'. Based on a French tune, 'Comme d'Attitude', with an anglicised lyric by former teen idol Paul Anka, 'My Way' seemed a fair summary of his life and times, reflecting as it did a romanticised vision of his trials and tribulations. Four years later, after a brief retirement, he returned with Ol' Blues Is Back (1973). Featuring his version of 'Send In The Clowns' from Stephen Sondheim's musical, A Little Night Music, he managed to make lines such as 'Isn't it rich?/ Isn't it queer?/ Losing my timing this late/ In my career' have a poignant resonance that in other hands could have been self-pitying, but in Sinatra's were wryly ironic – and palpably untrue. Then, in 1980, once again, he caught the zeitgeist with 'Theme From New York' ('New York, New York'). Upbeat and laden with bravado, it anticipated the mood of extravagance and hedonism that characterised the 1980s. And into the 1990s, with producer Phil Ramone, Sinatra cut a brace of albums featuring duets with star names including Bono of U2, Julio Iglesias, Willie Nelson and Barbra Streisand.

After a period of declining health, Ol' Blues died aged 82 in May 1998, but his immortality, as probably the greatest interpreter of the 20th century popular song, was guaranteed long ago.

SONGS FOR SWINGIN' LOVERS!
Capitol

FOR ONLY THE LONELY
Capitol

COME FLY WITH ME
Capitol

CD CHECKLIST

right: Jazz has constantly touched the popular music of the day; Cab Calloway with his 'Hi De Ho' novelty numbers was a case in point in the 1940s.

below: The Cotton Club in New York's Harlem was an early catalyst that saw jazz, mainly via Duke Ellington, attract mainstream 'pop' audiences.

bottom: Alto sax player and flautist David Sanborn has an emotive, blues-influenced sound which has made him one of the most accessible and biggest-earning jazz players of the past thirty years.

JAZZ

WITH THE DEMISE OF SWING AND THE BIG BAND AFTER THE SECOND WORLD WAR came a smaller, more economical ensemble that was eminently suited to the development of Bebop. Inspired by Basie's tenorman Lester Young and guitarist Charlie Christian, it represented a reaction against the regimented arrangements of Swing. Its most vociferous adherents were young Black musicians such as Charlie Parker, Thelonius Monk and Dizzy Gillespie, who were keen to break fresh ground by using unconventional rhythmic accents, arcane harmonies and convoluted phrases. Of equal importance was that it distanced jazz from the dominant dance band music of the period. This conferred upon it an artistic quality that had never been properly appreciated hitherto. Alto-saxophonist Parker, in particular, was a masterful exponent of Bebop, possessing an intuitive feeling for the blues while executing tumbling torrents of notes to create dramatic improvisations that were an inspiration to younger performers. Monk's advanced notions on harmony and

rhythm failed to ignite enthusiasts until the late 1950s when he worked with John Coltrane and Sonny Rollins.

As Bebop expanded its net, a cool school of Beboppers emerged on the West coast, such as Mulligan, Chet Baker, Stan Getz and Zoot Sims. They were followed by a new breed of big band such as Stan Kenton's and Billy Eckstine's. While experimentation was eagerly embraced by most, there was a mood among some that jazz had lost its way and a Dixieland revival ensued. In the UK, the traditional New Orleans jazz style of Ken Colyer and the mainstream jazz of Humphrey Lyttleton generated enough interest that saxophonist Ronnie Scott opened a club in London's Soho. The club continues to thrive today.

Back in the US a post-bop swing towards the avant-garde was spearheaded by John Coltrane, while bassist Charlie Mingus drew from the innate funkiness of R&B and early jazz styles to create a style that was as dynamic as it was intellectually challenging. Some of his compositions, such as 'Goodbye Porkpie Hat', have

NEWS

1943, APRIL: THE JEWS OF THE WARSAW GHETTO RISE UP AND FIGHT TO THE DEATH, REPELLING THEIR NAZI OPPRESSORS FOR A CONSIDERABLE TIME DESPITE BEING MALNOURISHED AND VASTLY OUTNUMBERED

TIME OUT Featuring TAKE FIVE BLUE RONDO A LA TURK
THE DAVE BRUBECK QUARTET
STRANGE MEADOW LARK · THREE TO GET READY · KATHY'S WALTZ · EVERYBODY'S JUMPIN' · PICK UP STICKS

left: Dave Brubeck's 1960 album Time Out, with each track featuring a different (usually tricky) time signature, would seem an unlikely way of breaking into the pop charts. But that's what happened with the single 'Take Five', the album also going on to become a best-seller worldwide.

acquired such currency that they have been covered by artists as diverse as rock guitarist Jeff Beck through to folk musicians like Bert Jansch. As the avant-garde picked up steam with players such as Archie Shepp and Albert Ayler following Coltrane's lead, the free jazz of Cecil Taylor and Ornette Coleman sparked controversy across the US and Europe. In Europe and the UK, young musicians such as drummer Han Bennink, saxophonists Peter Brotzmann and Evan Parker and guitarist Derek Bailey would take free form to the brink of cacophony in the name of improvisation. However, bandleader John Dankwork, with vocalist Cleo Laine, continued to straddle the divide between the formalism of mainstream jazz and the impressionism of the avant-garde; after composing soundtracks to films like The Servant, he pioneered a form of symphonic jazz.

At the end of the 1960s, the mood in jazz reflected the upheaval in attitudes in the rest of the music industry. As early as 1964, Duke Ellington had composed Far East Suite and the UK-based duo Joe Harriott and John

Mayer had incorporated Eastern influences with Indo-Jazz Fusion (1965), and so when Miles Davis started fusing jazz with rock idioms it was merely symptomatic. As Jazz Rock and Fusion took hold at the beginning of the 1970s, through Davis alumni such as keyboardists Chick Corea and Keith Jarrett, saxophonist Wayne Shorter and guitarist John McLaughlin, groups like Weather Report began drawing massive audiences. Soul stars such as James Brown, who had always employed musicians like 'Pee Wee' Ellis, with impeccable jazz credentials, helped break down the impression that jazz was only for intellectuals by bringing Funk onto the dancefloor. There was a certain irony in the fact that jazz was being returned to its place of origin by musicians such as Miles Davis, who had helped engineer its removal in the first place.

The upshot was that jazz, which had been becoming increasingly elitist, began embracing a new generation of musician such as Wynton and Branford Marsalis, Courtenay Pyne, Andy Sheppard and Bill Frisell. While many were nurtured by Davis and Art Blakey, jazz's return to the dancefloor enabled elements of rap, hip hop and reggae to impinge, creating new styles such as Acid Jazz. On a gloomier note, a bland form of Cocktail Jazz, stemming from the mainstream, drew massive audiences as performers like Kenny G cleaned up.

While jazz may have lost some of its ground-breaking qualities, individuals such as Sonny Rollins continue to cast their spell, creating a genuine mood of anticipation and expectation whenever they appear.

LATIN AMERICAN

ONE OF THE ENDURING IRONIES OF CONTEMPORARY MUSIC IS THAT THE GENERAL PERCEPTION OF LATIN AMERICAN MUSIC IS FOREVER SPLATTERED WITH THE SEQUINS AND FRILLS OF BALLROOM DANCING. For a quick squint through the disciplines of dance on offer in ballroom dancing will reveal that the tango came from Argentina, the rhumba from Brazil and the cha-cha from Cuba. That dance should be such a visible expression of South American music is less surprising in light of the Spanish colonisation that took place from the end of the 15th century and the concomitant importation of thousands of slaves from West Africa.

Much of the blame for this unfortunate stigma can be apportioned to performers like Carmen Miranda, who complete with baskets of fruit perched precariously on top of her head, shimmied and warbled her way through Hollywood musicals such as Down Argentine Way (1940), in which she sang 'South American Way', That

Night In Rio (1941), The Gang's All Here (1943), featuring Benny Goodman, and Copacabana (1947). Spanish bandleader Xavier Cugat was raised in Cuba, but moved to the US in 1921; his greatest success came during the 1930s and 1940s when his orchestra had hits with titles like 'The Breeze and I', featuring vocalist Dinah Shore. In the UK, Venezuelan Edmundo Ros moved to London in 1937 and became a regular fixture on radio and throughout the ballrooms, helping in no small way the popularity of Latin style.

However it was musicians such as guitarist Laurindo Almeida and bandleaders Machito and Tito Puente who were responsible for fusing Latin American rhythms with jazz. Starting his career in his native Brazil as a classical guitarist, Almeida saw Django Reinhardt on a visit to Europe. On his return to Brazil, he packed up and moved to Los Angeles where he joined the Stan Kenton Orchestra, before landing a recording contract with Capitol. In 1962, he recorded the wildly influential Viva Bossa Nova, which included Antonio Carlos Jobim's

NEWS

1944, JUNE 6: D-DAY ARRIVES, WITH ALLIED FORCES LANDING IN NORMANDY. HEAVY FIGHTING ENSUES AS THE ALLIES SUCCESSFULLY BREACH THE GERMAN LINES OF DEFENCE

above: The melodic quality of much Latin American music made it a highly successful format for entertainers like the pianist Dolores Ventura.

above right: The Buena Vista Social Club represents some of the finest talents on the Cuban music scene, with legendary players like the pianist Ruben Gonzalez collaborating with the American guitarist Ry Cooder.

MONGO SANTAMARIA
GREATEST HITS
Fantasy

TITO PUENTE
PUENTE GOES JAZZ
RCA

'The Girl From Ipanema'; in addition to winning a Grammy, it opened the door for Stan Getz's experimentation with Latin rhythms on the album Getz-Gilberto (1964). Jobim was to remain a central figure in the popularisation of Latin rhythms among jazz audiences, as Ella Fitzgerald, Gerry Mulligan, Dizzy Gillespie and Frank Sinatra all covered his material.

Machito was raised in Cuba, but moved to New York in 1937, where he worked with Cugat before establishing his own band. More fiery and impassioned than Cugat, Machito blazed a trail for later performers such as Puente, Celia Cruz and Tania Maria, who would use Afro-Cuban rhythms to create a style that was less commercialised and more dependent upon the percussive element in South American music. By the early 1960s, instrumentalists such as Ray Barretto, with 'El Watusi', and Mongo Santamaria, with 'Watermelon Man' (1963), had brought Latin rhythms to a much bigger audience. By the late 1960s, blues-based guitarist Carlos Santana, with his band Santana, brought

these same Latin cadences to rock audiences with a string of albums such as Abraxas (1971). Meanwhile, other performers such as Milton Nascimento, Ruben Blades and Gilberto Gil started to adapt traditional South American folk songs, often to reflect the parlous political climates.

While Latin styles are no longer confined exclusively to the ballroom or possess the MOR connotations that were foisted upon them during the 1960s, courtesy of Herb Alpert and Sergio Mendes, few audiences seem aware of the vitality of Afro-Cuban rhythms.

far left: Dean Martin in the Capitol recording studios with the top arranger Nelson Riddle.

far left, below: Dick Haymes was a quality singer, and the star of many movie musicals throughout the 40s, who in his time was a serious rival to the popularity of Bing Crosby and Frank Sinatra.

left: The showbiz romance that seemed made in heaven, between singer/actress Debbie Reynolds and the crooner Eddie Fisher.

below left: One of the longest-lasting careers of a ballad singer with his roots in the style of the 1940s and 50s has been that of Tony Bennett.

CROONERS

THE ARRIVAL OF SOUND IN THE MOVIES HERALDED A NEW REQUIREMENT IN A LEADING ACTOR OR ACTRESS: decent speaking voices, at least, and even sound singing voices. While overdubbing would be prerequisite in the early years, stardom was guaranteed for those who could sing, dance and act. Furthermore, as songwriting partnerships such as Rodgers and Hammerstein recognised the potential of the stage musical as vehicles for movies, allegiances were gradually transferred from Broadway to Hollywood. The growth in popularity of the Hollywood musical corresponded with the ascendancy of the Swing and big band era.

At first, big band leaders such as Paul Whiteman were reluctant to take on vocalists, but as the craze for dance bands and orchestras mushroomed vocalists were good distinguishing features. For not all the orchestras were as accomplished as Count Basie's or Duke Ellington's; many were virtually indistinguishable from one another. Furthermore, as a dance band rapidly became a fixture in any self-respecting hotel, a vocalist could provide character to the band's repertoire of covers from the popular hits of the day that were usually derived from stage or Hollywood musicals: the vocalists were the band's public face. To that end, vocalists were not obliged to be heavily stylised. Some, like Ella Fitzgerald, with Chick Webb's Band, or Billie Holiday, with Teddy Wilson's Orchestra, evolved their own highly distinctive styles more quickly than others, because they had the talent to do so in the first instance, but also

because, despite performing in front of affluent white audiences in clubs and hotels, they continued putting in the hours on the bandstand in front of small, discerning black audiences. It was this combination that made the careers of Holiday, Fitzgerald, Sarah Vaughan and Dinah Washington, among others.

Others such as Frank Sinatra, with Harry James and Tommy Dorsey; Anita O'Day, with Stan Kenton; Billy Eckstine, with Earl Hines; Bing Crosby, with Paul White-man; and Peggy Lee, with Benny Goodman, used the big band platform to forge their own styles. In so doing, a generation of vocalists known as crooners was spawned. Some of them such as Dick Haymes, Al Bowlly and Rudy Vallee attained the dizzy heights of super-stardom during the Swing era, only to find that once Swing had lost its zing their careers were all but finished. Others such as Doris Day, Perry Como, Jo Stafford and Kay Starr adjusted their vocal styles to adapt to market forces.

The big band stage was the ideal place for many fine singers to learn their trade. Furthermore bandleaders were well aware of the finishing school education they provided for their charges: when Sinatra left Dorsey, Dorsey demanded a third of Sinatra's future earnings. And that wasn't an isolated instance. As the crooners slipped from favour, stylists such as Nat 'King' Cole emerged to fill the vacuum. Soon, an up-and-at-'em school of vocalising, known as R&B, would begin to hog the airwaves. And before you could snat your fingers, rock'n'roll was banging on the door.

1945, AUGUST 6: THE US DROPS THE ATOMIC BOMB ON HIROSHIMA, CAUSING DEVASTATION ON AN UNPRECEDENTED SCALE. THREE DAYS LATER THEY DROP ANOTHER ON NAGASAKI. THE JAPANESE SURRENDER

POP INSTRUMENTAL

AN ENDURING MYSTERY IS WHY THE POP INSTRUMENTAL HAS ALWAYS TENDED TO BE REGARDED AS LITTLE MORE THAN A NOVELTY ITEM. Even when jazzmen such as Dave Brubeck ('Take Five'), Cannonball Adderly ('Mercy, Mercy, Mercy') and Herbie Hancock ('Rockit') have recorded titles that were totally representative of their extant output, the stigma of novelty has persisted. Initially, as bandleaders such as Paul Whiteman and Glenn Miller headed up bestseller lists, there was no suggestion of novelty: charts were reflecting popular tastes. After World War II, as independent labels proliferated, any ruse to generate sales was fair game. Consequently R&B musicians such as Earl Bostic and Bill Doggett managed to score sizeable hits with bright, sassy tunes that gave a general indication of their abilities. Then, gradually, MOR instrumentalists such as Al Hirt ('Java'), Perez Prado ('Cherry Pink And Apple Blossom') and Herb Alpert ('Lonely Bull') began cutting singles, both to stimulate album sales and to promote a stylistic variant: Herb Alpert's Tijuana Brass marked a resurgent interest in music with a Latin American or Hispanic inflection. Novelty persisted though.

Even during the rock'n'roll era, Bill Justis's 'Raunchy' had a gimmick: guitarist Sid Manker picked out the melody on the bass lines. From that gimmick, though, the career of Duane Eddy was launched. Using Manker's gimmick, with loads of reverb, Eddy cranked out a string of hits, including 'Rebel Rouser', 'Because They're Young' and 'Peter Gunn'. As a consequence, a plethora of guitar-led instrumentals followed from groups such as The Shadows ('Apache', 'F.B.I.', 'The Man Of Mystery', 'Wonderful Land', 'Guitar Tango' and 'Dance On'), The Ventures ('Walk Don't Run', 'Pefidia' and 'Ram-Bunk-Shush') and Johnny and The Hurricanes ('Red River Rock', 'Beatnik Fly' and, even, 'The James Bond Theme').

In the UK, the bi-product of The Shadows' success was the instrumental duo. Guitarist Jet Harris and drummer Tony Meehan — both former members of The

NEWS

1948, JANUARY 30: HAVING HELPED TO ACHIEVE INDIAN INDEPENDENCE FROM BRITISH COLONIAL POWER, MAHATMA GANDHI IS ASSASSINATED BY HINDU EXTREMIST NATHURAM GODSE

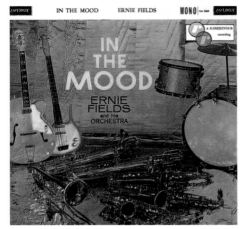

far left: Organ star Bill Doggett with 'Honky Tonk' and alto supremo Earl Bostic with sides like 'Flamingo' stormed the jukeboxes and R&B charts in the 40s and 50s.

left: Ernie Fields and his Orchestra made a trademark rock'n'roll instrumental sound with their raucous reworkings of such standards as the Glenn Miller favourite 'In The Mood'.

Shadows – scored hits with 'Diamonds' and 'Scarlet O'Hara'. Decca producer Joe Meek, inspired by the topicality of the space-race, took Billy Fury's backing group, The Tornados, under his wing, and cut 'Telstar' and then 'Globetrotter'. Apart from The Shadows, none of these groups lasted long, but they were early manifestations of the move away from the domination of the solo vocalist to the phenomenon of the Beat group. Similarly, in the US, the Beach Boys-led surf craze spawned its fair share of instrumentals, with The

Surfaris' 'Wipe Out' and Dick Dale – the architect of the surf sound – with 'Let's Go Trippin' and 'Miserlou'.

While these groups may have transcended novelty for a spell, the ephemeral nature of the instrumental is best exemplified by the impact of movies and television upon record makers. 'The James Bond Theme' by The John Barry Seven has survived most of the films. In 1998, keyboards techno-file Moby unleashed a trip-hop version of it. There is no getting away from it, the pop instrumental seems destined to remain a novelty.

left: In the 40s Progressive Jazz bandleader Stan Kenton had huge instrumental hits with numbers like 'The Peanut Vendor' and 'Unison Riff'.

right: The Surfaris were a teenage outfit who came in on the surf music boom of the early 1960s with a sole instrumental smash 'Wipe Out'.

RAMSEY LEWIS TRIO
GREATEST HITS
Chess

HERBIE MANN
MEMPHIS UNDERGROUND
Atlantic

CD CHECKLIST

RHYTHM AND BLUES

above: An advertisement for a so-called 'rock'n'roll' package film which featured a host of stars including Nat Cole, Dinah Washington and rhythm and blues names Ruth Brown, Joe Turner and The Clovers.

above right: The guru of New Orleans rhythm and blues, who influenced everyone from Fats Domino to Doctor John, Roy Byrd aka Professor Longhair.

MUCH HAS BEEN MADE, QUITE RIGHTLY, OF THE IMPACT OF RHYTHM AND BLUES UPON THE DEVELOPMENT OF CONTEMPORARY POPULAR MUSIC. That impact reached its zenith in the early 1960s in the UK when a plethora of groups such as The Beatles, The Rolling Stones, The Yardbirds, Manfred Mann and Them started covering songs by R&B musicians and bluesmen like Chuck Berry, Muddy Waters, Bo Diddley, John Lee Hooker, Willie Dixon and Lightnin' Hopkins. This was not only the catalyst for the R&B explosion, but also generically what is now perceived as guitar-based rock, which has been the dominant strain of contemporary popular music for the last 40 years.

Evolving from the blues and gospel, rhythm and blues was derived from the big band jazz of the late 1930s, which, as big bands became too expensive to run, slimmed down to small five- or six-piece combos. Drawing a fine line between the purism of jazz and the blues and reaching its zenith in the 1950s with performers as different, stylistically, as Fats Domino and Louis Jordan or Dinah Washington and The Coasters or Ray Charles and James Brown, R&B was all about entertainment: the honking horn section embodied the implicit showmanship of R&B. That showmanship was integral to rock'n'roll. Indeed rock'n'roll and R&B can be deemed synonymous, the differences being entirely perceptual and governed more or less by a record or an artist's ability to crossover from an exclusively Black audience market to include a young white audience.

Furthermore, producers Dave Bartholomew and Willie Dixon and bandleader Johnny Otis – himself a white man – have all noted that rock'n'roll and rhythm and blues were exactly the same.

Through that crossover, R&B attracted a wider audience and influence and, ironically, it was young white kids in the 1940s and 1950s who, hearing R&B records, were fired with the determination that they too would become musicians.

Guitarist and producer Steve Cropper of Booker T & The MGs once noted that, when he was growing up in the South during the 1950s and he went to see visiting bands, because segregation was still a fact of life, the white members of the audience were required to watch the show from the gallery. In later years, he recognised that the only way he could get close to where the real action was, was by being a musician on the bandstand: there was no segregation amongst musicians on the bandstand. That enthusiasm triggered the likes of Cropper and many others to become musicians in the first place. And it is they who, through the years, have managed to keep the flame of R&B burning brightly today by inspiring further new generations of musicians and performers.

As rock's domination continues unchallenged, it is musicians such as Van Morrison, Georgie Fame, Duke Robillard and Jools Holland, who have paid homage to the spirit of R&B by utilising comparable arrangements. And as for survivors such as Ray Charles and James Brown, their influence just continues to grow.

LOUIS JORDAN
THE BEST OF...
MCA

left: Probably the most famous publicity shot of Hank Williams, taken at the peak of his career before his drinking problem began to take its toll.

right: The influence of Hank Williams continues to be felt in country music and popular music generally, nearly half a century after his death.

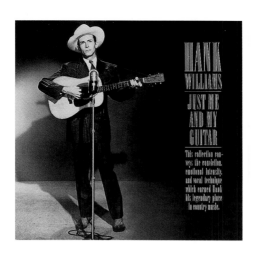

HANK WILLIAMS JUST ME AND MY GUITAR

This collection conveys the conviction, emotional intensity, and vocal technique which earned Hank his legendary place in country music.

HANK WILLIAMS

THE INFLUENCE OF HANK WILLIAMS UPON SUCCESSIVE GENERATIONS OF PERFORMERS IS OF SUCH MAGNITUDE THAT THERE ARE FEW WHO HAVEN'T BEEN TOUCHED IN SOME WAY BY HIS MUSIC. When New Country reared its head in the mid-1980s, many of the young turks clamouring to be heard cited Williams and the naturalism of his songs as their inspiration. He was born Hiram King Williams on September 17, 1923, in Georgiana, Alabama, and joined the local church choir in 1929. By 1936 he had won a talent contest in Montgomery – singing 'WPA Blues' – which prompted him to form The Drifting Cowboys. For the next ten years he fronted The Drifting Cowboys on WSFA, Montgomery, and was then signed by the Sterling label in December 1946, where he was backed by The Willis Brothers. The following year, he was signed by Frank Walker to the MGM label, and became a regular on the Louisiana Hayride.

From 1949, in tandem with his producer and occasional co-writer Fred Rose, he started a run of hits with 'Lovesick Blues', which was followed by 'Wedding Bells', 'Mind Your Own Business', 'You're Gonna Change', 'My Buckets Got A Hole In It', 'I Just Don't Like This Kind Of Living', 'Long Gone Lonesome Blues', 'Why Don't You Love Me', 'Why Should We Try Anymore', 'Moaning The Blues', 'Cold Cold Heart', 'Howlin' At The Moon', 'Hey Good Lookin'', 'Crazy Love', 'Baby We're Really In Love', 'Honky Tonk Blues', 'Half As Much', 'Jambalaya', 'Settin' The Woods On Fire' and 'I'll Never Get Out Of This World Alive'. He

also adopted the pseudonym of Luke The Drifter for a number of monologues.

Despite his formidable popularity, he was beset by personal problems: he was fired from the Grand Ole Opry in August 1952 because of excessive drinking, and the same problem caused his wife, Audrey Shepherd, to divorce him the same year. On January 1, 1953, he was booked into a gig in Canton, Ohio, and, with a chauffeur driving him, fell asleep in the back of the car. He died of a heart attack en route.

After his death, MGM issued 'Your Cheatin' Heart', 'Take These Chains From My Heart', 'I Won't Be Home No More' and 'Weary Blues From Waiting', all of which became big hits. His band, The Drifting Cowboys, went on to back Ray Price, who proved himself to be a good interpreter of Williams's songs. In the years since his death Williams's reputation has increased several-fold, with performers of all musical persuasions covering his material, and some – like Gram Parsons and Keith Whitley – emulating his life-style and following him to an early death. His songs remain as poignant and touching today as they did 40 years ago, and have been covered by Ray Charles, Dwight Yoakam, Randy Travis, Mitch Miller, Tony Bennett and Jo Stafford, among others. He was elected to the Country Music Hall Of Fame in 1961, and the biopic Your Cheatin' Heart was made in 1964, with George Hamilton playing the part of Williams, and his son, Hank Williams Jr, singing on the soundtrack. Several biographies have appeared: Chet Flippo's Your Cheatin' Heart (1981) is probably the best.

40 GREATEST HITS
Polydor

LOW DOWN BLUES
Mercury

CD CHECKLIST

1949, OCTOBER 1: MAO TSE-TUNG FORMS THE COMMUNIST PEOPLE'S REPUBLIC OF CHINA, WITH HIMSELF AS CHAIRMAN

TV & WIDE OF

right: Connie Stevens had a couple of pop hits based on the success of the TV show Hawaiian Eye in which she starred with Eddie Byrne.

below, left: Surfers Jan and Dean attempted to cash-in on the Batman craze prompted by the 60s cult television series.

below, right: Count Basie played, and had a minor hit with, the theme from the 50s Lee Marvin TV series M Squad.

opposite: Piano entertainer Liberace owed his fame largely to the 1950s US television show which launched his career.

THE POPULARITY OF THE CINEMA was seen to be under threat right from the late 1940s onwards as television caught the ears and eyes of the public at large, and likewise the emergence of the video as a marketing tool was widely seen as a threat to the survival of radio as the dominant vehicle. As it transpires, cinema has reasserted itself in the closing years of the century, and radio too has struggled back from the edge of the abyss to overtake video as the most potent weapon in the PR's armoury. Both television and video have acquired the cosy aura of warmth and respectability that would have been unimaginable only ten years ago.

JAN AND DEAN BATMAN

THE MUSIC FROM M Squad

RCA VICTOR

LIBERACE

COMPLETE LIFE STORY

CHILDHOOD

FAMILY

ROMANCES

CAREER

TELEVISON'S RELATIONSHIP WITH POPULAR MUSIC, PARTICULARLY TEEN-ORIENTED POPULAR MUSIC, HAS ALWAYS BEEN PRODIGAL. While middle-of-the-road tastes have been reasonably catered for through variety programmes and showcase specials of the major names ranging from Sinatra to Barbra Streisand, rock music and such has been far less sympathetically dealt with. Certainly, Dick Clark, from 1956 until the 1960s, with American Bandstand, endeavoured to present a view of pop music that would not be ingratiating, but by calling himself 'the world's youngest teenager' he appeared patronising in the extreme. Similarly, the UK's attempts to win over youth markets seemed somewhat hollow when Top Of The Pops first came to the screens in the early 1960s, but it has survived to become an object of affection as much as anything else. Specialist programmes about pop or rock have always been subject to the fickle finger of fashion: in Britain Ready, Steady, Go! created a formula in the mid 1960s that TV producers have endeavoured to replicate ever since. Likewise in America the era was marked by shows like Hullabaloo and Shindig that purported to have the finger on the pulse of the public. And things don't seemed to have improved much over the years.

WHILE TERRESTRIAL TELEVISION HAS GRAPPLED WITH MUSIC PROGRAMMING, the cable and satellite revolution has had no such problems, for they were quick to latch upon the video as the key component. MTV (Music TeleVision) has flourished through programming non-stop videos, or producing documentary features around bands with a new release. Geared specifically to rock audiences at first, MTV responded to criticisms that Black performers were given insufficient coverage by airing videos from Michael Jackson's album, Thriller, on heavy rotation, which contributed to making it the biggest-selling album of all time; MTV's sister operation, VH-1, has concentrated upon niche markets of rock. TNN (The Nashville Network) has made country music the boom genre of the 1990s.

Despite the enduring popularity of cable and satellite, music programming remains lazy for the most part, with few production companies willing to do anything other than feast upon the crumbs that record companies throw in their general direction. Until cable and satellite television can prove that they are willing to mount productions comparable in scale to those of terrestrial stations, they will remain the poor relation. If terrestrial TV can show entire operas or the Glastonbury Festival, why can't cable and satellite invest in original programming?

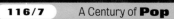

left, top: Johnnie Ray, whose gimmick was to break down in tears onstage, was dubbed by the press variously as 'The Cry Guy', 'Nabob of Sob' and 'The Prince of Wails'.

left, 2nd top: Patti Page 'The Singing Rage' had many hits in the early 50s, like 'I Went To Your Wedding' 'Tennessee Waltz', and 'How Much Is That Doggie In The Window'.

left, 2nd bottom: Strident singer Teresa Brewer hit the jackpot with 'Music! Music! Music!' in 1950, followed by a string of smashes worldwide.

left, bottom: Georgia Gibbs' biggest hits were in cover versions of mid-50s black R&B songs including 'Tweedle Dee', 'Dance With Me Henry' and 'Jim Dandy', all of which made the US R&B charts as well as the national pop listings.

POST-WAR POP

After World War II, the US was beset by an even graver threat to its prosperity: Communism. If the flagwaving jingoism of the war years had made entertainers such as The Andrews Sisters and crooner Bing Crosby international icons, the aftermath yielded a strong conservatism and an overt staunchness in the upholding of the American way of life. That was, after all, the reason why they had entered the war. So, although singers such as Crosby, Frank Sinatra and Dick Haymes continued to exert influence, it was vocalists like Johnny Ray ('Cry'), Al Hibbler ('Unchained Melody'), Kay Starr ('Wheel Of Fortune'), Al Martino ('Here In My Heart'), Doris Day ('It's Magic') and Guy Mitchell ('My Heart Cries For You'), who presented a clear, cleancut image of Americana in its various forms. That it was anodyne made it eminently more palatable to most tastes in light of the growing influence of frenetic black styles such as be-bop jazz and R&B.

1950-1960

CHICAGO BLUES

WHILE LOS ANGELES HAD ITS APPEAL FOR BLUESMEN FROM THE SOUTH-WEST LIKE T-BONE WALKER, CHICAGO WAS THE MOST OBVIOUS DESTINATION FOR SOUTHERN BLUESMEN. Chicago and Detroit were the twin peaks of the industrial heartland of the Midwest, offering employment on car assembly lines and a flourishing club circuit. And it was clubs like The Macomba on Chicago's South side that were the catalyst for what is known as Modern Blues.

Owned by two Polish emigrés, brothers Leonard and Phil Chess, The Macomba attracted the biggest names in jazz and R&B, such as Lionel Hampton, Louis Jordan, Ella Fitzgerald, Billy Eckstine and Louis Armstrong. By 1946, the Chess brothers had diversified by opening a record label. Called Aristocrat, initially, it was changed to Chess and, operating from a store front, the Chess brothers started to record artists such as Muddy Waters, Howlin' Wolf, Memphis Slim, Willie Mabon and Sonny Boy Williamson. As Muddy Waters

right: Guitarist Buddy Guy – particularly in his association with bass player Willie Dixon – was one of the mainstays of the Chicago blues scene.

above: The British R&B boom meant that Chicago stars like Chuck Berry were to be found touring the UK with English beat and blues groups.

above, centre: Belfast's Them, with Van Morrison (2nd right), were one of the hundreds of UK groups influenced by the Chicago blues sound.

above, right: John Mayall's Blues Breakers with Eric Clapton (2nd left) were a catalyst in British R&B.

would later say to historian Arnold Shaw: 'We're doing the stuff like we did way years ago down in Mississippi.' However it wasn't quite the same, because now the bands were amplified and, despite the presence of horn sections, it was the electric guitars that were the centrepieces of these blues bands.

Muddy's deft chording and restrained lyrical solos inspired reverence and his compositional talents were awesome, with titles like 'I Got My Mojo Working', 'I'm Ready', 'I Can't Be Satisfied', 'Rolling Stone', 'Rollin' & Tumblin'' and 'Hoochie Coochie Man' forming the backbone of the Electric Blues. Furthermore, his band came to resemble a who's who of the Chicago blues scene with Little Walter and James Cotton on harmonica, pianist Otis Spann, guitarists Jimmy Rogers, Hubert Sumlin, Buddy Guy, Luther Allison and Luther Johnson and the eminence gris of the Chess label, bassist and producer Willie Dixon, all passing through the ranks at one time or another.

While Chess and Muddy represented one side of the coin, John Lee Hooker understood instinctively how the blues should feel: 'Crawlin' Kingsnake', with the rhythmic tapping on the sounding board, a fractured chord here and there and the mesmerising tapping of the foot, created an atmosphere of foreboding sufficient to make the flesh creep and the teeth tingle. When the blues slipped out of fashion in the 1950s, Hooker just kept on doing what he had been doing all along.

By the time the 1960s dawned, the blues – courtesy of enthusiasts like Alexis Korner and

producers Bob Koester and Sam Charters – was undergoing a renaissance with R&B bands such as The Rolling Stones, The Pretty Things, The Yardbirds, Manfred Mann, John Mayall's Bluesbreakers, Georgie Fame and The Blue Flames forming in the UK and bands like The Paul Butterfield Blues Band coming together in the US. As a consequence, a new breed of superhero was launched upon the public: the guitarist. Among those to endure were Eric Clapton, Mike Bloomfield, Elvin Bishop, Jimmy Page, Jeff Beck and Peter Green. Not all survived unscathed though, as Bloomfield died in 1981 and Green spent many years in obscurity endeavouring to come to terms with his success. In later years, guitarists such as Jimi Hendrix, Duane Allman and Stevie Ray Vaughan all died prematurely.

As for Hooker, he has – along with BB King – assumed the mantle of elder statesman, with any number of musicians paying homage at his court. This has resulted in a plethora of reissues and some impressive new recordings, including The Healer (1990), Mr Lucky (1992) and Don't Look Back (1997), featuring famous fans such as Clapton, Bonnie Raitt, Van Morrison, Pete Townsend, Robert Cray and Larry McCray. While Hooker has helped maintain the current financial well-being of the blues, label owners such as Bruce Iglauer at Alligator, Chris Strachwitz at Arhoolie, producer Mike Vernon and vocalist/radio DJ Paul Jones have all nurtured new bands and young musicians, ensuring that the legacy of the blues remains intact.

1950, JUNE 25: THE KOREAN WAR, INVOLVING US AND UNITED NATIONS FORCES, IS TRIGGERED BY NORTH KOREA INVADING SOUTH KOREA

right: Patsy Cline in the furs and jewels that were a long way from the subsequent image of the female Country star.

PATSY CLINE

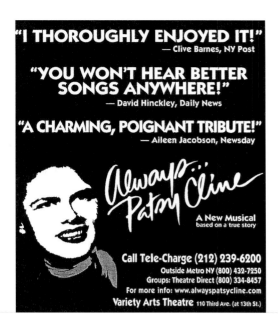
IN 1997, AN OLD TAPE OF A PATSY CLINE CONCERT AT THE CIMARRON BALLROOM IN TULSA IN 1961 WAS DISCOVERED. It served as a timely reminder of why Patsy Cline remains such a pivotal influence upon not just Country vocalists, but also stylists of any cultural background.

For Cline was very much her own woman. Not, perhaps, through her espousal of any especially feminist rhetoric, but more because she lived her own life the way she chose to do so. This individuality and unwillingness to be typecast suffused Cimarron performance, as she covered unlikely songs such as 'Bill Bailey, Won't You Please Come Home?', the Connie Francis hit 'Stupid Cupid', 'Shake Rattle and Roll' and 'When My Dreamboat Comes Home', making her impact on performers such as k.d. lang, Mary Chapin Carpenter, Tammy Wynette, Lucinda Williams and Reba McEntire that much more credible. Possessed of a voice and an emotive 'crying' vocal style that set the tone for her inheritors, Patsy Cline has become the ad-man's embodiment of Country, combining maudlin lyrics with a tragic demise.

She was born Virginia Patterson Hensley in Winchester, Virginia, on September 8, 1932. Displaying considerable precocity, she was an accomplished tap dancer by the age of four and had learnt to play the piano by the age of eight. After singing in local clubs, she auditioned for a trip to Nashville in 1948, where she appeared on the club circuit. Influenced by Rose Maddox and Kitty Wells, she won an Arthur Godfrey

Talent Scouts Show in 1957 with her rendition of 'Walking After Midnight'. This was then recorded and released by Decca. It was the first of a number of hits for that label that included 'I Fall To Pieces', 'Crazy' , 'Who Can I Count On' (1962), 'She's Got You', 'Heartaches', 'Strange' (1962) and 'When I Get Thru' With You' (1962). This spate of hits guaranteed her a spot at the Grand Ole Opry and established her as the Queen of Country Singers, supplanting Kitty Wells – a position that was reinforced by other hits, including 'Imagine That' (1962), 'So Wrong' (1963) and 'Leavin' On Your Mind' (1963).

On March 5, 1963, she was killed in an air crash near Camden, Tennessee, when returning home from a benefit concert in Kansas City; Hawkshaw Hawkins and Cowboy Copas were also killed in the crash. In subsequent years, her mystique and popularity have grown out of all proportion to that which she enjoyed during her lifetime.

Her posthumous hits include 'Sweet Dreams (Of You)', 'Faded Love', 'When You Need A Laugh', 'He Called Me Baby' and 'Anytime'. She was belatedly elected to the Country Music Hall of Fame in 1973, and in 1981 she was cited in the film Coal Miner's Daughter as having been an influence on Loretta Lynn. In 1985 Jessica Lange played Cline in Sweet Dreams, a film based on her life story. And more recently there has even been a Broadway musical dedicated to her music. Although she died over thirty years ago, the Patsy Cline legend is intact and looks set to run and run.

right: With hits like 'Ain't That A Shame' and 'Blueberry Hill', Fats Domino took the sound of New Orleans rhythm and blues into the pop charts worldwide.

below: 'The Killer' Jerry Lee Lewis was the wild man of 50s rock'n'roll with his pumping boogie piano and off-the-wall vocals best remembered in numbers like 'Whole Lotta Shakin'' and the immortal 'Great Balls Of Fire'.

ROCK'N'ROLL

IN PINPOINTING THE TRANSITION FROM R&B TO ROCK'N'ROLL, THE ONLY REAL DISTINCTION SEEMS TO LIE IN THE ICONOGRAPHY: CARS JOINED SEX AND DRINKING AS THE PRIME SUSPECTS. For many the distinction was purely semantic: Fats Domino had been playing with some success since the early 1950s. When rock'n'roll replaced R&B as the buzz phrase, Domino became inextricably associated with this style: no longer was he described as R&B, he was dubbed a rock'n'roller. As Domino's producer and arranger Dave Bartholomew was moved to observe: 'rock'n'roll and R&B are the same thing, but they (the whites) stole it from us (the blacks).' Johnny Otis – a white man – says much the same thing. So rock'n'roll was less to do with a style, more the product of a good marketing man's fevered imagination: in this instance that marketing man was Alan Freed. Rumour has it that Freed attempted to copyright the term; here he was a bit slow on the uptake, as registering it as a trademark would have been far more lucrative.

For all the assertions that rock'n'roll was exclusively a bi-product of black music, there are grounds for suggesting that country music played as big a part in the genesis of rock'n'roll as R&B. This too needs clarification as nowadays the Country-influenced strain of rock'n'roll is dubbed Rockabilly. At its peak no such distinction was drawn, as Elvis Presley and Carl Perkins were routinely lumped together with Little Richard as purveyors of the all-encompassing rock'n'roll genre. Furthermore, it would be a mite too simplistic to suggest that just the black performers brought R&B to the party and white performers brought Country: Chuck Berry was heavily influenced by Country music, and Elvis Presley was as influenced by the blues as by Country. The real point at issue, though, is that from the rock'n'roll era, a range of artists and performers who, quite reasonably, might have described themselves as R&B musicians became purveyors of rock'n'roll, as distinct from R&B. Semantics, again? Perhaps, but the case for Little Richard would be that he adapted the potency and emotional commitment of gospel to rock'n'roll.

While musically there were few intrinsic differences between R&B and rock'n'roll, those that did exist were glossed over by marketing men or more importantly producers. Both Leiber & Stoller and George Goldner were experts in their own way of taking R&B vocal groups and adapting their sound to meet the requirements of rock'n'roll. And so it

rock'n'roll

was that the dominant R&B musicians to bestride the rock'n'roll arena benefited from producers or label owners that were far-seeing enough – or just that cute – to master the cross-generational and cross-racial imagery of rock'n'roll. Or if one wishes to be absolutely brutal about it and perhaps over-simplistic: those that were perceived as rock'n'roll were those who were signed to record labels that had the distribution to make the records available nationally. Lew Chudd at Imperial in Los Angeles knew perfectly well that Fats Domino appearing in a variety of films such as The Girl Can't Help It could do more to stimulate record sales than any number of appearances on Dick Clark's American Bandstand could achieve. Similarly, it was common knowledge at Chess that appearances on the Alan Freed Moondog Balls would stimulate record sales.

Therefore it was producers such as Dave Bartholomew, Johnny Vincent and Allen Toussaint in New Orleans, Bumps Blackwell in Los Angeles, and the Chess brothers – Phil and Leonard – with Willie Dixon in Chicago, and Herb Abramson, Ahmet Ertegun and Jerry Wexler in New York who turned R&B into rock'n'roll. It was ironical that the rough-hewn vigour of rock'n'roll was, in turn, diluted to present the more consumer-friendly synthesised pop music at the Brill Building and, more contentiously, at Motown.

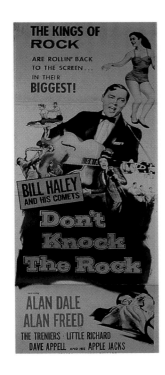

above: The first glimpse most teenagers had of their rock'n' roll idols was in low-budget movies made to cash in on the craze that Hollywood obviously thought would never last.

right: Little Richard, another singer/pianist, whose gospel-style shout and roaring sax accompaniment made 'Tutti Frutti' and 'Long Tall Sally' true anthems of rock'n'roll.

right: Johnny Burnette (centre) and seminal Rockabilly outfit The Rock'n'Roll Trio with Paul Burlison (left) and brother Dorsey Burnette on bass.

below: As composer of 'Blue Suede Shoes', Carl Perkins' place in rock'n'roll history was assured, though a car accident meant fellow Sun Records prodigy Elvis Presley stepped into the sneakers chart-wise.

ROCKABILLY

IN CARL PERKINS' SELF-PENNED 'BLUE SUEDE SHOES', ROCKABILLY ACQUIRED ITS DEFINING MOMENT. Falling somewhere between rock'n'roll and Hillbilly (as the contraction may suggest), Rockabilly's moment of glory lasted for just three years from around 1954 until 1957. While with 'Blue Suede Shoes', Perkins summed up the poverty that could inspire such pride in a new pair of shoes, it subliminally espoused the hopes engendered by the post-war economic consumerism. For just as doo-wop groups had been inspired by the success of groups like The Ink Spots and The Mills Brothers, so the emergence of Elvis Presley had a comparable effect on the white working classes of the South. As Perkins once said about his upbringing, 'you either worked the dirt or you owned it, and we worked it'.

Although Rockabilly quickly became out-dated, its influence was far-reaching and enduring. For the supercharged inventiveness of Gene Vincent's group, The Blue Caps, whose guitarist Cliff Gallup matched Presley's Scotty Moore in the ambitiousness of his solos, or 'The Rumble' (1954) by the super-cool guitarist Link Wray from Fort Bragg, North Carolina, contrived to make as big an impact on young musicians such as The Beatles as R&B or the blues: George Harrison's guitar solos suggested the influence of Perkins, Moore or Gallup instead of, say T-Bone Walker or Muddy Waters, while 'The Rumble', with its frenetic distorted tone, inspired The Who's Pete Townshend.

Similarly, Rockabilly – with writers such as Perkins, Jack Scott, Charlie Feathers, Mac Curtis and Johnny Burnette – contributed to the notion that music was a form of expression that did not require formal training: anyone with application and – perhaps – talent could learn how to play a musical instrument or write their own material themselves. While that was in no way prerequisite, it helped establish rock'n'roll beyond the US. For up until the emergence of The Beatles, rock'n'roll was perceived as, exclusively, a bi-product of American culture and British artists were always following in the footsteps of their American counterparts. Despite The Beatles and others looking to 50s rock'n'roll for inspiration initially, they were soon able to add their own cultural experience to create their own distinctive hybrid. In that spirit Rockabilly continued to exert its influence upon later generations: the seasoned accomplishment of Dave Edmunds, Ry Cooder and Creedence Clearwater Revival's John Fogerty; the uncompromising garage bands of the

rock'n'roll

ROY ORBISON
AND THE TEEN KINGS

BILLY PAR ELLIS   JAMES MORROW   JACK KENNELLY

ROY ORBISON   JOHNNY " PEANUTS " WILSON

above: The independent Imperial label had a fine roster of Rockabilly artists like The Strikes on its books.

right: Roy Orbison in his pre-dark glasses Rockabilly days.

1960s; and the raw energy of punk. Furthermore, revival groups such as Sha-Na-Na, The Flamin' Groovies, The Stray Cats and The Darts variously prospered during the 1970s and 1980s, while performer Robert Gordon teamed up with Link Wray for a brace of albums (Robert Gordon with Link Wray, 1977, and Fried Fish Special, 1978) that possessed the visceral energy and stylistic accuracy of Rockabilly's halcyon days. Even the UK's Jools Holland with his Rhythm and Blues Orchestra slips the odd Rockabilly tune into the repertoire; and guitarist Jeff Beck, accompanied by The Big Town Playboys, recorded an entire album – Crazy Legs (1993) – celebrating the style of Cliff Gallup. And as for Link Wray, he continues touring, attracting to his performances some of the best-dressed audiences around.

CARL PERKINS
THE SUN YEARS
Sun

JOHNNY BURNETTE
THE BEST OF JOHNNY BURNETTE
MCA

CD CHECKLIST

1954, MARCH 1: THE US TEST H-BOMB ON THE PACIFIC ISLAND OF BIKINI ATOLL. THE BOMB IS FIVE TIMES MORE POWERFUL THAN THE ATOMIC BOMB WHICH DESTROYED HIROSHIMA IN 1945

right: Loving You was one of Elvis' late-50s movies which retained some credibility as rock'n'roll vehicles.

far right: Elvis in 'Las Vegas' mode in the 70s, with white studded suit, but before corpulence took its toll.

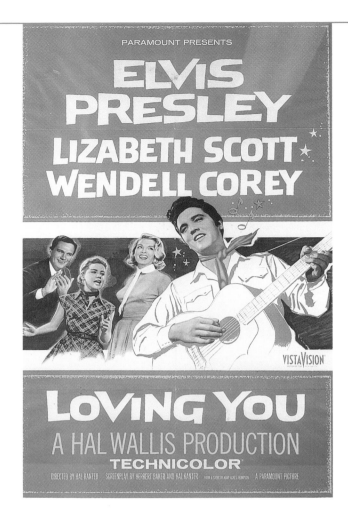

PARAMOUNT PRESENTS

ELVIS PRESLEY
LIZABETH SCOTT
WENDELL COREY

VISTAVISION

LOVING YOU
A HAL WALLIS PRODUCTION
TECHNICOLOR

DIRECTED BY HAL KANTER SCREENPLAY BY HERBERT BAKER AND HAL KANTER FROM A STORY BY MARY AGNES THOMPSON A PARAMOUNT PICTURE

ELVIS PRESLEY

WHEN SUN RECORDS BOSS, SAM PHILLIPS, AVERRED THAT IF HE COULD FIND A WHITE GUY WHO COULD SING LIKE A BLACK MAN, HE WOULD MAKE A FORTUNE, LITTLE COULD HE HAVE KNOWN HOW PRESCIENT THAT COMMENT WOULD TURN OUT TO BE. For Elvis Presley with those early Sun recordings quite literally drew from his roots. And those roots were to be found in gospel, blues and Country.

Born Elvis Aaron Presley on January 8, 1935, in Tupelo, Mississippi, the son of a sharecropper, his parents moved to Memphis in 1948 and encouraged him to sing at revival meetings and the local church. After graduating from Humes High School in 1953, he started truck driving for the Precision Tool Company. That same year he

1950 -1960

rock'n'roll

made his first visit to Sam Phillips' Memphis Recording Services, to cut a song as a birthday present to his mother, Gladys. As a consequence, in early 1954 Elvis met Phillips and they cut some demos together with guitarist Scotty Moore and bassist Bill Black. Despite the crudeness of these demos, Phillips was sufficiently impressed to organise more sessions. In July, 1954, they cut Bill Monroe's 'Blue Moon Of Kentucky' and Arthur Crudup's 'That's All Right, Mama'. Possessing the same rough-hewn vigour of Elvis's other Sun records, such as Roy Brown's 'Good Rockin' Tonight', Kokomo Arnold's 'Milkcow Boogie' and Arthur Gunter's 'Baby Let's Play House', this was the template of rock'n'roll, as well as Rockabilly.

Initially managed by Scotty Moore, and then Bob Neal, Elvis's career took off with the arrival of Colonel Tom Parker, the manager of Country singers Hank Snow and Eddy Arnold, who booked him onto the Hank Snow Jamboree. In August 1955 his final Sun single 'Mystery Train' was released, and later that year his contract with Sun was bought out by RCA for $35,000, with Parker assuming full managerial control of his career.

Over the next three years, with guitarist/producer Chet Atkins, Elvis cut a string of hits that included 'Heartbreak Hotel', 'Blue Suede Shoes', 'Don't Be Cruel', 'Hound Dog', 'Love Me Tender' (1956), 'All Shook Up' (1957), 'Jailhouse Rock' and 'King Creole' (1958). Although these hits marked him out as the authentic voice of rock'n'roll, they also suggested a versatility that would kick with a vengeance once he hit Hollywood. For by 1958, Elvis had appeared in three films, Loving You, Jailhouse Rock and King Creole. Even the intervention of a spell in the army could not diminish his appeal, although his records became progressively more tame as Hollywood assumed control of the image that was now known as The King. That is not to say they were bad records, for songs such as 'One Night' and 'I Got Stung' (1958) recalled some of the vigour of the early Sun sides, while ballads such as 'It's Now Or Never', 'Are You Lonesome Tonight' and 'Can't Help Falling In Love' possessed a conviction that transcended the often maudlin sentiment of the lyrics.

After eschewing live performances in favour of a series of less-than-inspiring movies, in 1968 he began to make strides towards relaunching his career as a serious rock'n'roller with an NBC-TV special, Elvis, backed by Scotty Moore, Charles Hodge and D.J. Fontana. This 'special' proved beyond any doubt that Elvis still encapsulated the spirit of rock'n'roll and that his voice was as strong as ever, as did From Elvis In Memphis, recorded the following year with producer Chips Moman. Armed with a backing band that included Rick Nelson's former guitarist James Burton and former Cricket Glen D. Hardin on keyboards, with backing vocals by the Sweet Inspirations, Elvis started a series of dates in Las Vegas that predicated his position as a showman par excellence.

Throughout the 1970s, as he declined physically – becoming overweight, emphasised by a flamboyant dress-sense – his popularity was unassailable: an estimated audience of 1.5 billion tuned in for his 1973 TV special, Aloha From Hawaii. However his deterioration appeared irreversible, and in 1975 he was hospitalised with a stomach disorder, which was treated with cortisone: the most notable side-effect of this treatment is to cause bloatedness. On June 26, 1977, he performed at the Market Square Arena in Indianapolis, Indiana, but within six weeks he was dead, having died of heart failure on August 16, 1977.

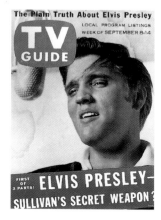

top: The 'million-dollar quartet' tapes with Elvis, Cal Perkins, Jerry Lee Lewis and Johnny Cash were only available on a bootleg for many years.

above: From 1956 to 1959 Elvis Presley was simply the most famous face in the world.

THE KING OF ROCK & ROLL: THE COMPLETE 50s MASTERS
RCA

ALL TIME GREATEST HITS
RCA

GREAT COUNTRY LOVE SONGS
RCA

CD CHECKLIST

1955, OCTOBER: THE 'BIG FOUR' SUMMIT IS HELD IN GENEVA WITH THE WORLD'S FOUR MOST POWERFUL NATIONS IN ATTENDANCE – THE US, BRITAIN, FRANCE AND THE SOVIET UNION

right: The diminutive Frankie Lymon (centre) and The Teenagers took Doo-Wop into the pop charts via the film Rock, Rock, Rock.

below: The Leiber & Stoller sides penned for The Coasters were the best-known epitome of Doo-Wop.

DOO-WOP

45 RPM
ATCO RECORDS
45-6132
Pub., Tiger, BMI
Time: 2:12
CAL C-461
CHARLIE BROWN
(Leiber-Stoller)
THE COASTERS
Division of ATLANTIC RECORDS, New York, N.Y.

THE BLACK DOO-WOP VOCAL GROUPS OF THE EARLY 1950s INITIALLY TOOK ON THE CHARACTERISTICS OF THE BARBER SHOP QUARTETS, but where barber shop quartets tended to draw their material from music hall, vaudeville and light opera, the black vocal groups drew from their own cultural heritage, using elements of gospel and blues. Many adopted the vocal purity of tone and phrasing associated with gospel, while others adopted the vernacular of the ghetto. It was the success of The Ink Spots and The Mills Brothers that galvanised the growth of vocal groups more than any other factor. This was peer pressure in its most undiluted form. Early groups such as The Mississippi Sheiks were unable to match the impact of The Ink Spots and The Mills Brothers, despite laying a reasonable claim to being the tradition's legitimate progenitors, as they did not try to dilute their music.

Groups such as The Orioles, The Moonglows (who incidentally were the catalyst for the term Doo-Wop through their use of 'blow harmonies'), The Drifters and The Five Royales retained a rough-hewn flavour that drew in equal measure from gospel and R&B. Initially the Doo-Wop groups' popularity tended to be ghettoized, reflecting the environment whence they sprung. Therefore crossover into the white pop markets was restricted and tended to be regarded as little more than a novelty. But by 1954, Doo-Wop groups were no longer regarded as novelty acts, although Leiber & Stoller, with The Coasters, would take the concept of novelty to another level with their witty vignettes. Consequently groups were constantly forming, endeavouring to reach the middle-ground market between R&B and pop (this would later describe itself as rock'n'roll). However what was to happen with greater frequency was the incidence of the one-hit wonder. Although that was to become a very 'rock'n'roll' concept in itself – cut a record and bang it out with maximum publicity – the intensity of the competition ensured that good material with a crossover potential was at a premium.

Soon producers such as Leiber & Stoller and George Goldner would get hip to the idea of forming groups – or labels come to that – just to record a song; among those to benefit from the Goldner method were The Harptones, The Crows, The Flamingos, The Isley Brothers, Little Anthony & The Imperials, and in the 60s girl groups like The Shangri-La's and The Dixie Cups. But it was Phil Spector who took the process a

rock'n'roll

stage further. Spector, with Brill Building writers such as Ellie Greenwich & Jeff Barry, Cynthia Weil & Barry Mann and Gerry Goffin & Carole King and groups such as The Crystals and The Ronettes, elaborated vast, grandiose productions on titles such as 'Then He Kissed Me' and 'Be My Baby'. Simultaneously, Berry Gordy at Motown signed groups one after another, and each were assigned to their own team of writers and producers. During the 1970s, Gamble & Huff in Philadelphia signed groups such as The Three Degrees, The O'Jays and Harold Melvin & The Blue Notes and created their own 'house' style. Now, in the 1990s, the legacy of Doo-Wop resides in the plethora of vocal groups, whose vocal purity and harmonising has reasserted traditional values like quality of composition above technological expertise.

above: Another vocal group catapulted to fame via a movie vehicle – Rock Around The Clock – The Platters.

CD CHECKLIST

NEWS

1956, NOVEMBER 4: SOVIET TROOPS ENTER BUDAPEST, CRUSHING AN UPRISING IN HUNGARY

LEIBER & STOLLER

SINCE THEIR FIRST MEETING IN 1950, the songwriting and production partnership of Jerry Leiber (born in Baltimore on April 25, 1933) and Mike Stoller (born on Long Island on March 13, 1933) has infused the rock'n'roll era with a knowing, but affectionate, mockery. While many white writers such as Dan Penn, Spooner Oldham, Willie Nelson and Chips Moman have contributed very successfully to the canon of R&B and Soul, few achieved it with as much panache, variety and consistency as Leiber & Stoller. At first, with the assistance of talent scout, producer and bandleader, Johnny Otis, they encapsulated the raw sexual urgency and visceral energy of rhythm & blues when they wrote and produced 'Hound Dog' for Big Mama Thornton in 1953. Later Elvis Presley recorded 'Hound Dog', along with 'Jailhouse Rock' and 'Love Me',

rock'n'roll

and showed that not only were they attuned to the urgency of rhythm & blues, but also they could tap into rebellious, anti-establishment impulses that propelled rock'n'roll. Where they really showed their mettle was in their work with black vocal groups, such as The Robins and The Coasters.

In 1951 Los Angeles-based vocal group, The Robins, were teamed up with Leiber and Stoller by Johnny Otis. Under this arrangement, The Robins scored hits with 'Riot In Cell Block #9' and 'Smokey Joe's Cafe'. However, their success distanced them from the conservatism of gospel-inspired vocal groups such as The Orioles. For Leiber and Stoller's utilised the argot of the street: these songs were not about the sanctity of love, they were the stories behind the newspaper headlines. Such was Leiber and Stoller's success that they were offered a deal by the influential independent, but New York-based, Atlantic label. Moving East from Los Angeles, two members of The Robins, Carl Gardner and Bobby Nunn, went along with Leiber and Stoller and started a new group called The Coasters.

Despite a constantly changing line-up ,The Coasters, under the auspices of Leiber and Stoller, notched up a whole string of hits such as 'Searchin'' and 'Youngblood' (1957), 'Yakety Yak' (1958), 'Charlie Brown', 'Along Came Jones' and 'Poison Ivy' (1959) and 'Little Egypt' (1961). As with The Robins before them, The Coasters managed to get straight to the heart of black American music by utilising the vernacular of the streets in their lyrics.

While The Coasters were undoubtedly their primary concern, they found time to expand their interests working with Elvis Presley, Wilbert Harrison and notably The Drifters. As rock'n'roll became progressively tamer, Leiber and Stoller tended to concentrate more upon Soul, nurturing the talents of The Drifters ('There Goes My Baby' and 'On Broadway') and their former lead vocalist Ben E. King ('Spanish Harlem' and 'Stand By Me'), and harnessing the seemingly inexhaustible supply of young writers currently streaming out of Broadway's hit factory, the Brill Building. These included Gerry Goffin and Carole King, Barry Mann and Cynthia Weil, Jeff Barry and Ellie Greenwich, and Doc Pomus and Mort Shuman.

In 1964 Leiber and Stoller co-founded the Red Bird label with producer George Goldner. While Goldner's reputation as a producer and svengali-figure was legendary throughout the music industry, he was incapable of sustaining interest for too long. The race tracks and casinos held far more allure for Goldner. Even so the label's first release was 'Chapel Of Love' by The Dixie Cups: it went to #1 and stayed there for three weeks. After selling their share of the label in 1966 they diversified, working throughout the late 1960s and early 1970s with artists such as Peggy Lee, Procol Harum, Stealers Wheel and Elkie Brooks.

During the 1980s Leiber and Stoller diversified still further with projects such as Hound Dog, an animated film feature, and an autobiographical documentary entitled Yakety Yak. In 1980 they put together the musical, Only In America, which included thirty of their more celebrated compositions. Then during the 1990s they ventured further into the territory of the musical, as their stage show, Smokey Joe's Café, generated huge acclaim on both sides of the Atlantic. Although both are now in semi-retirement, the partnership has endured longer than most marriages and it is not inconceivable that even at this moment they are not confecting some new extravaganza to titillate the taste-buds.

below: An earlier musical based on Leiber & Stoller songs was Only In America, produced in the 1970s.

THE COASTERS
THEIR GREATEST RECORDINGS
Atlantic

1957, OCTOBER 11: THE WORLD'S LARGEST RADIO TELESCOPE IS UNVEILED AT JODRELL BANK, UK

right: An early snapshot of Holly c.1954 (left) with Larry Welborn and Bob Montgomery as the trio Buddy and Bob.

below: The image of the bespectacled Holly which John Lennon claimed made wearing glasses seem cool.

BUDDY HOLLY

BUDDY HOLLY DIED OVER FORTY YEARS AGO: HE HAS BECOME A ROLE MODEL FOR MORE GROUPS THAN ONE COULD POSSIBLY MENTION. Buddy Holly and The Crickets were the first truly self-contained group: they wrote, they played all the instruments on their records and they performed live. Holly's compositional powers were intuitive, the trademark hiccups were spontaneous, and the instrumental prowess of The Crickets came from years of assimilating country music – an assimilation which was combined with a somewhat notional interpretation of rock'n'roll.

Charles Hardin Holley (the 'e' was dropped when he signed his first recording contract) was born in Lubbock, Texas, on September 7, 1936. During his childhood he mastered the piano and the guitar, and listened to the blues, Country & Western and R&B; he later teamed up with a fellow schoolboy, Bob Montgomery, and broadcast over KDAV as Buddy & Bob, with Sonny Curtis in the line-up. In 1955 they got their first break by opening for Elvis Presley and Ferlin Husky, among others, and Holly was signed to Decca as a result.

In 1956 Holly travelled to Nashville and cut some sides with producer Owen Bradley; while these sides included an early version of 'That'll Be The Day', Bradley's slick approach did little for Holly, and he was dropped by Decca. After this setback, Holly formed a new band with Jerry Allison (drums), Niki Sullivan (guitar) and Joe Mauldin (bass), and went to Clovis, New Mexico, to cut some sides with producer Norman Petty, who had recently made his mark with 'Party Doll' for Buddy Knox.

Petty negotiated two separate deals: one for The Crickets (the name the group had settled upon during a recording session) with Brunswick, and another one for Holly with Coral. The sides Holly cut as a member of The Crickets included 'That'll Be The Day', 'Oh, Boy!', 'Maybe Baby' and 'Think It Over'. His solo sides included 'Peggy Sue', 'Listen To Me', 'Rave On', 'Early In The Morning' and 'Heartbeat'. By October 1958, Holly and the Crickets had separated, with Holly (who had moved to New York) pursuing a solo career with a new group that included Waylon Jennings (bass), Carl Bunch (drums) and Tommy Allsup (guitar). In January 1959 they started a nationwide package tour, but midway through the tour, on February 2, after playing at the Surf

rock'n'roll

above: The Crickets with Buddy Holly (bottom), Jerry Allison (left), Joe Mauldin (top) and Niki Sullivan (right).

Ballroom in Clear Lake, Iowa, the light aeroplane in which they were travelling crashed just minutes after take-off, killing Holly, the Big Bopper (DJ JP Richardson), Ritchie Valens and all the other passengers.

After his death, material culled from Holly's final recording sessions in New York, and unreleased material from the Norman Petty sessions, gradually began to see the light of day, including 'It Doesn't Matter Anymore', 'True Love Ways', 'Reminiscing', 'Brown-Eyed Handsome Man', 'Bo Diddley', 'Wishing' and 'Love's Made A Fool Of You'. The 1978 film biography The Buddy Holly Story, starring Gary Busey as Holly, was greeted with critical acclaim rare for a rock biopic, and the musical Buddy is running to this day in London's West End.

1958, FEBRUARY: IN BRITAIN, THE ANTI-NUCLEAR WEAPONS CAMPAIGN FOR NUCLEAR DISARMAMENT IS FORMED, ATTRACTING THE YOUNG ON AN UNPRECEDENTED SCALE

right: 'Genius + Soul = Jazz' had Ray Charles with the cream of the Count Basie band and arrangements by Quincy Jones and Ralph Burns.

centre: Dubbed 'The Genius', Charles was a cult figure in Europe – particularly France – before he broke though into the pop charts.

far right: With albums like What'd I Say on the Atlantic label, Ray Charles summed up the marriage of blues and gospel that became Soul.

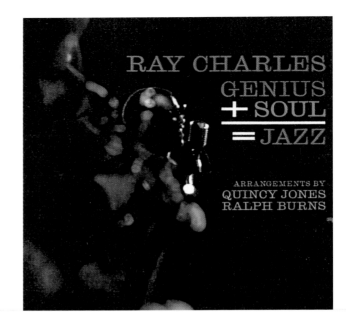

RAY CHARLES

GOSPEL PROVIDED MUCH OF THE GALVANISING FORCE AS RHYTHM & BLUES SLID SEAMLESSLY INTO THE SOUL ERA. But it was the efforts of performers such as Ray Charles and James Brown who cemented that transition. Moreover, both sought to control his musical destiny: Charles led – and still leads – his own orchestra and was one of the first black musicians to set up his own record label, Tangerine. While the prime motivation may well have been a perfectly natural desire to control and, therefore, reap as many of the financial rewards as possible, there was the subtext of ridding himself of the white man's shackles: ever since the emergence of R&B in the 1940s, white performers had capitalised with anodyne covers. The combination of gospel and R&B was too powerful to replicate and Charles recognised that in gospel there were vocal techniques that could be employed within a secular discipline.

Raymond Charles Robinson was born in Albany, Georgia, on September 23, 1930. When he was seven he contracted glaucoma and became blind; he was sent to study piano and clarinet at the Deaf and Blind School in Florida. By the time he was sixteen he was earning his living playing in various bands in and around Florida. In 1948, he moved to Seattle, where his next-door neighbour was Quincy Jones. After forming the McSon Trio, with guitarist G. D. McGhee and bassist Milton Gerred, he was signed to Downbeat Records in 1949, who released his first published composition, 'Confession Blues'. By 1952 he had

changed his name to Ray Charles and been signed to Atlantic for $2,500.

Overnight, the emphasis in his repertoire changed from a jazz-tinged flavour to a much harder R&B sound. One of the earliest recordings was 'Mess Around', which was followed by 'It Should Have Been Me' in 1954, the first in a string of R&B hits that included 'I've Got A Woman' and 'Hallelujah! I Love Her So'. In 1957 his first album, Ray Charles, was released; it was followed in November by his first major national hit, 'Swanee River Rockin' (Talkin' 'Bout that River)'. In 1958 he appeared at the Newport Jazz Festival; his performance was recorded and released as Ray Charles At Newport. Then came the release of 'What'd I Say': at the time it was his calling card, and with Charles' whoops and yells and 'sanctified' call-and-response vocals exchanged with his prototype vocal group The Raelettes, it still distills the essential ingredients of R&B, gospel and hip small band jazz – his recipe for Soul.

After signing a three-year contract with ABC-Paramount in 1959 – Atlantic retained the rights to all material, issued or unissued, cut during his tenure with the label – Charles altered the ground rules by making his debut a thematically linked album. Entitled The Genius Hits The Road (1960), all the song titles related to place names in the US and one of them, 'Georgia On My Mind', hit the top spot; the following year, Charles was duly rewarded with four Grammies. Others may have wondered how to follow that, but Charles had no such problem. Enlisting the help of Quincy Jones as arranger,

NEWS

1959, JANUARY 2: FIDEL CASTRO PROCLAIMS A NEW REVOLUTIONARY GOVERNMENT IN CUBA HAVING OUSTED THE DICTATOR BATISTA

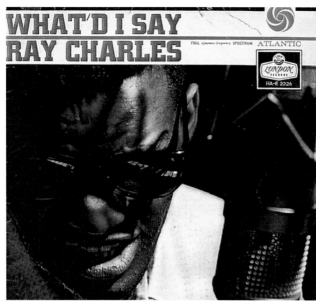

he released Genius + Soul = Jazz (1961). This album gave a clear indication that while he was happy playing Soul, he certainly intended to keep alive the traditions of the big band sound that were just as much a part of his musical heritage as anything else.

The following year he sparked considerable controversy by recording Modern Sounds In Country & Western (1962), featuring 'I Can't Stop Loving You', and Modern Sounds In Country & Western, Volume 2 (1963), with Hank Williams' 'Your Cheating Heart'. While these albums provoked a hysterical response, they highlighted Charles's strong associations with, and affection for, Country music. His next stop-over was for Ingredients In A Recipe For Soul (1963), which gave him yet another Grammy-winning hit, 'Busted'.

Thereafter, the chart-action slowed down and his output became slightly patchy. Every so often he released an album such as The Volcanic Action Of My Soul (1971), which recaptured some of the visceral energy of the Atlantic material. Furthermore, some of his auxiliary roles, such as his duet with Aretha Franklin at the Fillmore West (1971), the reworking of George Gershwin's Porgy & Bess (1976), with Cleo Laine, and the contribution to Quincy Jones's Back On The Block (1989), show him at his most imaginative and powerful. In 1992 he returned with his most complete album in years, My World, which confounded all the sceptics who had written him off for good. Charles may not have the abundance of vitality of bygone years, but he can still dazzle. If he feels like it.

THE BEAT BOOM

At the end of the 1950s, UK pop music was undergoing a sea change. Hitherto, it had been a pale alternative to its American counterpart. The BBC was the only broadcasting company in the British Isles, and consequently the BBC held a monopoly over tastes in popular music – and it seemed to believe, despite the advent of rock'n'roll that had revolutionised public taste, that sanitised singers like Tommy Steele and Cliff Richard were the acme of cool.

However there was the club circuit, which catered to both jazz and folk audiences, and there were the teen-oriented coffee bars. And it was in the jazz clubs that R&B began to take root through blues devotees such as Alexis Korner and 'trad' (Dixieland) jazz bandleader Chris Barber. Barber was a catalyst for not only did he help develop skiffle – a bi-product of folk and R&B – but also he encouraged blues men like Muddy Waters to tour Britain. Gradually, a blues and R&B circuit evolved with groups like The Rolling Stones, Manfred Mann and The Graham Bond Organization spearheading the charge in London. Up north, in cities like Newcastle and Liverpool, groups such as The Animals and The Beatles formed. The Beat groups had arrived, bringing with them a style that could match their American counterparts.

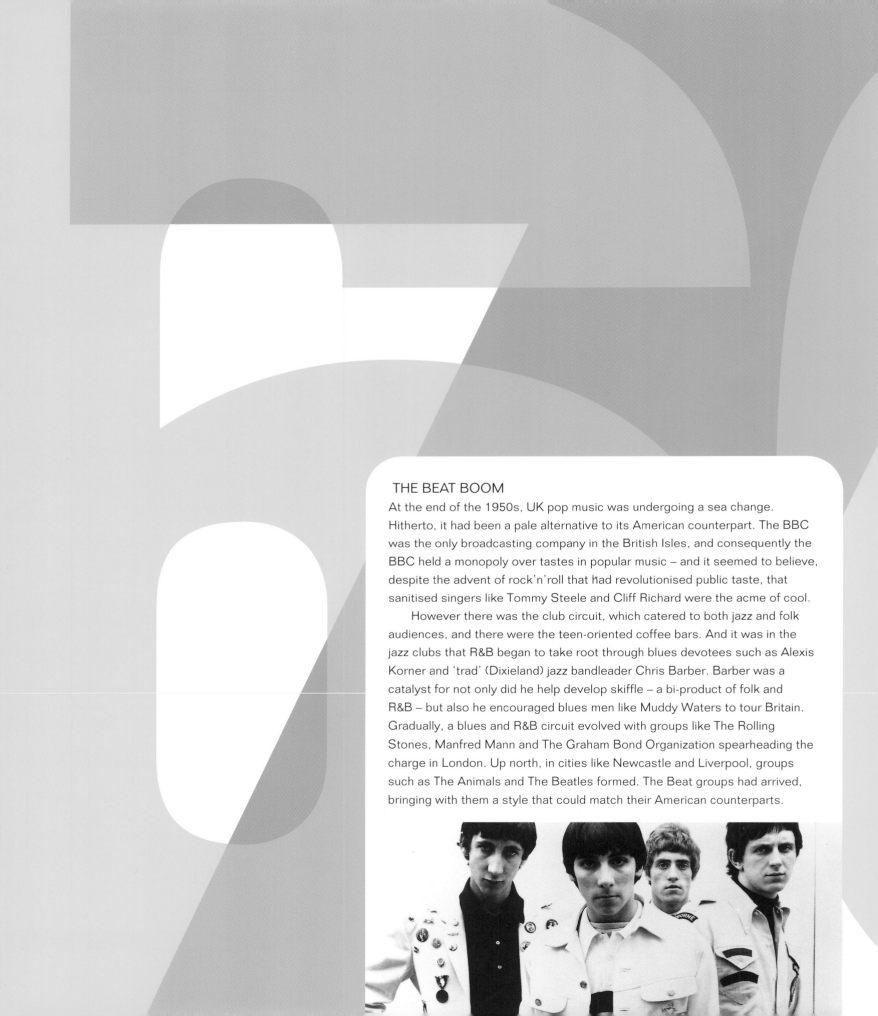

1960-1970

left: The 1987 album Trio featured three top names in a unque collaboration – Dolly Parton, Emmylou Harris and Linda Ronstadt.

below: Willie Nelson, along with Waylon Jennings, spearheaded the tough new approach to Country in their Outlaws album of 1976 which was the first manifestation of a 'New Country' emerging.

COUNTRY

COUNTRY MUSIC HAS ALWAYS BEEN A HYBRID, CONSTANTLY MUTATING AND EVOLVING, REFLECTING PERHAPS AS ACCURATELY AS ANY OTHER INDIGENT MUSICAL FORM THE SOCIETY FROM WHENCE IT SPRANG.

While there has always been an associational link with the Appalachians and Southern States of the US, this hybrid – hillbilly music, as it was formerly designated – evolved through a synthesis of Anglo-Celtic ballads, dances and folk songs and East European folk music, which had been transplanted by immigrants. Gradually this started to assimilate Afro-rooted influences, as the blues and gospel began to cross-pollinate. Within this hybrid, one of the most American of all indigent genres evolved, that of the 'cowboy song'. With the addition the cowboy song, the folk ballad or saga song began to take on a rather different face, and hillbilly music – with its shadings of Bluegrass – was described as Country & Western. However, Hillbilly, Country & Western or indeed Bluegrass were the musical reflections of essentially agrarian rural communities. Country was – and still is – regarded as a pejorative term denoting the simplistic musical expression of poorly educated, working class: more simplistically it was the the white man's blues.

With the emergence of rock'n'roll, the life styles of venerated Country performers such as Hank Williams were crucial to the perception of what a rock and roll star should be: both Elvis Presley and Johnny Cash

NEWS

above: Hank Snow always managed to straddle the fine line between commercialism and traditional styles.

centre: From the rockabilly environment of Sun Records, Johnny Cash has become a trancendental figure who for many epitomises country music.

far right: With songs like 'You're My Best Friend', Don Williams helped C&W cross over into the MOR mainstream during the 1970s.

VARIOUS ARTISTS
THE OUTLAWS
RCA

MERLE HAGGARD
THE VERY BEST OF
Capitol

CD CHECKLIST

were in varying degrees anti-authoritarian. For the heart of Country music, as exemplified by the Grand Ole Opry in Nashville, remained deeply conservative, reflecting the simple hopes and aspirations of its adherents.

The head-on collision between rock'n'roll and Country yielded the mutant rockabilly, with performers such as Buddy Holly and Carl Perkins utilising Country-styled arrangements, but with their lyrical imagery aimed at young audiences.

Even teen-idols such as Ricky Nelson, with his guitarist James Burton, drew from the Country stylings of Merle Haggard and Buck Owens. Both Owens and Haggard had migrated westwards and settled in Bakersfield, the most southerly tip of the San Joaquin Valley, in the late 1940s. And going against the accepted trends of Country music – almost exclusively acoustic, although instruments towards the end of the 1940s began to be electrified and amplified – the Bakersfield sound was characterised by the use of Fender Telecaster guitars with the volume cranked up.

By the 1960s, as well-educated college kids started to embrace traditional music, Country found aficionados in performers such as Gram Parsons and Chris Hillman. While both were erstwhile members of Folk Rock group, The Byrds, both brought their love of Country music into a broader context, paving the way for what was to be described as New Country. Before New Country emerged though, Country Rock had its day. Notably through groups such as The Eagles and The Flying Burrito Brothers, Country Rock was a blessing and a curse. For on the one hand it pioneered a soft, melodic form of rock that was radio-friendly to the point of being bland. On the other hand, it created an audience among affluent thirty-somethings who had never been exposed to orthodox Country music a such, but had grown up against a background of performers such as Bob Dylan and The Beatles. The consequence of this strange turn of events was a plethora of singer-songwriters with more angst and literacy than musical savvy, but it was this curious synthesis that engendered New Country.

OWN ENTERTAINMENTS PAPER

MERSEY BEAT

NEMS
WHITECHAPEL AND GREAT
CHARLOTTE STREET

THE FINEST RECORD
TIONS IN THE

Open until 6-0 p
(Thursday and Sat

JANUARY 4-18, 1962   Price

"Don't Forget:
"KLAATU
BARADA NIKTO"

Beatles Top Poll

FULL RESULTS INSIDE

Cover photograph by Albert Marrion

HERMAN'S HERMITS
SATURDAY, JUNE 12th

THE DAVE CLARK 5
FRIDAY, JUNE 18th

FIRST AMERICAN CONCERT
The Kinks & the Moody Blues
SATURDAY, JUNE 19th

THE BEATLES
SUNDAY, AUG. 15th
SHEA STADIUM

THE FIRST NEW YORK FOLK FESTIVAL

4 DAYS: JUNE 17th thru JUNE 20th
AT CARNEGIE HALL

THE BEATLES

above: A few months before they secured a recording contract (and sacked drummer Pete Best, far right) the Beatles were voted No 1 in the local Liverpool music paper Mersey Beat.

far right and centre: The many later solo efforts of individual Beatles included the perennial favourite 'Happy Xmas (War Is Over)' from John Lennon, and Ringo's less memorable take on the 50s sci-fi epic The Day The Earth Stood Still.

WHILE THE BEATLES HAVE GONE FROM STRENGTH TO STRENGTH AS PART OF THE MYTHOLOGY OF THE 1960s, the success of the 3-volume Anthology series in 1995-6 predicated not only their commercial status, selling around 26 million units worldwide, but also their immeasurable part in the evolution of contemporary music. Indeed, the term 'Beatle-esque' has come to assume much broader connotations, not only to a recent era of music, but also to a style of harmonizing: groups ranging from the contemporaneous exponents of Folk Rock, The Byrds, through the genre-jumping pure pop of The Bee Gees and the galumphing tunefulness of The Electric Light Orchestra to the tabloid-baiting antics of Oasis – have all doffed their hats in the direction of The Beatles.

However, with The Beatles, not only could they boast a songwriting team in John Lennon and Paul McCartney that would have been prodigious in any epoch, they had the visceral energy and inquisitiveness essential to the deveopment of any aspiring musician. In

George Harrison they had a guitarist who was as intuitive as he was inquisitive – it was he after all who acquired and used a sitar, triggering a widespread interest in Indian music in the process. Furthermore George's under-exploited compositional abilities provided a stylistic counterpoint to that of Lennon and McCartney. In Ringo Starr, they possessed a drummer whose lack of flash disguised a rhythmic steadiness that was the backbone to the group's overall sound.

As performers the Beatles changed the landscape for budding musicians, appearing initially in clubs such as Liverpool's Cavern, their performances combined energy with an amateurish enthusiasm. The group's willingness to grow up on stage, making mistakes and trying out fresh things before an audience, was ground-breaking in itself. When manager Brian Epstein took control of the group, he persuaded them to step out of the jeans and leather jackets into smooth, neat suits. In a sense this well-groomed image harked back to bygone eras and soon – controversially – groups such as The

left: The Beatles' entourage visiting the Maharishi (sitting at back), including (front row, 2nd left to right) Jane Asher, Paul McCartney, George Harrison, Pattie Boyd, Cynthia Lennon and John Lennon.

centre: Along with other British beat groups, the Beatles took America by storm. Here, framed now as valuable memorabilia, a flyer and ticket for their Shea Stadium date on August 15, 1965.

Rolling Stones and The Pretty Things showed the way forwards with their studied scruffiness. In that respect, Epstein got it wrong. By the end of the decade, any self-respecting musician was too preoccupied with their music to show anything but contempt for such minor issues as how they looked.

By the time The Beatles played their final gig in San Francisco on August 28, 1966, they had set another benchmark in the development of rock music: albums were now the order of the day. If both Rubber Soul (1965) and Revolver (1966) suggested that albums were of comparable importance to that of singles, Sergeant Pepper's Lonely Hearts Club Band (1967) certainly predicated that surmise. Costing around £25,000 and taking around 700 hours to record, Sergeant Pepper made it clear that rock music could not only be taken seriously, it was the medium of the moment. Had it not been for The Beatles and Sergeant Pepper, musicians certainly would not have been allowed to go into the studio for months on end to see

what they could come up with. Furthermore, the success of Sergeant Pepper heralded the cult of the Record Producer. While George Martin had guided The Beatles' career from their first sessions at EMI's Abbey Road Studios, encouraging them to use fresh ideas at every stage – they were the first rock group to use a string quartet ('Yesterday') – his success showed record companies the virtues of employing technical wizards who could complement and enhance the music they were recording. In other words, as had happened the previous decade with Elvis Presley, The Beatles and Rock music weren't expected to last: everyone thought that soon something would knock them – and it – off the collective pedestal at any second.

When The Beatles split up in 1970, it was because of personal differences in the group. Anyone thinking that once they had gone, popular music would resume the staid demeanour of the late 50s and early 60s were in for a big surprise, because the musical landscape had changed irrevocably. Rock music was now accorded serious consideration among academics – even if that consideration was often sententious and patronizing.

In the years since the group's demise, rumours of a reunion abounded. These were finally laid to rest in late 1980 when John Lennon was shot dead outside the Dakota Building in New York. While George and Ringo have distanced themselves from the day to day to business of making records, Paul – now Sir Paul – continues to make albums with as much enthusiasm and relish as he did all those years ago, back in the 1960s.

WITH THE BEATLES
Parlophone

REVOLVER
Parlophone

SGT PEPPER'S LONELY HEARTS CLUB BAND
Apple

ANTHOLOGY
Apple

CD CHECKLIST

1961, APRIL 12: THE SOVIET UNION PUT THE FIRST MAN INTO SPACE, THE RUSSIAN COSMONAUT YURI GAGARIN, NINE MONTHS BEFORE THE UNITED STATES FOLLOWED SUIT WITH ASTRONAUT JOHN GLENN

right, top: Mark Knopfler with the country-folk tinged English band Dire Straits.

right, below: Richie Furay's search for his musical roots took him from Buffalo Springfield to (pictured) Poco.

right, 2nd below: Fairport Convention with (l to r) Dave Pegg, Bruce Rowland, Dave Swarbick and Simon Nicol.

right, bottom: Simon and Garfunkel during a UK TV show in the mid-1960s.

FOLK ROCK

THROUGH THE MCCARTHY ERA OF THE 1950s, GUTHRIE, PETE SEEGER, RAMBLIN' JACK ELLIOTT AND CISCO HOUSTON BROUGHT FOLK MUSIC INTO CONTACT WITH A NEW YOUTHFUL AUDIENCE, WHO WERE UNIMPRESSED WITH THE NOTION OF 'REDS UNDER THE BED'. Soon the East-coast coffee bar and club circuit had spawned a whole host of aspiring writers and college drop-outs that included Bob Dylan, Joan Baez, Fred Neil and Jim McGuinn, among others. Similarly in the UK, folk entered the rock mainstream through the skiffle of Lonnie Donegan, with his reading of 'Rock Island Line', 'Cumberland Gap' and other songs from the Guthrie/Ledbetter repetoire in the mid-50s.

In 1964 McGuinn, now working on the West coast, had teamed up with songwriter Gene Clark to form The Byrds, with David Crosby, Chris Hillman and Michael Clarke. When The Byrds topped the charts on both sides of the Atlantic with Dylan's 'Mr Tambourine Man', folk rock announced its birth after a long and often uncertain pregnancy. While The Byrds took a leaf out of The Beatles' book, emulating their harmonies, The Byrds were able to go just a few steps further, for Crosby's vocal range gave them harmonic choices that others could only dream of. In 1966, Dylan caused uproar when he recorded with session men such as Mike Bloomfield (guitar) and Al Kooper (keyboards) and then toured with The Hawks – better known as The Band; Dylan had 'gone Electric'.

Meanwhile, in the UK, folk singer and guitarist Martin Carthy inadvertently boosted the career of

left, top: The Flying Burrito Brothers with (centre, front) Gram Parsons.

left, below: New England-born Buffy Sainte-Marie, best know for her song 'Universal Soldier'.

left, 2nd below: Folk-based singer-songwriter Tim Buckley.

left, bottom: The Lovin' Spoonful with (centre) leader John Sebastian, jug-band style rock for the optimistic 60s.

another aspiring American singer Paul Simon in the early 60s by introducing him to the traditional English Folk song, 'Parsley, Sage, Rosemary & Thyme'. When Simon teamed up with his old friend Art Garfunkel, as 'Scarborough Fair' the song became one of their biggest hits. Simon's own finely honed songs – with Art's sublime harmonies – touched upon the travails of urban life in the twentieth century and in the process broached an extraordinary level of mainstream popularity. Furthermore, like Dylan, Simon was prepared to employ arrangements from all facets of contemporary music from all corners of the world.

If Carthy failed to reap many rewards for his advice to Simon, he remained in the vanguard of Anglo-Celtic folk music, nurturing interest on the club circuit and creating an environment where groups such as Fairport Convention, Steeleye Span and The Albion Country Band could flourish. With a lineup that now reads like a who's who of Folk rock, Fairport Convention introduced a hitherto unknown Canadian writer called Joni Mitchell to UK audiences through their cover of 'Chelsea Morning' on their debut, Fairport Convention (1967). Later albums such as What We Did On Our Holidays (1968) and Leige & Leif(1969) combined traditional English folk songs, 'Matty Groves' and 'Tam Lin', with material by Dylan along with self-penned compositions. Furthermore, with vocalist Sandy Denny and fiddler Dave Swarbrick joining the group, they edged closer to traditional sources for material.

In the US, Folk Rock was less cut and dried. Despite the influence of Dylan and the initial success of The Byrds,

groups such as Buffalo Springfield, featuring Stephen Stills, Neil Young and Richie Furay, spawned Crosby, Stills and Nash and Poco, with Young starting a solo careeer before hooking up with Stills to make Crosby, Stills, Nash and Young. Furay showed where the real sensibilities of Americans wishing to discover their roots lay by starting the country-influenced Poco. McGuinn and Hillman had followed a similar route earlier with Sweetheart Of The Rodeo.

While Fairport became the template for other folk rock bands in England, in Ireland and Scotland, meanwhile, groups such as Planxty and Horslips plugged in and started updating their indigent folk music. By the mid-1980s, Irish groups such as The Pogues had brokered a deal with the mainstream, encouraging a spate of folk bands such as Altan, who were acoustic in origin and inspiration, but were quite prepared to utilise the benefits of technology where appropriate. Similarly, in Scotland, the chunky anthemic chords of groups like Simple Minds, The Waterboys and Big Country encouraged others such as Runrig and Wolfstone to expand the traditional rock band format, integrating Bag-Pipes and other traditional instruments into a basic rock format.

1961, AUGUST 17: THE WALL INBERLIN IS ERECTED, DIVIDING THE CITY INTO TWO HALVES BETWEEN ITS EASTERN AND WESTERN SECTORS

BOB DYLAN

top: Bob Dylan's debut album in 1962, fresh-faced with the cap that was his Greenwich Village folk-singer trademark briefly.

above: Good As I Been To You (1992) marked a return to the solo acoustic sound of his debut album with versions of traditional folk songs.

EMPLOYING IMAGERY IN HIS SONGS THAT IN ANOTHER EPOCH WOULD HAVE BEEN PUBLISHED IN VERSE FORM, DYLAN PROVED THAT THE SONGWRITER'S VERNACULAR WAS LIMITLESS AND THAT SACRED COWS WERE THERE TO BE DEMYTHOLOGISED.

Born Robert Allan Zimmerman, near Duluth, Minnesota, on May 24, 1941, Dylan played with The Golden Chords, before joining The Shadows, while at high school. In 1959 he enrolled at the University of Minnesota and started to play on the college folk-club circuit, changing his name to Bob Dylan (the name derived from the television cowboy character Matt Dillon, while the spelling paid homage to the Welsh poet Dylan Thomas). By 1960 he had dropped out of college and become immersed in the local counter-culture of radical politics and Beat poetry, fuelled by the folk songs of Woody Guthrie and Leadbelly and the blues of Robert Johnson.

In late 1960 he went to New York to visit Guthrie, and started to play the Greenwich Village club circuit, where he was spotted and signed to the Columbia label by the legendary A&R man John Hammond. His debut, Bob Dylan (1961), was a mélange of diverse styles and influences; it displayed his ability as a songwriter with the coolly laconic 'Talking New York' and 'Song To Woody'. The following year, his alignment with the civil rights stimulated his growth as a songwriter. Over the next two or three years albums such as The Freewheelin' Bob Dylan (1963) – featuring the wry 'Blowin' In The Wind', which was an accurate barometer of the mood of

pessimism among America's youth, and the fatalistic love-song, 'Don't Think Twice, It's Alright' – The Times They Are A-Changin' and Another Side Of Bob Dylan, backed up by appearances at the Newport Folk Festival, established him as the voice of American youth with his trenchant swipes at the establishment.

In 1965, he changed from predominantly acoustic instrumentation to electric, cutting Bringing It All Back Home and Highway 61 Revisited. When released as a single, 'Like A Rolling Stone' from Highway 61 Revisited caused more of a stir for its length at over six minutes than for its bittersweet lyrics. Even so it established new standards for what was deemed suitable for the singles market. While these albums were lambasted by folk purists, they marked the development of Folk Rock.

After teaming with The Hawks – later The Band – for a UK tour, he cut the double album Blonde On Blonde. On completion of the album, Dylan was injured in a motorbike accident and he immured himself in Woodstock with The Band, cutting the Basement Tapes, which were not issued until 1975. In 1967 he went back to Nashville and cut the Country-ish John Wesley Harding. While it intimated the stark simplicity of Freewheelin' with the gentle 'I Pity The Poor Immigrant' and the allegorical 'All Along The Watchtower', it suggested a growing interest in Country, which came full circle with Nashville Skyline (1969). In the early 1970s, Dylan's output varied wildly: from the fragmented feel of Self Portrait (1970), through the pastoral idyll of New Morning (1970), to Planet Waves (1973) and the live Before The Flood (1974).

NEWS

left: A poster for the film by D.A. Pennebaker of Dylan's 1965 UK tour Don't Look Back, which was made in black-and-white and released in 1967.

right: Bob Dylan as he appeared on the cover of the country-influenced album Nashville Skyline.

In the mid-1970s he took part in the Rolling Thunder Revue with a bunch of friends, including Joni Mitchell, Joan Baez, Roger McGuinn, Mick Ronson and poet Allen Ginsberg. While the edited highlights of the tour later appeared on the album Hard Rain, it was sandwiched between two of his finest efforts, Blood On The Tracks (1975) and Desire (1976). Street Legal (1978) and Bob Dylan At Budokan (1979), with the latter documenting his 1978 world tour, marked the end of a phase, as with Slow Train Coming he claimed to have converted to Christianity – a theme he returned to on Saved (1980) and Shot Of Love (1981).

Throughout the 1980s Dylan's studio albums were varying in consistency, but what became almost a never-ending tour continued through the 1990s, during which time three studio albums, Oh Mercy (1989), Good As I Been To You (1992) and Time Out Of Mind (1997), showed that while he certainly isn't mellowing, he has reached that platform of inscrutability where he can be all things to all men – and women.

PSYCHEDELIC ROCK

above: Although basically a blues band, Big Brother and the Holding Company with Janis Joplin came in on the wave of late-60s psychedelic groups.

FIRST BANDIED AROUND IN SAN FRANCISCO IN 1965–66, THE TERM PSYCHEDELIA WAS APPLIED TO THE DRUG CULTURE THAT GREW UP AROUND GROUPS SUCH AS JEFFERSON AIRPLANE AND THE GRATEFUL DEAD. Using drugs with hallucenogenic properties, such as LSD and mescalin, the Psychedelic experience evolved from Ken Kesey's Acid Tests, where chemist Stanley Owsley dispensed his own prescription of LSD to all-comers as bands such as the Grateful Dead played protracted sets against back-projected light shows. For many participants, the euphoria engendered by the ingestion of acid in tandem with the Dead's long sets induced a spirit of 'oneness' and camraderie. The Beatles, after their first of several visits to Haight-Ashbury – the epicentre of Psychedelia – were quick to associate the supposed spiritual benefits of LSD with their growing interest in Eastern mysticism, which they championed by following mystic and guru Maharishi Mahesh Yogi. All but George Harrison were quick to dismiss the Maharishi as a charlatan as soon as question marks about his probity were raised. Harrison, though, remained, and remains, a committed adherent of Eastern spiritual practices.

However, before the Maharishi had made his timely entrance into the lives of the Fab Four, Harrison had been sufficiently interested in Indian classical music to buy himself a sitar as early as 1965, which was used on Revolver, and also to befriend sitar maestro Ravi Shankar, who became Harrison's mentor and teacher; Harrison was by no means the first to demonstrate interest in Indian

Classical music – the British-based jazz musicians Joe Harriott and John Mayer assembled Indo-Jazz Fusions in the mid-1960s, largely inspired by saxophone giant John Coltrane's interest in Eastern music.

For a short while, in the wake of The Beatles' fascination with all things Indian, other groups such as Notting Hill-based Quintessence endeavoured to apply some of the rudiments of Indian classical music to rock. Psychedelia flourished as groups such as Pink Floyd performed with light-shows, utilised elements of electronic music, and wrote lyrics with space-age imagery, thus pioneering what was to be described as Progressive Rock. Back in San Francisco, while Psychedelia was diluted with followers being dubbed 'hippies' or more appallingly 'flower children' – due to their devotion to such concepts as love and peace – bassist Phil Lesh of the Grateful Dead, and guitarist Jorma Kaukonen and bassist Jack Casady of Jefferson Airplane, drew extensively from the forms and rhythmic patterns of Indian classical music.

Inevitably, once The Beatles had turned their backs on Eastern mysticism and the media had got their hands on the twin concepts of 'hippies' and 'flower children', the potential for spiritual enlightenment while 'tripping' was down-played. By the 1970s, Psychedelia had passed into history and Progressive Rock. Certainly in San Francisco, the Dead and The Airplane continued in much the same way as before, but as the decade wore on, psychedelic bands were seen as products of a bygone era.

Towards the middle of the 1980s, ecstasy replaced LSD as the bespoke drug. Immediately it gained

---

JEFFERSON AIRPLANE
SURREALISTIC PILLOW
RCA

KULA SHAKER
K
Sony

NEWS

1962, AUGUST 5: MARILYN MONROE IS FOUND DEAD IN HER BUNGALOW NEAR HOLLYWOOD, CONSPIRACY THEORIES RAGING FOR YEARS TO COME

below: Psychedelic poster art defined the era visually; a poster for a London Queen Elizabeth Hall date by the Incredible String Band.

centre: A flyer for an album by The Grateful Dead.

right: A poster for a Filmore Auditorium gig by the Jimi Hendrix Experience.

popularity, ostensibly inspiring feelings of uncontrollable good-humour and boundless energy. The only apparent way to absorb this elation was by dancing endlessly. While there were similarities with the Psychedelic culture of the late 1960s, nobody could possibly pretend that that had been dance-oriented. Acid House emerged from synthesising elements of Chicago House style with that of European disco, which had found its feet on the dance-floors of clubs in Ibiza. Although dance was pivotal to this new spin on Psychedelia, groups such as The Orb evolved

ambient House, which had parallels with Pink Floyd; The Prodigy boy-wonder Liam Howlett imbued the rave culture with a wit and flair that belied its superficial hedonism; and The Shamen entered the spirit of the drug culture with a dedication and conviction worthy of the Grateful Dead.

By the mid-1990s, as melodic guitar-led bands such as Oasis dominated the airwaves, Kula Shaker, drawing much of their lyrical imagery from eastern religion and mysticism, seemed to bridge the gap that the rave culture had engendered.

above: The Jimi Hendrix Experience's defining album, their 1967 debut Are You Experienced with (l to r) Redding, Hendrix and Mitchell.

right: The art of psychedelic graphics seemed particularly apt for the swirling, mind-blowing music of Hendrix.

right: Hendrix has often been judged a young, hedonistic character whose lifestyle directly led to his demise.

JIMI HENDRIX

above: Lost in space, Hendrix made the guitar speak in ways simply never heard before.

OF ALL THE PERFORMERS TO EMERGE DURING THE 1960S, HENDRIX WAS ONE OF THE MOST INFLUENTIAL. His technical prowess as a guitarist far exceeded the flamboyant showmanship for which he was mostly known. While Hendrix was an innovator, there was nothing faddish about his technique or indeed showmanship: as early as the 1940s, guitarist T-Bone Walker had been playing a jewel-encrusted guitar behind his head; later still Guitar Slim and Johnny 'Guitar' Watson employed similar tactics to attract attention.

It all started in 1954 when he was given an electric guitar, which he learnt to play by listening to records by R&B artists such as B.B. King and the Chicago blues of Muddy Waters and Elmore James. After a spell in the army he became a session guitarist, under the pseudonym Jimmy James, backing artists like King, Sam Cooke, Jackie Wilson and Little Richard, which was followed by stints with the Isley Brothers and Curtis Knight's Kingpins. By 1965 he had launched out on his own and was beginning to pull the disparate strands together that would make his style the most widely copied since that of jazz guitarist Charlie Christian in the late 1930s.

The formation of the Jimi Hendrix Experience, with drummer Mitch Mitchell and bassist Noel Redding, provided the framework for a number of records – 'Hey Joe', 'Purple Haze' and the debut album Are You Experienced (1967) that made the average guitarist sound as if they were auditioning for the annual village fete. On June 18, 1967, the group appeared at the Monterey Pop Festival on the same bill as Otis Redding and Janis Joplin;

Hendrix's performance – as near as damn it – blew all others off stage, gobsmacking the crowd: deconstructing 'The Star Spangled Banner' was tantamount to sedition. His grasp of technique and bluesy lyricism on titles like 'Little Wing', 'The Wind Cries Mary' and 'Burning Of The Midnight Lamp' was a revelation to those who believed technique was all about playing as many notes as possible, as fast as possible.

After Axis: Bold As Love (1967), he cut Electric Lady-land (1968), featuring 'Voodoo Chile', among others, with assistance from Al Kooper and Steve Winwood: its style anticipated Jazz Rock. Twenty-five years later, it is still as fresh today as it was then, prompting those who had been raised on jazz to view rock with a more appraising eye. Ultimately this caused many young jazzmen – from guitarists John McLaughlin and John Scofield to bassists Stanley Clarke and Jaco Pastorius – to look at technique as if it were a lump of putty, instead of a lump of concrete; and for successive generations of black funksters such as James Brown, Sly Stone, George Clinton and Prince to view rock with the acquisitive eye for detail of a diamond merchant. Naturally there was a down-side to his impact, as heavy metal became the mainstay of Sports Stadia across the US.

Despite his premature death in London on September 18, 1970, he managed to cram enough into his short career to last most people a lifetime, and his willingness to play anywhere, anytime, with anyone, ensured a staggering body of work that influenced all that came within its compass.

1963, NOVEMBER 22: PRESIDENT JOHN F.KENNEDY IS GUNNED DOWN DURING A MOTORCADE THROUGH DALLAS, TEXAS

SOUL

above: One of the greatest individual voices of soul music, Motown's Marvin Gaye.

SOUL IS A SYNTHESIS OF R&B AND GOSPEL: THE TESTIFYIN' TRADITIONS OF GOSPEL FUSED WITH THE SECULAR TRADITIONS OF R&B. THE HYBRID IS SOUL. Thus one of the first soul records was 'I Gotta Woman' by Ray Charles: the call-and-response style of Charles' vocals can be traced back to gospel, while the lyrical imagery dealt with the minutiæ of everyday life. Sam Cooke was Soul's first true sex symbol. When he was a member of The Soul Stirrers the adulation his performances inspired had little or nothing to do with religious zeal: his ability to work a congregation up into a frenzy was born out of his awareness of his own sexuality and his instinctive showmanship. When he left The Soul Stirrers to become a 'pop singer', Cooke took the inflections and intonations of church music with him.

During the 1960s the inexorable rise of Motown delineated a pattern in the rising popularity of Black American music. For the success of Motown represented the mainstream acceptance by white audiences that Black culture was a force in itself. Through this popularisation by Motown, the more earthy facets of Soul music began to impinge overtly upon white culture: white guitarist Steve Cropper of Booker T & The MGs once asserted that the only reason he had started playing was that in the segregated South of his upbringing, the only desegregated place was on the bandstand. This culture crash came to a head with the success of the Stax and Atlantic labels. Both were owned initially by white men, but both sought to develop acceptance of Black American music in its purest and most unadulterated form. Atlantic, for example, signed Aretha Franklin,

soul

creating under the nominal tutelage of producer Jerry Wexler a body of work – including songs by Brill Building writers Gerry Goffin and Carole King – that embraced the secular with all the fervour and commitment of a revivalist meeting. Otis Redding, in the months before his death in an aeroplane crash, seemed set to crossover and achieve major appeal among white audiences after his appearance at the Monterey Pop Festival alongside Rock artists such as Jimi Hendrix and Janis Joplin. However it was James Brown that made the single biggest impact, bringing Funk into a wider context.

During the 1970s Soul achieved a universal appeal through at first Gamble and Huff's Philadelphia label and then through the ubiquitous and often spurious benefits of disco. While disco endorsed the rhythmic qualities of Soul, it tended to devalue the emotional content. Nevertheless the emergence of singers such as Luther Vandross and Teddy Pendergrass (former lead vocalist of Harold Melvin & The Blue Notes) harked back to the Sam Cooke era, for they were unafraid to deploy the melisma of gospel in a secular context. However, it was the march of technology that had the greatest effect on Soul, as synthesizers and drum-machines became standard issue. Moreover rap artists and hip hop groups were not above using samples of chord sequences or rhythm tracks or snatches of vocals from great Soul records and repackaging them within different settings. Now, in the 1990s, the practice of sampling has become just another facet of record production, and so the basic principles of Soul have tended to re-assert themselves with vocal superiority and emotional content defining the prerequisites.

above: Soul man Billy Stewart had a huge hit with a radical version of 'Summertime' in 1966. He was to die with three of his band in a 1970 car crash.

left: The undisputed Queen of Soul, Aretha Franklin.

1964, JULY 2: THE CIVIL RIGHTS ACT MADE LAW, MAKING RACIAL DISCRIMINATION ILLEGAL THROUGHOUT THE UNITED STATES

JAMES BROWN

ON DECEMBER 17, 1988, A SOUTH CAROLINA JUDGE SENTENCED
JAMES BROWN, 'THE HARDEST WORKING MAN IN SHOW BUSINESS',
to six years in prison on a variety of charges, including resisting arrest and carrying
firearms without a licence. Thus a career that had spanned 33 years came to a temporary
halt; he was released in 1991. However, in purely statistical terms, he has notched up
114 appearances in the US charts, which is more than any other black artist.

Born in Barnwell, South Carolina, on May 3, 1928, and raised in Augusta, Georgia,
Brown, with Bobby Byrd, who were both members of the Gospel Starlighters, formed
The Famous Flames in 1954. By 1956 Brown had signed with the Federal label, a
subsidiary of King, and recorded 'Please Please Please'; that it was described by Syd

Nathan, the owner of King, as 'a piece of shit', said more about Nathan's eloquence than it did about the record. Although it was a very minor hit in the US, it possessed the dramatic sense of timing that was to become Brown's hallmark. In 1959, having signed with the booking agency, Universal Attractions, he took the 'James Brown Show' out on the road and began a practice that would earn him a reputation as one of the most exciting performers in the world.

Throughout this period he released new singles such as 'Think' and 'Night Train' every couple of months, while maintaining the unflagging work schedule that was already his trademark. In 1962 he released Live At The Apollo, which captured the raw unbridled energy of his show where elements of Soul, gospel and R&B were fused. The success of this album gave him the requisite muscle to form his own production company, Fair Deal, with Ben Bart, owner of the booking agency Universal Attractions. After a brief spell with the Mercury subsidiary, Smash, which resulted in legal action with Nathan, Brown cut 'Out Of Sight' (1964).

This clearly indicated the direction in which Brown was moving: the juddering bass line punctuated by staccato blasts from the horns and the extraordinary rhythmic intensity of guitarist Jimmy Nolen pioneering a dance-oriented Funk that would prepare the ground for countless imitators. Despite the legal wrangling with Nathan, Brown demanded, and got, a higher royalty rate and greater artistic control.

Over the next few years, Brown issued a string of records that changed the map: 'Papa's Got A Brand New Bag', 'I Got You (I Feel Good)', 'It's A Man's, Man's, Man's World', 'Cold Sweat', 'I Got The Feelin'' and 'Say It Loud – I'm Black And I'm Proud'. Furthermore, as Ray Charles had done in the 1950s, so Brown was to do in the 1960s by being both a catalyst and a commentator upon the growing Civil Rights movement. Although Martin Luther King was quoted as saying that he viewed Brown's support as potentially hazardous, this did not stop Brown from appearing to appeal for calm on national TV following King's assasination on April 4, 1968, and the ensuing rioting in over thirty cities.

During the 1970s, more hits followed, including 'Get Up I Feel Like Being A Sex Machine', 'Super Bad' and 'Get Up, Get Into It, Get Involved', and albums such as the live Sex Machine (1970) and Revolution Of The Mind (1972), but it was his support of younger musicians such as bassist Bootsy Collins that illustrated his talent for leadership, not altogether dissimilar from the approach of both trumpeter Miles Davis and pioneering 'soul jazz' drummer Art Blakey. In common with other Black performers such as Marvin Gaye and Bobby Womack, Brown collaborated with Fred Wesley of the JB's (who had replaced The Famous Flames in 1971) on the scores of Black Caesar and Slaughter's Big Rip-Off (1973). While these 'blaxploitation' movies were routine, they reiterated the extent of Brown's influence.

Although the hits decreased, James Brown continued to exert a strong hold upon his audiences wherever he appeared. Nowhere was this influence more keenly felt than in the volatile atmosphere of clubland, where by the 1980s and 1990s his earlier ground-breaking records were being sampled and remixed by DJs. To date, Brown has been sampled in this way more than any other single artist. That his new records released during that corresponding period have been erratic or non-existent is irrelevant, for despite the odd entanglement with the law, his live show remains, as ever, an absolute object lesson in stagecraft.

above: A Soul classic and one of the most sensational live albums of all time, from 1962 James Brown Live At The Apollo.

1965, MARCH: PRESIDENT LYNDON JOHNSON SENDS THE US MARINES INTO THE SCALATING CONFLICT IN VIETNAM

MOTOWN

WHEN BERRY GORDY SET UP MOTOWN RECORDS IN 1959, HE CREATED A TEMPLATE THAT MANY BLACK BUSINESSMEN AND WOMEN HAD ENDEAVOURED BUT FAILED TO ACHIEVE PREVIOUSLY, THROUGH LACK OF FINANCE, FORMAL EDUCATION OR SINGLE-MINDEDNESS. By the end of the 1960s, Motown was the largest black-owned corporation in the USA, and had achieved a crossover to white middle-class audiences.

Gordy was born on November 28, 1929, in Detroit, Michigan. After a successful career as a boxer and three years in the army in Korea, he returned to the USA in 1953 and opened the 3-D Record Mart. The record shop didn't last long and went bankrupt in 1956. The following year, after a spell working for General Motors, he formed a songwriting partnership with Billy Davis, the boyfriend of his sister Gwen, and they started to write for one of his former boxing colleagues, Jackie Wilson. In 1958 they had their first hit, 'To be Loved'; it was followed by 'Lonely Teardrops', 'I'll Be Satisfied' and 'Reet Petite'. With the royalties he earned from Wilson's records, he set up his own production company, leasing Marv Johnson's 'You Got What It Takes' to United Artists. His motives for this step were undoubtedly governed by a desire to make money, but also he had taken exception to the way Brunswick had produced the songs he had written for Wilson, swamping them with lavish string arrangements.

By 1960 Gwen had set up her own label, Anna, which had Barrett Strong, Joe Tex, Lamont Dozier and the Spinners under contract. In the meantime, Gwen had met former

soul

far left: He started as a twelve year-old child prodigy at Motown, and developed into a legend – Stevie Wonder.

left: One of Motown's greatest, and a founding artistic father of the company, Smokey Robinson (far left) with his group The Miracles.

Moonglow and producer Harvey Fuqua, whose own label, Harvey, had Junior Walker and Marvin Gaye under contract. Fuqua sold the Harvey label to Gordy. In March 1960, Barrett Strong scored a big hit with the Gordy-penned 'Money', which prompted Gordy to set up the Tamla Motown label.

While there can be little doubt about Gordy's business acumen – the voracity with which he set about accumulating publishing rights was breathtaking – he had a remarkable nose for talent and, like all good managers, the ability to delegate. He set about employing under contract teams of musicians, writers, producers, engineers and arrangers to service the requirements of his fast-developing roster of artists; it was they who pioneered the Motown Sound. A former friend, Smokey Robinson, who with his group, The Miracles, gave Motown its first million-seller with 'Shop Around', was the only artist afforded any latitude within the strict hierachy, although Marvin Gaye and Stevie Wonder were later allowed to break the mould, after Gaye's phenomenal success with 'I Heard It Through The Grapevine'.

By the mid-1960s, Gordy had assembled a roster of artists such as The Supremes, The Four Tops, The Temptations and Stevie Wonder. Although some critics maintained that Gordy tailored the Motown Sound to the requirements of the white middle-class, a large percentage of Motown's output was just as feisty and raw as anything that came out of the Stax or Fame studios.

In 1971 Gordy relocated Motown to Los Angeles. Some artists, like The Four Tops, chose to remain behind in Detroit. Furthermore, artists and technicians, who had become increasingly resentful over the niggardly rates of pay and lack of credit, gradually drained away to other labels where – or so they thought – they would be better rewarded. However, unlike its main competitor of the 1960s Stax, Motown continued to thrive throughout the 1970s and 1980s, signing artists like The Jackson Five, Lionel Richie, The Commodores and Boyz II Men.

In 1982 Gordy signed a distribution deal with MCA, which culminated in the selling of the entire company to an entertainment conglomerate, Boston Ventures, with MCA acquiring 20 per cent of it. In the early 1990s, Motown was acquired by Polygram; Gordy however retains significant publishing rights.

top: The Supremes with (l to r) Florence Ballard, Diana Ross and Mary Wilson

above: An advertising logo for the single 'Please Mr.Postman' by the Marvellettes.

1966, AUGUST 13: CHAIRMAN MAO TSE TUNG TRIGGERS THE CULTURAL REVOLUTION, DESTABILISING ALL ASPECTS OF CHINESE SOCIETY

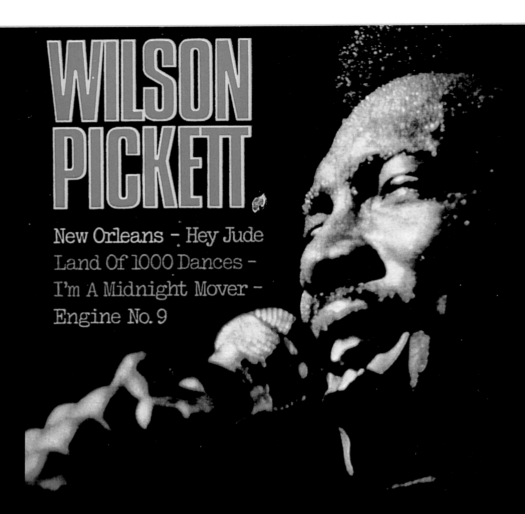

WILSON PICKETT

New Orleans – Hey Jude
Land Of 1000 Dances –
I'm A Midnight Mover –
Engine No. 9

STAX

SUPER Soul On Tour
Ben E. King
Sister Sledge
Jimmy Castor Bunch
Detroit Spinners
ATLANTIC

IN 1961 JIM STEWART FOUNDED THE STAX LABEL. Throughout the 1960s the name Stax was synonymous with Soul and R&B. It differed from its counterpart, Motown, in Detroit, who seemed to be more adept at penetrating the white mainstream, by aiming at the black markets. Despite the fact that Stewart was white, as were most of the producers and session musicians, Stax managed to draw from the rich traditions of Southern styles, incorporating elements of gospel and blues, as well as Country.

Stewart was born in Middleton, Tennessee, in 1930. After graduating from Memphis State University he went into banking, but played the fiddle in a country-swing band in his spare time. In 1957 he recorded the Country tune 'Blue Rose'. The following year, he and his sister Estelle Axton formed their own record label, Satellite. In 1958 Chips Moman, a session guitarist, teamed up with Stewart and produced most of the records that were issued by Satellite.

In 1960 Moman spotted an old cinema called the Capitol on East McLemore Avenue, Memphis; Stewart rented it for $100 a month. He knew that in order to survive it was necessary to have the co-operation of the local radio stations. He approached John Richbourg of the Nashville station, WLAC, which had a predominantly black audience, and made over to him a percentage of the royalties of a song he had written. The song was 'Cause I Love You', recorded by Carla Thomas, the daughter of Rufus Thomas, who was a DJ on the Memphis station, WDIA; Rufus persuaded another DJ, Dick Cole of WLDK, to play the record. After it had sold fifteeen thousand copies locally it came to the attention of Atlantic producer Jerry Wexler, who leased it from Stewart for $1,000 for national release on the Atlantic label; this was the first money Stewart had earned for Stax. The record featured Steve Cropper on guitar and Booker T. Jones on baritone sax, who –- as members of the house band, The Mar-Keys, later known as Booker T & The MGs – became pivotal to the Stax 'sound'. That year they changed the name of the label from Satellite to Stax: the name 'Stax' was a contraction of the first two letters of the names Stewart and Axton.

Throughout the early 1960s Stewart set about establishing the company; signings like William Bell and Otis Redding began to develop the reputation of the label. In 1965 he enlisted the services of Al Bell, as head of promotion. With Bell in place he had a man who was quite prepared to use his blackness in the same way as Motown's Berry Gordy: to inspire racial loyalty. By 1968, despite the loss of Redding in a plane crash in 1967, Stax had accumulated a roster of artists such as Eddie Floyd, Sam & Dave, Johnnie Taylor and blues guitarist Albert King that was the envy of many of the major companies.

In 1968 Stewart signed a deal with Gulf & Western, the owners of Paramount Records. It was the first of a series of decisions that signalled the beginning of the end for Stax. As part of the deal Stax was required to deliver 27 albums to Paramount to cement it. That they were able to fulfil this commitment within a month showed an admirable proficiency, even though the quality was variable. The biggest seller was Hot Buttered Soul by Isaac Hayes. In 1972 Stewart sold his share of the company to Bell, but remained as president.

Throughout the early 1970s, as tales of gross mismanagement and financial irregularities proliferated, Stax underwent a series of changes that precipitated its eventual demise in 1976. Despite that, the Stax catalogue remains a crucial link in the evolution of black music in the twentieth century.

right: The Stax house band, Booker T. and the MGs, with (l to r) Donald 'Duck' Dunn, Steve Cropper, Al Jackson and (seated) Booker T. Jones.

far right: Otis Blue, the seminal album collection from the great Otis Redding.

1967, OCTOBER 9: HERO OF THE CUBAN REVOLUTION CHE GUEVARA IS KILLED CONDUCTING A GUERRILLA CAMPAIGN IN BOLIVIA, THEREBY ACHIEVING INSTANT CELEBRITY WITH YOUNG PEOPLE ACROSS THE GLOBE

EVINS-KIRSHNER DEBUTS **DIMENSION RECORDS**

WITH
ITS FIRST SINGLE
HEADED UP THE TRACK
TO NUMBER ONE!

LITTLE EVA

Produced by
JERRY GOFFIN
or NEVINS-KIRSHNER

LOCO-MOTION

DIMENSION #1000

ontact:
IIL LA VIOLA
50 Broadway,
ew York, N.Y.
6-6490

LOU ADLER
6515 Sunset Blvd.
Hollywood, Calif.
HO 6-5188

DIMENSION RECORDS
A Division of Kevins Kirshner Assoc.

Distributed by

AMY-MALA

BRILL BUILDING

above: Little Eva was actually Carol King's baby sitter until she steamed into the big time via King and Goffin's 1962 dance craze hit 'The Locomotion'.

'THEY SAY THE NEON LIGHTS ARE BRIGHT/ ON BROADWAY.' THUS WENT THE OPENING COUPLET OF ONE OF THE DRIFTERS' BIGGEST HITS, 'ON BROADWAY'. And nowhere did those lights shine as bright as from the Brill Building on Broadway. For a brief spell during the late 1950s and early 1960s, the Brill Building embodied Tin Pan Alley. For the level of productivity and creativity emanating from this anonymous façade established it as the hub of the music business. Every songwriter of note gravitated to the Brill

Building at one point or another – some to find the lyricist to match his or her tunes (or vice versa), some as formed partnerships in search of that elusive deal, or others who had tried careers as performers but failed to make the grade. Once admitted, writers were put in cubicles with a desk and a piano. Here they composed the soundtrack for teenage dreams: this was the era of Kennedy and dreams were attainable with this wunderkind in the White House.

Music publisher Don Kirshner ruled the roost, forming Aldon Music. Kirshner was raised in New Jersey and met

1968, MAY: RIOTING STUDENTS AT THE BARRICADES BRING PARIS TO A STANDSTILL, AND ALMOST BRING DOWN THE FRENCH GOVERNMENT

above: Neil Sedaka, Brill Building songsmith who had hits in his own right, forging a career as a MOR performer for many years to come.

centre: Carol King's album Tapestry confirmed her status as both singer and writer nearly a decade after the Brill Building days.

right: The Chiffons, best remembered for 'He's So Fine', just one of the many girl vocal groups whose repetoire relied heavily on song writing talents based in the Brill Building.

Bobby Darin in 1956. Together they wrote jingles and songs until Darin was signed to Atlantic. In 1958, with Al Nevins – formerly of The Three Sons – Kirshner formed Aldon Music, with the express idea of supplying songs for the teenage market, which, fuelled by a combination of fast-food and TV, especially Dick Clark's show American Bandstand, had the potential to boom. Signing writers such as Goffin & King ('Oh No Not My Baby' for Maxine Brown; 'One Fine Day' for The Chiffons; 'Some Kind Of Wonderful', 'When My Little Girl Is Smiling' and 'Up On The Roof' for The Drifters; 'The Locomotion' for Little Eva; and 'Will You Love Me Tomorrow?' for The Shirelles), Barry Mann & Cythia Weil ('Uptown' and 'He's Sure The Boy I Love' for The Crystals; 'Walkin' In The Rain', with producer Phil Spector, for The Ronettes; 'You've Lost That Lovin' Feeling' and '(You're My) Soul And Inspiration' for The Righteous Brothers; 'Come On Over To My Place', 'I'll Take You Home' and 'On Broadway', with Leiber & Stoller, for The Drifters), Neil Sedaka & Howie Greenfield ('Stupid Cupid' for Connie Francis and 'I Go Ape', 'Calendar Girl' and 'Oh Carol', which Sedaka himself performed) and Neil Diamond ('Sunday and Me' for Jay & The Americans and 'I'm A Believer' for The Monkees), the Brill Building quickly became synonymous with high quality pop music.

Kirshner's success encouraged other music publishers to come and set up shop with Lieber & Stoller – Jeff Barry & Ellie Greenwich ('Be My Baby' and 'Baby I Love You', with Phil Spector, for The Ronettes; 'Da Doo Ron Ron' and 'Then He Kissed Me', with Phil Spector, for

The Crystals; 'Today I Met The Boy I'm Gonna Marry', with Phil Spector, for Darlene Love; 'Chapel Of Love' for The Dixie Cups; 'Do Wah Diddy' for The Exciters; and 'Leader Of The Pack' for The Shangri-Las) and Doc Pomus & Mort Shuman ('Teenager In Love' for Dion & The Belmonts; 'Save The Last Dance For Me', 'I Count The Tears', 'This Magic Moment' and 'Sweets For My Sweet' for The Drifters; and 'A Mess Of Blues', 'Little Sister', 'His Latest Flame' and 'Surrender' for Elvis Presley). In particular the strengths of this production line lay in the synergy that existed between producer and writer, with Phil Spector being the exemplar.

Despite its eventual demise as an arbiter of teenage taste, the Brill Building launched the careers of Carole King and Neil Diamond. Indeed King had anticipated the direction of her career back in 1962 by scoring a hit in her own right with 'It Might As Well Rain Until September'. In 1970 she helped establish the popularity of the singer-songwriter genre, which now spans country, folk and rock, with her second solo album, Tapestry (1970) – it sold in excess of 15 million copies.

right: The great Martha and the Vandellas, a girl group out of the Motown stable.

below: An advertisement for two Red Bird releases, both pure pop classics, by The Jelly Beans and The Shangri-Las.

PURE POP

THE 60S, AS WELL AS BEING THE ERA THAT SAW ROCK MUSIC HAVING PRETENSIONS TO BECOMING SOMETHING MORE THAN MERE POP MUSIC, was also the golden age of pure pop, music that was unashamedly commercial, instant and disposable – but often highly memorable in retrospect.

The decade began with a pop scene that was dominated by pretty boys – saccharine singers like Bobby Vee, Fabian and, in the UK, Cliff Richard and Adam Faith. On the female side, names included the teenage Brenda Lee and Connie Francis, all putting out perfectly respectable, but often ineffectual, single releases aimed straight at the charts – and their aim was true. It was also the era of the last great dance craze, The Twist, spearheaded by Chubby Checker and Joey Dee and The Starlighters.

The epitome of pure pop came in the form of the ubiquitous girl groups who sprang up in the wake of the Brill Building songwriters and Phil Spector's production 'stable' – outfits like The Shirelles, Chiffons, Crystals and Ronettes, serving a teen-oriented repertoire of dance crossed with angst. And talking of angst, it didn't come any more dramatic than the talk-over classics of The Shangri-Las, including 'The Leader of the Pack', 'Remember (Walking In The Sand)' and 'Past Present and Future', produced by George 'Shadow' Morton. Simultaneously in Detroit, Berry Gordy's Tamla Motown featured girl groups prominently in its burgeoning roster, including Martha and the Vandellas and The Supremes.

Manufactured, maybe, but three-minute classics all the same. Likewise later in the decade with The Monkees, a group literally put together for a TV series aimed at jumping on the Beatles bandwagon, but who nevertheless came up with pure gems in the studio including the great Neil Diamond-penned 'I'm A Believer'. Rumour had it the guys themselves didn't play the actual session that produced the hit, but that wasn't really the point – the end product was the seven-inch piece of plastic, and the sounds therein, and that was justification in itself.

NEWS

1968, APRIL 4: US CIVIL RIGHTS LEADER MARTIN LUTHER KING JNR IS ASSASSINATED IN MEMPHIS, TENNESSEE

left: Chubby Checker, whose rise to fame and subsequent fall from favour coincided with that of the Twist.

left: Spector's ultimate creation – The Ronettes, with Ronnie (bottom) who went on to marry Phil Spector.

right: The Teddy Bears, with Phil left, Spector's hit-making high school group from 1958.

far right: Phil Spector looking enigmatic, a characteristic of his style throughout his career.

PHIL SPECTOR

WHILE THERE HAVE BEEN MANY PRODUCERS WHO HAVE EXERTED A MAJOR INFLUENCE UPON THE DEVELOPMENT OF POPULAR MUSIC AND THE WAYS OF TREATING IT, NONE HAS ENJOYED QUITE SUCH A HIGH PROFILE AS PHIL SPECTOR.

Born on December 26, 1940, in the Bronx, New York City, he first came to prominence as a member of The Teddy Bears, with 'To Know Him Is To Love Him'. By 1961, having recorded for the Imperial label and worked as a producer with Lee Hazelwood in Los Angeles, he moved back to New York, where he became an assistant to Leiber & Stoller and wrote with Gene Pitney. That same year he set up his own label, Philles, with Lester Sill. His innovative approach to production paid scant attention to cost or feasibility. Using top-class session men such as Hal Blaine and Earl Palmer (drums), Joe Osborne (bass), Leon Russell, Hal Battiste and Mac Rebennack (keyboards) and Steve Douglas (saxophones) as well as Brill Building writers like Ellie Greenwich, Jeff Barry, Cynthia Weil and Barry Mann, Spector produced confabulations that explore the whole gamut of teenage emotion. The formula paid dividends immediately as all-girl groups such as The Crystals, with 'There's No Other (Like My Baby)', 'Uptown', 'He's A Rebel', 'Da Doo Ron Ron' and 'Then He Kissed Me', and The Ronettes, with 'Be My Baby', 'Baby, I Love You', '(The Best Part Of) Breaking Up', 'Do I Love You?' and 'Walking In The Rain', and session singers like Darlene Love, with '(Today I Met) The Boy I'm Gonna Marry' and 'Wait 'Til My Bobby Gets

Home' notched up a string of hits. At Christmas, in 1963, Spector issued what remains the definitive Christmas album, A Christmas Gift For You: this has subsequently become known as Phil Spector's Christmas Album.

In 1964, Spector, now calling his production style The Wall of Sound, hooked up with The Righteous Brothers. The result was another string of hits that included 'You've Lost That Lovin' Feeling', 'Just Once In My Life', 'Unchained Melody' and 'Ebb Tide'. Then, in 1966, he retired from production work – seriously miffed – when 'River Deep, Mountain High' by Ike & Tina Turner bombed in the US. In 1969 he tried to relaunch the career of his wife, Ronnie, the former Ronette, by setting up the Phil Spector International label, through A&M. His only real success was with 'Black Pearl' by Sonny Charles and The Checkmates. As such, the new label was not a great success, but it gave him the necessary impetus to revive his career and led to an association with the disintegrating Beatles, particularly John Lennon and George Harrison, both of whom he worked with on various solo projects for the Apple label. In later years he produced The Ramones, Leonard Cohen and Cher. In 1997, Spector won a legal battle with EMI, which gave him full contractual right to all the recordings he created in the early 1960s.

While rumours surrounding Spector's health and his authoritarian approach to those with whom he worked proliferated, Spector elevated the public perception of the role of the producer. No longer was the producer just a backroom boffin, he was worthy of as much respect as the artists with whom he was working.

VARIOUS ARTISTS
BACK TO MONO
ABKCO

CD CHECKLIST

1969, JULY 20: US ASTRONAUT NEIL ARMSTRONG, WITH PARTNER 'BUZZ' ALDRIN, IS THE FIRST MAN TO SET FOOT ON THE SURFACE OF THE MOON

POP WILL EAT ITSELF

Pop music in the 70s was developing into a many-headed beast. Mainstream rock was taking itself increasingly seriously, even acquiring the connotation 'Progressive' for a while, with an academic-style school of 'music journalism' emerging to complement its navel-gazing. It still filled stadiums of course – increasingly so – and sold albums by the million, but the day of the singles-oriented pop act seemed numbered. As a backlash, and filling a more immediate commercial need, came a whole plethora of teenie-oriented bubble gum acts ranging from The Osmonds in America to Suzi Quatro in the UK, who once more saw the singles charts as their goal. And bridging the seemingly unbridgable gap between these two camps was Glam Rock, the glitterati led by David Bowie, The New York Dolls and Marc Bolan who strode both stages in their platform boots at the same time.

Then, from off the streets and cellar clubs of New York's Bowery and London's Soho came Punk; bands like The Ramones and The Sex Pistols stuck a finger in the air to just about everyone in the perceived pop establishment, and things were never to be the same again. Once again pop had eaten itself, and this time it followed the feast with a loud burp.

1970-1980

right: Jim Morrison with the Doors carried the rebellious ethos of late 60s rock into the 1970s – albeit briefly.

below: With The Faces, and then solo, Rod Stewart came to epitomise British stadium rock by the mid 70s.

opposite: The Rolling Stones, and Mick Jagger in particular, took to playing the spectacular stadium gig like it was the local rhythm and blues club.

ROCK

above: As the presentation of rock, both live and on record, became more and more flamboyant, so did its publicity and marketing image.

WHILE THE ROCK ERA GENERATED CHANGE IN THE MARKETING STRATEGIES OF THE RECORD INDUSTRY, THE WHOLE RECORDING PROCESS UNDERWENT A RADICAL CHANGE. Before the success of The Beatles, the record producer was seen as an unglamorous technician in a white coat who oversaw the mixing and engineering of a record. Many producers determined what their charges would play and therefore by extension, determined what a record would sound like. With The Beatles' producer, George Martin, that changed, as he became a catalyst for the group's creativity. Martin's approach of assisting in the creative process altered the perception of the producer, enabling other talented technicians such as Bob Johnston, Tom Wilson, Jimmy Miller and Glyn Johns, among others, to adopt a more wide-ranging view.

As a consequence, by the end of the 1960s, young rock musicians were broadening their horizons, fusing rock with classical, jazz, folk and country influences. Advances in technology with the development of the Moog synthesiser by Robert Moog and the mellotron enabled keyboard specialists such as Keith Emerson of The Nice – and then Emerson, Lake and Palmer – and then Rick Wakeman the opportunity to simulate effects comparable in range to an entire symphony orchestra; Pink Floyd, who had started around the birth of the Psychedelic era in the late 1960s, also embraced the new technology, drawing in references to exponents of electronic music such as Terry Riley and John Cage. Although these Progressive bands undoubtedly helped

to break down barriers, they created a mood in the 1970s that rock music was beginning to acquire the studied seriousness of classical music: in other words, rock music was endeavouring to attain levels of musical literacy and accomplishment that was an anachronism.

Towards the end of the 1970s in the UK, Punk redeemed rock with a visceral and often vituperative energy that had been lacking since the mid-1960s. Punk bands such as The Sex Pistols and The Clash gave fresh impetus to a stale rock scene, encouraging a host of

NEWS

1970, SEPTEMBER 12: PALESTINIAN ARAB GUERRILLAS BLOW UP THREE AEROPLANES AT DAWSON'S FIELD, AMMAN, HERALDING A DECADE FRAUGHT WITH INTERNATIONAL TERRORISM

young aspiring musicians with little or no formal expertise to go through their training on stage. However in the US, rock – now a multi-billion dollar industry which continued to flourish with heavy metal bands dominating the live music circuit – was mainly centred around sports arenas and a burgeoning international festival circuit. Although the guitar-based heavy metal represented one side of the coin, the other side saw the establishment in the mainstream of writers like Bruce Springsteen and country-rock bands such as The Eagles. The success of The Eagles spawned an entire sub-genre of Soft Rock bands, who were lyrical and melodic above all – if sometimes lacking in that vital element of surprise and immediacy: Fleetwood Mac's album Rumours became the biggest-selling album of all time until it was eclipsed by Michael Jackson's Thriller in the 1980s.

Throughout the late 1980s and early 1990s the dominant motif in the continued evolution of rock music was its cross-pollination with the dance culture, where Afro-Caribbean rhythms held sway and the emergent idioms of hip hop, House, rap, reggae and Jungle were pervasive. To that end, despite the popularity – but comparative orthodoxy – of bands such as Radiohead, Blur, Pulp and Oasis, who were maintaining the traditions of The Beatles and The Kinks, it was groups such as The Prodigy, U2 and Afro-Celt Sound System whose pan-cultural influences did more to erode barriers. This in conjunction with the continued development of independent record labels created a mood in rock music where anything might happen.

right: Leonard Cohen became the stereotype of the poetic troubadour, his songs full of personal angst that alienated many but ensured him a loyal following for over thirty years.

SINGER-SONGWRITERS

OVER THE LAST TEN YEARS OR SO, THE STAR OF THE SINGER-SONGWRITER HAS BEEN IN THE ASCENDANT, AS RECORD COMPANIES, recognising their apathetic attitude to the genre during the CD boom of the 1980s, have endeavoured to redress the imbalance by signing up as many artists as possible who write their own material. No area of contemporary music has been quite as fertile as the singer-songwriter genre, for it has permeated country, folk and rock in equal measure.

While Bob Dylan must be accorded a share of the blame – or thanks – for showing that it was possible to write what one felt without resorting to the cheesy gimmickry of Tin Pan Alley, communications played their part as well. For as radio, in the US, came to reflect all facets of contemporary music, esoteric folk music ceased to be the exclusive preserve of the diehard enthusiast. Consequently the late 1960s saw the escalation in popularity of a plethora of songwriters such as Tom Paxton, Tom Rush and John Sebastian of

above: With initial support from The Beatles' George Harrison, James Taylor emerged as a leader in the 70s singer-songwriter stakes.

centre: The Hissing Of Summer Lawns (1975); Joni Mitchell made the charts with the eco-single 'Big Yellow Taxi' in 1970 and is now respected as one of America's finest.

right: With a night-weary, bruised voice and lyrics to match, Tom Waits brought a beat-poetry sensibility to his jazz-tinged material.

The Lovin' Spoonful. By the early 1970s, songwriters such as Carole King, with Tapestry (1971), James Taylor, with Sweet Baby James (1970), and Jackson Browne, with For Everyman (1973), had consolidated the commercial base of the singer-songwriter. But it was three Canadians that took Dylan's template and expanded the genre.

Poet Leonard Cohen, with The Songs Of Leonard Cohen (1968), brought a quiet intensity with songs such as 'Suzanne' and 'The Sisters of Mercy' that became the soundtrack for the growing pains of the young. As Cohen's career has developed, the existential gloom has been replaced by a laconic acerbity. Joni Mitchell penned the anthem of the generation with 'Woodstock', while her eloquent reflections upon the vicissitudes of life possessed a sharpness many of her contemporaries lacked. In later years Mitchell was to distance herself from the Folk Rock arrangements that were the norm, edging more towards jazz, which culminated with Mingus, a tribute to the great bassist. Neil Young's idiosyncratic style with Buffalo Springfield and Crosby, Stills, Nash & Young showed a guitarist of the highest calibre, at home in any contemporary genre. When his solo career started in 1969, Young displayed the full range in his songwriting palette, with albums such as Everybody Knows This Is Nowhere (1969) and After The Goldrush (1970). In later years, his inventiveness showed little sign of letting up as he became the putative Godfather of Grunge and then toured with the former Stax house band Booker T & The MGs.

Equally delivering from a tough rock'n'roll stance not usually associated with the archetypal singer-songwriter was Bruce Springsteen, who suffered during the 70s by being variously branded as the next 'big thing', or – more impossibly – the next Bob Dylan. Notwithstanding such ill-advised hype, his 1975 album Born To Run was rightly regarded as a classic, followed by Darkness On The Edge Of Town (1978) which included, as well as the title track, other concert favourites like 'Badlands' and 'The Promised Land'.

Elsewhere, the Belfast Cowboy, Van Morrison, formerly of Them, began to lay the foundations for his solo career with the jazz-influenced, epochal Astral Weeks (1969). Influenced by Ray Charles, R&B and the blues, Morrison's eclecticism has enabled him – in later years – to draw overtly from the traditions of Irish folk song without radically altering his overall style. Christy Moore, too, has used the traditions of Celtic folk song to forge a style, where passionate intensity and emotional integrity are transcendent.

Now as singer-songwriters proliferate, some like Steve Earle retain a vital edge by allowing their various influences to coalesce, creating a style that is as direct as it is honest. In the end, though, all roads seem to lead back to Dylan, despite the attempts by other writers such as Paul Simon to harness styles from other cultural milieus. It is worth reflecting upon the words of the Texan songwriter Townes Van Zandt, who was inclined to comment: 'There are only two sorts of songs – the blues and zip-pa-dee-doo-dah.' He wasn't wrong.

right: With a background in both music and the theatrical fringe, David Bowie was a natural architect of glam rock.

centre: Starting his career as a mod, then archetypal hippy, Marc Bolan's most successful identity was that of the ultimate glam rock teen idol.

far right: Elton John, about whom the phrase 'over the top' would be an understatement, came to epitomise glam.

GLAM ROCK

THAT GLAM ROCK CAME ABOUT AT ALL WAS DUE MAINLY TO THE EXCESSES OF PROGRESSIVE ROCK. In a sense it anticipated, in a less overt fashion, Punk. For purveyors of Progressive Rock were noted for their lack of dress sense, which contrasted sharply with their penchant for musical overstatement. Consequently, artists such as David Bowie and Marc Bolan were key instigators in the return to a less bombastic, more direct style of song. Furthermore, by adapting the early kitsch style of rock'n'roll, with lashings of glitter and lamé, they sought to highlight just how passé old hippies such as Pink Floyd in their T-shirts and flared jeans had become. Bowie, in full make-up, assumed a camp, androgynous role, with guitarist Mick Ronson as his foil, cutting albums such as The Man Who Sold The World (1970), Hunky Dory (1971), The Rise and Fall Of Ziggy Stardust (1972) and Aladdin Sane (1973). Produced by Tony Visconti, Bowie's output reflected a sexual ambiguity that found a receptive audience in adolescents, who felt

out of kilter with contemporary society. Visconti, too, had earlier revived the career of Marc Bolan. Initially an acoustic guitarist with a penchant for fey tales about pixies and elves, Bolan reinvented himself in the early 1970s as a guitar-toting teen idol. In the former role he had limited success; in the latter he broke out with a series of finely wrought, exciting singles such as 'Ride A White Swan', 'Hot Love', 'Get It On', 'Metal Guru' and 'Telegram Sam' that counteracted the prevailing trend of pomposity among Progressive bands. While his guitar work was effective rather than accomplished, the simple chord structure of his songs opened up fresh vistas.

Naturally enough other producers such as Mike Leander and Phil Wainman found ready and willing converts in Gary Glitter and The Sweet, respectively. Even Roy Wood, formerly of The Move and The Electric Light Orchestra, formed Wizzard, whose homages ('See My Baby Jive' and 'Ball Park Incident') to the simple pleasures of the rock'n'roll era contrasted sharply with the elaborate productions of The Electric Light

NEWS

1972, SEPTEMBER 5: ARAB TERRORISTS KILL 11 ISRAELI ATHLETES AT THE MUNICH OLYMPICS, CASTING A PALL OVER THE ENTIRE GAMES

Orchestra, under Jeff Lynne. Slade, too, managed to embrace the spirit of Glam Rock with their robust, but melodic sing-a-longs. Others though, such as Roxy Music, lead by vocalist Bryan Ferry, contrived to harness the visual spectacle of Glam Rock with the experimentalism of Progressive bands such as King Crimson. In guitarist Phil Manzanera and synthesiser specialist Brian Eno, Roxy Music brought facets of the avant-garde to the brink of the mainstream without sacrificing any of their musical identity.

In the US, Glam Rock never quite caught on, as such. However, it didn't stop the grand guignol theatrics of Alice Cooper and The Tubes harnessing elements of the genre. Later on, heavy metal band Kiss adopted 'full make-up' to provide the visual distinctiveness that their music often lacked. Indeed, it could be said that the combination of spandex and leather – the standard-issue uniform for any aspiring heavy metal outfit – was derived from the Glam Rock period. By the mid-1970s, Glam Rock as such had disappeared as Bowie reinvented

himself briefly as The Thin White Duke, purveying a Funk-driven blend of blue-eyed Soul, before disappearing to Berlin with Brian Eno to start the next chapter of his career. Bolan died in a car crash in 1977, just as Punk was picking up momentum. Gary Glitter continues to tour, recreating his role as the 1970s answer to Liberace.

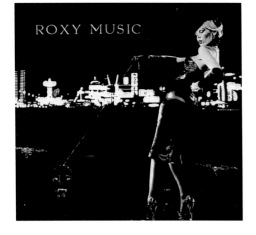

PROGRESSIVE ROCK

IF THE BEATLES, AND THEIR SGT PEPPER ALBUM IN PARTICULAR, WERE THE CATALYST, THE DEVELOPMENT OF THE SYNTHESISER BY ROBERT MOOG FACILITATED THOSE WITH SIGHTS SET ON MORE GRANDIOSE WORKS. Keyboardist Keith Emerson of The Nice showed the way with his flamboyant stage act and his rendering of titles like 'America' from Leonard Bernstein's musical West Side Story; later, in Emerson, Lake and Palmer, Emerson would adapt Mussorgsky's Pictures At An Exhibition

(1971). Later other groups such as Yes and Barclay James Harvest endeavoured to match ELP in harnessing a compositional standard previously restricted to the milieu of classical music. Indeed Jon Lord, the keyboards player at the helm of Deep Purple, went a stage further by composing Concerto For Group and Orchestra (1970). Despite their popularity among certain audiences, none of these groups acquired the status they might have felt were commensurate with their achievements. However, in 1973, Mike Oldfield achieved far-reaching commercial

NEWS

1973, JANUARY 27: A PEACE TREATY IS SIGNED IN PARIS, RESULTING IN A CEASEFIRE AND WITHDRAWAL OF US TROOPS FROM VIETNAM. THE WAR BETWEEN NORTH AND SOUTH, HOWEVER, CONTINUES

above: King Crimson; Robert Fripp (right) led the group before exploring more esoteric techno-driven areas towards the end of the 1970s.

appeal with Tubular Bells. Playing all the instruments himself, Oldfield applied standards of composition that were more commonly found in classical music.

Where rock began to become seriously Progressive was in the hands of musicians such as Pink Floyd, whose grasp of electronics and composition enabled them to put on performances that were audio-visual extravaganzas, and guitarist Robert Fripp of King Crimson. Fripp's technical expertise enabled him to utilise elements of the avant-garde, especially modal and tonal ideas from composers such as Luciano Berio and Karl-Heinz Stockhausen. In the US, the term Progressive never entered the vernacular to quite the same extent, even though The Velvet Underground, as early as 1965/6, under the auspices of painter Andy Warhol, were involved in The Exploding Plastic Inevitable, a multi-media package that combined music, film, light-shows and dance. Frank Zappa, with The Mothers Of Invention, was also Progressive, but he – like his sometime protégé, Captain Beefheart – was too experimental for most palates: Beefheart's Trout Mask Replica remains a pivotal influence almost 30 years after its release. However, Clive Davis, during his tenure as supremo of Columbia, initiated a far-reaching programme of signings that included nominally Progressive outfits such as Blood, Sweat & Tears, Chicago and Flock.

Elsewhere, there were big US pop chart hits for bands like Kansas, Styx, Boston, Supertramp and REO Speedwagon, Progressive groups who successfully

plugged into the emergent mainstream AOR – adult oriented rock – market.

Curiously, Europe, where composition with the aid of computers and synthesisers was regarded as something interesting and not something to be feared, was more receptive with German groups such as Can and Amon Duul II adopting rock idioms within a genuinely experimental context; Can's debut Monster Movie (1969) is a benchmark for Techno enthusiasts. While Can remained an acquired taste, others such as Tangerine Dream and the Dutch group Focus developed significant audiences because they were more accessible. Similarly, Jean-Michel Jarre broke through with the album Oxygene (1976), which was a large-scale composition for synthesisers.

By the mid-1970s, as groups such as Roxy Music became more popular, former Roxy-technophile Brian Eno worked with Robert Fripp and then David Bowie on a trio of albums – Low (1977), Heroes (1977) and The Lodger (1979) – that detailed an affinity with the post-industrial minimalism present in the Can's Holger Czukay. During the 1980s, groups such as Heaven 17 and Orchestral Manoeuvres In The Dark, who, in the 1970s, might have been considered Progressive by virtue of their dependence on technology, had become the mainstream of contemporary pop music. Consequently, where initially the term Progressive was used to denote a certain adventurousness, by the 1970s it had become a euphemistic blanket covering anything that was bombastic or pretentious.

YES
CLOSE TO THE EDGE
Atlantic

KING CRIMSON
IN THE COURT OF THE CRIMSON KING
EG

right: There's A Riot Going On by Sly and The Family Stone was considered dangerously militant in 1971 – and the No 1 hit track 'A Family Affair' even used a drum machine!

far right: The incomparable Bootsy Collins with Bootsy's Rubber Band, part of the George Clinton-inspired glam approach to funk.

FUNK

opposite, top: Inspired where George Clinton might be deemed indulgent, Earth, Wind And Fire were a soul dance band to whom a 'funky' sound was as natural as breathing.

opposite, below: After early 60s hits with 'Shout' and 'Twist and Shout' the Isley Brothers progressed through Motown ('This Old Heart Of Mine') to being major players on the 70s disco/funk scene.

FUNK HAD BEEN A POPULAR ADJUNCT OF MAINSTREAM JAZZ THROUGHOUT THE 1950s, when organists such as Jimmy Smith, Brother Jack MacDuff and Jimmy McGriff had trademarked the style. Others such as Charlie Mingus – especially a brace of albums for the Atlantic label, Blues & Roots and Oh Yeah! – embodied Funk. But the term seemed inherently pejorative: it smacked of simplification. And that was probably a part of its appeal to James Brown. Did he describe himself as funky? Or was it a collective acknowledgement that the way James and The Famous Flames played was funky? Who can say? The point is that from about 1965, Brown was a purveyor of Funk. One of the key ingredients was the guitarwork of Jimmy Nolen. The incisive, chattering chops of Nolen, sometimes embellished with the odd bit of wah-wah, added another dimension to Soul.

For Funk, with its clipped polyrhythms, may have alluded subliminally to Afro-Cuban styles or the music of the townships, but it was its suitability for development into extended grooves that helped to promulgate it. While improvisation had always been a fundamental characteristic of jazz, Funk enabled Black bands such as Sly & The Family Stone, The Isley Brothers, Earth, Wind & Fire, The Ohio Players and George Clinton's Funkadelic/Parliament collective to deploy themselves in the manner of rock bands such as Cream or The Jimi Hendrix Experience. Even Motown took up the baton as The Temptations – with producer Norman Whitfield – scored significant hits with 'Psychedelic Shack', 'Cloud

Nine' and 'Papa Was A Rolling Stone'; later The Commodores with 'Machine Gun' provided a springboard for the MOR success of the songwriter Lionel Richie.

However, if any moment best sums up Funk, it was guitarist Wah-wah Watson's introduction to Isaac Hayes's 'Theme From Shaft'. In those few bars, the image of Black music in the early 1970s was formed: from the threads and the afro-hairstyles to the lifestyles. The film, Shaft, triggered a series of movies with soundtracks by key figures such as Marvin Gaye (Trouble Man), James Brown (Slaughter's Big Rip-Off), Bobby Womack (Across 110th Street) and Curtis Mayfield (Superfly).

That they were dubbed 'blaxploitation' movies suggested that they were not usually taken seriously by Hollywood, but the broader agenda reflected an expanding power-base in the American entertainment industry. Funk, with its strutting and preening machismo, predicated James Brown's earlier call-to-arms, 'Say It Loud – I'm Black And I'm Proud'. With the success of the movies and the concomitant soundtracks Funk entered the musical mainstream as groups such as Kool & The Gang and the Miami-based KC and The Sunshine Band flourished.

The ascendancy of Funk found its natural milieu on the dance-floor, where the extended instrumental necessitated ultimately the introduction of the 12-inch single, which was the response to demands from DJs for a format that was more user friendly than the

FUNKADELIC
ONE NATION UNDER A GROOVE
Warner Bros.

NEWS

1974, AUGUST 8: US PRESIDENT NIXON RESIGNS FROM OFFICE AS A RESULT OF THE WATERGATE SCANDAL

traditional 7-inch single format. After the introduction of the 12-inch single, the evolution of a style specifically designed for the dance-floor was but a beat away: enter disco and the cult of the DJ.

For the growth in importance of the DJ provided a back-drop for many of the key developments in Black music since the 1970s, when rappers such as Grandmaster Flash and The Sugarhill Gang began to add rap vocal tracks to existing instrumental backing tracks. In the 1990s Funk has enjoyed a renaissance on its own merits, instead as merely a constituent in the make-up of now traditional styles such as hip hop, House and Techno.

Moreover, the style of movie soundtracks such as Shaft has influenced a move towards a longer and thematic style in composition, that is more closely allied with the approach of both classical and jazz composers of film music. In the final analysis, all this goes to suggest that the boundaries between styles are becoming less and less distinct.

PUNK

PUNK WILL FOREVER BE ASSOCIATED WITH THE SEX PISTOLS AND THEIR UNRULY DECLAMATORY THAT STYLE TOOK NO PRISONERS – LEAST OF ALL TV INTERVIEWERS. The roots of Punk are ideological, more than musical. When Punk first reared its head in London in the 1970s, there was a mood of decline and discontent in the country as a whole. Unemployment, strikes and wage restraint were the order of the day, while outbreaks of rioting were common-place. On top of this, rock groups such as Yes, Led Zeppelin, Pink Floyd and Genesis, with their grand stage-shows, had become alienated from a new, young generation that had grown up without the dubious benefit of the 'love-and-peace' rhetoric of the Woodstock generation. Therefore the best way to rebel against existing musical

punk / new wave

left: The Sex Pistols' Johnny Rotten (John Lydon) in a typical punk-provocative pose.

far left: Siouxie (left) and The Banshees were central to the club-based scene of London punk c.1976-1977.

attitudes was by doing exactly the opposite. As rock concerts became ever more expensive, so an alternative pub circuit emerged; as rock groups became ever more bombastic and overstated, so groups started knocking out songs of two or three minutes in duration; and as standards of musicianship increased, so basic ability – or indeed total inability – to play an instrument was no let or hindrance to a musical career. History was merely repeating itself: Elvis Presley had had no formal musical training – he sang what he knew; and The Beatles flouted conventions by playing Little Richard material, before penning their own songs. Indeed, in the mid-1960s in the US, Garage bands such as Mitch Ryder and The Detroit Wheels, The Standells and ? and The Mysterians had briefly made inroads with their brash, pugnacious celebrations of disenchantment. Towards the end of that decade, both MC5 and The Stooges would provide a sardonic antidote to the superficial optimism of the Woodstock generation. As the Woodstock generation were deflowered, a new wave started to emerge in New York. With father figures such as David Bowie and Lou Reed of The Velvet Underground, the clubs CBGB's and Max's Kansas City put on gigs by groups such as Richard Hell & The Voidoids, The New York Dolls, The Ramones and Talking Heads. By the mid-1970s, the New York New Wave had achieved its own momentum, as poets such as Patti Smith articulated the mood of antipathy and disenchantment.

Similarly, in the UK, the pub circuit had created openings for writers such as Graham Parker, Elvis Costello and Nick Lowe and bands like Dr Feelgood. As the number of venues proliferated around the UK, so independent record labels such as Stiff and Chiswick sprung up. But down in Chelsea, entrepreneur Malcom McLaren, with fashion designer Vivienne Westwood, gave Punk its focus by creating a visual identity that included straight-leg (not flares) bondage-style trousers. This was, as writer George Melly said, 'Revolt Into Style'. With the image sorted, all McLaren needed was a band. And he found the nucleus of them at his clothes shop, Sex, on the King's Road. Naming them The Sex Pistols, they spawned countless imitators, but more importantly, they fostered a mood of attainability: anything was possible. Other groups such as Siouxsie and The Banshees, The Jam and The Clash were signed up by record labels, causing a feeding frenzy among record company A&R men. While Punk, as a style, remained hot for only a few short years, it caused a change in the mapping of the musical landscape. Once again it seemed that anyone could be in a band with little or no musical knowledge. And anyone could run a record label too. Of late, there has been a sort of revival; forgetting the embarrasing come-back tour of the Sex Pistols, neo-punk bands Green Day and Rancid have both topped the US charts!

left: One of the more musically literate bands to come out of UK punk, Ian Dury and The Blockheads merged spikey lyrics with an energetic style tinged with jazz/funk.

below: Patti Smith brought a background in performance poetry to bear on her impact on the New York punk scene.

DO IT YOURSELF
IAN DURY & the BLOCKHEADS

SEX PISTOLS
NEVER MIND THE BOLLOCKS
Virgin

MC5
BACK IN THE USA
Atlantic

CD CHECKLIST

1975, APRIL 30: THE COMMUNIST FORCES OF NORTH VIETNAM REACH SAIGON. THE SOUTH VIETNAMESE GOVERNMENT SURRENDERS

NEW WAVE

WHEN PUNK PICKED UP MOMENTUM IN THE UK IN THE MID-1970s
IT HAD A DESIRABLE KNOCK-ON EFFECT THAT CAUSED A TEMPORARY
UPHEAVAL IN THE RECORD BUSINESS. Much of this was manifest in a
plethora of new artists getting signed to record labels. Bands such as The Police were
emblematic of the spirit of Punk, but they achieved their ends through the sheer
professionalism of their live act and through the crafted songs of bassist Sting (aka
Gordon Sumner); these included 'Roxanne', 'Can't Stand Losing You', 'Message In A
Bottle' and 'Don't Stand So Close To Me'. Their immediate success in the US was as
much due to Andy Summers' incisive guitar solos that were in stark contrast with
prevailing trends among guitarists where as many notes as possible were squeezed out
in random order. Despite the success of their singles, albums like Outlandos d'Amour
(1978) and Regatta de Blanc (1979) shifted in lorry loads.

Others such as Elvis Costello immediately caught the ear with early records like
'Less Than Zero', 'Alison' and 'Watching The Detectives'. Signed to the independent
Stiff label by Jake Riviera in 1977 after DJ Charlie Gillett aired some of Costello's
demos on his Honky Tonk radio show, his distinctive, slightly hectoring vocals poured
scorn on the establishment. DJ Charlie Gillett was the catalyst for the career of Dire
Straits, with guitarist Mark Knopfler. While Dire Straits were a million miles in style
from the aggressive posturings of Punk, they represented a return to a more melodic
and lyrical brand of bluesy, country-tinged rock, the like of which had not been seen
since The Grateful Dead first started playing back in the 1960s; Dire Straits eventually
came into their own with Brothers In Arms, the album that made the CD the dominant
format, thereby deposing the vinyl disc.

The Stranglers, too, with Dave Greenfield on keyboards, created a sound that was
eerily redolent of The Doors. While they were not above indulging in some of the
antics more commonly associated with Punk, they were totally dissimilar stylistically to
The Clash or The Sex Pistols. However, Joy Division, with the songs of bleak despair
of Ian Curtis, summed up the true mood of the young where feelings of isolation and
alienation were endemic. Joy Division recorded two albums, Unknown Pleasures
(1979) and Closer (1980), before Curtis hung up himself in 1980. The group

---

BLONDIE
PLASTIC LETTERS
Chrysalis

ELVIS COSTELLO
THIS YEAR'S MODEL
Rykodisc/ Demon

CD CHECKLIST

reconstituted itself, becoming New Order, one of the most important bands to come out of the UK in the 1980s.

Similarly, in New York, groups such as Talking Heads, with David Byrne, and Television, with Tom Verlaine, led a return to a more organic form of rock. While Talking Heads, with albums such as Talking Heads 77 (1977), More Songs About Buildings and Food (1978), Fear Of Music (1979) and Remain In Light (1980), reflected Byrne's avant-garde leanings, they embraced African influences alongside. Blondie, in contrast, with lead vocalist Debby Harry, combined the group's art-school background with a deft pop sensibility that brought them a string of hits that included 'Denis Denis', 'Sunday Girl', 'Heart Of Glass', 'Rapture' and 'Call Me'; with both 'Heart Of Glass' and 'Call Me', Blondie anticipated the assimilation of dance rhythms in much the same way as Madonna would later do.

Meanwhile, in Los Angeles, groups such as Tom Petty and The Heartbreakers seemed to pay homage to the city's golden age when The Byrds and Buffalo Springfield ruled the roost, with a bunch of self-penned compositions that included 'American Girl', 'Breakdown', 'Don't Do Me Like That', 'Refugee', 'Don't Come Around Here No More' and 'I Won't Back Down'. By and large though, the city of Los Angeles remained impervious to any kind of New Wave. For the streamlining and airbrushing of styles was what had made Hollywood great in the first place.

right: With bass player Sting (right) coming from club jazz, The Police helped promote the emergent reggae sound in their most popular songs.

far right: Blondie's second album, Plastic Letters, before Debbie Harry went from punk pin-up to international icon.

right: American design school graduates David Byrne, Chris Frantz and his girlfriend Tina Weymouth, and keyboard player Jerry Harrison, debuted with Talking Heads '77, then followed with More Songs About Buildings And Food in '78.

far right: Named after the girl members' beehive hair-dos, like The Talking Heads the quirky kitsch material of The B-52s was launched via CBGB's club in New York's Bowery.

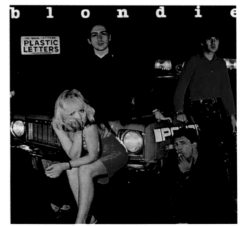

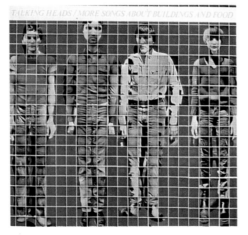

1976, JUNE 16: SOUTH AFRICAN POLICE KILL A 13-YEAR-OLD BOY WHEN THEY BRUTALLY BREAK UP A DEMONSTRATION BY 2,000 SCHOOL CHILDREN IN THE SOUTH AFRICAN TOWNSHIP OF SOWETO. RIOTS ENSUE

PRODUCTION LINE POP

Jackson Five

SUPERFICIALLY, THE 1970s WERE THE DECADE WHEN GLAM ROCK, DISCO AND PUNK WERE THE DOMINANT GENRES, but examination of the charts reveals a slightly different story. For the 1970s was the decade when pop music started to take stock of its recent history and to begin repackaging itself. Consequently, Roy Wood and Wizzard employed the theatrics of Glam Rock, while quietly engineering a rock'n'roll revival, which picked up momentum in the UK with groups such as Showaddywaddy and Darts; later The Stray Cats would come along and infuse the revival with a touch of Rockabilly-styled respectability. Producer Mickie Most, the man who had given the world 'The House Of The Rising Sun' and a bunch of other R&B-styled hits for The Animals, felt that groups like Mud, Racey and Smokie were worthy successors. However he did spread the burden of responsibility by enlisting writers Nicky Chinn and Mike Chapman to provide the material for many of his acts. Chinnichap, as they were known, had proved their mettle with Phil Wainman's protégés, The Sweet.

PRODUCER JONATHAN KING launched the Bay City Rollers upon an unsuspecting public with an updated version of The Gentry's 'Keep On Dancin'' in 1971. The Rollers moved on to the tender mercies of Phil Coulter and Bill Martin, who gave them such pearls as 'Shang-a-Lang' and 'Summerlove Sensation'; then it was on to Phil Wainman, who provided them with 'Bye Bye Baby', among others. Although the Rollers may not have been particularly interesting on any counts at all, they served to prove that the popularity of 'boy bands' in the 1990s does have its precedents.

Meanwhile Mike Leander, formerly an A&R man at Decca, where he had worked with The Rolling Stones and Billy Fury, created Gary Glitter, triggering a string of hits such as 'Rock And Roll' and 'Do You Wanna Touch Me (Oh Yeah!)' and Glam Rock. Such was Glitter's success that his backing band, The Glitter Band (later The G Band), instigated a parallel career with a string of hits such as 'Angel Face'.

BACK IN THE USA, The Partridge Family TV series produced David Cassidy, who followed with a solo career, hoards of young girls proving susceptible to his not displeasing warblings. Consequently, between 1971 and 1974, Cassidy scored hits with 'Cherish', 'Rock Me Baby' and 'Daydreamer', among others. That most of his hits stemmed from pop's illustrious archives did not deter his fans one jot, as many had not been born when they were first hits. Likewise under the tutelage of the opportunist Mike Curb at MGM Records, The Osmonds were intended to compete with Motown's teeny-bop contenders The Jackson 5, with hits like 'One Bad Apple' and 'Crazy Horses'. The singles-driven pop production lines were roaring into action again, and nothing could stop them.

ONE STEP BEYOND...

below: Jimmy Cliff was a leading songwriter on the Kingston scene, hits including 'You Can Get It If You Really Want' for Desmond Dekker and 'The Harder They Come' recorded by Madness.

REGGAE

NOW THOROUGHLY ACCEPTED AS THE STANDARD APPELLATION FOR THE STRAIN OF AFRO-CARIBBEAN MUSIC EMANATING FROM JAMAICA, REGGAE'S INFLUENCE HAS NEVER BEEN ACCORDED ITS FULL DUE. First heard in the UK in the 1950s as immigrants began to settle, it was originally known as Bluebeat or Ska. During the 1960s, entrepreneurs such as Chris Blackwell, who would later go on to found Island Records, began importing singles from Jamaica to sell to specialist record shops in London. Among the records Blackwell was selling were productions from the Coxsone Dodd empire. After working in the US, Dodd returned to Jamaica in 1954 and set up his first sound-system. Employing figures like Lee Perry and Prince Buster, Dodd recorded local musicians and cut acetates to use on his sound-system. By 1961, he had moved on and was pressing copies of these acetates for general release on his own Studio One label. With Clancy Eccles cutting the first release, 'Freedom', other signings included The Vikings (later known as Toots and The Maytals) and Alton Ellis. Within two years, Dodd had not only his own studio, but also a pressing plant. Using The Skatalites – who were to have hits with 'Guns Of Navarone', among others – as backing band, Dodd recorded early sides by Bob Marley and The Wailers. After the departure of Marley and the break-up of The Skatalites, Jackie Mittoo became Dodd's number-one assistant By now, Studio One records were leased to the Trojan label in the UK, which had been established by Blackwell in partnership with Lee Gopthal in 1968; Trojan was to provide a variety of hits for artists like Desmond Dekker and Jimmy Cliff.

By 1968, Lee Perry had established his own Upsetter label. Reggae had now firmly supplanted Bluebeat and Ska and Perry was its most active purveyor. Cutting over a hundred singles between 1968 and 1974, Perry worked with Marley and produced hits by Junior Murvin and Max Romeo. Furthermore, he worked with toasters such as U-Roy, Denis Alcapone and Big Youth, who anticipated the popularity of rap, and King Tubby, the man who arguably created Dub. With the instrumental Dub versions, Perry and King Tubby laid out the ground-plan for the drums'n'bass of Jungle. Throughout the early 1970s, as Philadelphia Soul dominated the charts, Perry responded with lover's rock and artists such as John Holt and Susan Cadogan duly cleaned up.

reggae

left: Madness were the most successful of the new ska-influenced British pop bands.

right: Prince Miller with the most famous reggae rhythm section , drummer Sly Dunbar (left) and bass player Robbie Shakespeare (right).

As reggae's popularity, both in the UK and in Jamaica, flourished, performers such as Dennis Brown and Gregory Isaacs began to draw attention along with The Wailers and Toots and The Maytals. Furthermore the dreadlocks of Rastafarianism began to symbolise not only cultural differences, but also the philosophical distances endemic in British society. Icons of Rastafarianism, such as groups like Burning Spear and the images of the Lion of Juda and Emperor Haile Selassie of Ethiopia, the spiritual home of Rastafarians, became potent symbols in the late 1970s, engendering affinities with the similarly alienated Punk movement. Producer Perry was to collaborate with The Clash on 'Complete Control'.

At the end of the 1970s, reggae experienced a ground swell of respect from British bands such as UB40, which was followed by a Ska revival, courtesy of bands like Madness, The Specials and The Selecter. If these feelings of kinship espoused by young white British bands were not fully reciprocated initially, it provided a backdrop for the integrated bands of the 1980s and 1990s who would find expression through the emergent dance culture, with ragga – the combination of rap and reggae – being the most clearest visible manifestation in the clubs of Britain. For as Punk made way for other trends, reggae was to crop up time and again through groups like Big Audio Dynamite, who would themselves metamorphose into Dreadzone, and the prodigiously ambitious Afro-Celt Sound System. Still mutating, reggae continues to be a vital link, commanding interest right across the board.

BURNING SPEAR
MARCUS GARVEY
Island

1976, SEPTEMBER 9: MAO TSE-TUNG, CHAIRMAN OF THE PEOPLE'S REPUBLIC OF CHINA AND INSTIGATOR OF THE INFAMOUS CULTURAL REVOLUTION, DIES AT THE AGE OF 82

right: The 'best of' collection Legend was the only Bob Marley album to make the British No 1 spot when it was released three years after his death, in 1984.

below: Bob Marley in the red, gold and green which denoted Rastafarianism, and became a trademark colour combination for genuine rastas, and reggae musicians and fans generally.

BOB MARLEY

STILL EXTRAORDINARILY UNDER-RATED, THE SONGS OF BOB MARLEY SEAMLESSLY BLENDED ELEMENTS OF ROCK, GOSPEL AND R&B, OVERLAID BY THE DOMINANT AFRO-CARIBBEAN RHYTHMS OF REGGAE. Where Marley differed from many of his counterparts lay in his ability to harness the ideology and theology of Rastafarianism in readily accessible lay-terms.

Born in St Ann, Jamaica, on February 6, 1945, Marley moved with his mother to the Trenchtown district of Kingston in 1957. At the age of 15, under the eagle-eye of vocalist Joe Higgs, he formed a vocal group with Peter Tosh, Bunny Livingston and Junior Braithwaite. While the group was inspired initially by the sounds of Black American vocal groups such as The Impressions, soon they started forging their own style. In 1962, Marley was introduced to Leslie Kong, who produced Marley's first record, 'Judge Not', for the local Beverly label. The following year, Coxsone Dodd, who had built a recording studio, signed Marley's group, now known as The Wailing Wailers. Using Ska band, The Skatalites, as backing band, The Wailing Wailers strung together a sequence of hits that included 'Simmer Down', as well as a cover of Bob Dylan's 'Like A Rolling Stone'.

By 1967, the group had broken away from Dodd, following a dispute over unpaid royalties. Starting their own label, Wailing Soul, with producer Clancy Eccles, they cut sides such as 'Hypocrite' and 'Stir It Up'. Although these sides were popular local hits, poor distribution militated against international acclaim. Even so, these sides were the template for the emergent style of the group, where the emphasis was upon reflecting life in Trenchtown. When the label folded, the group was signed to singer Johnny Nash's publishing company. Cutting stacks of demos, the group's career seemed to be stalled. A brief spell with Kong followed, which, in turn, was followed by sessions with the legendary producer Lee 'Scratch' Perry. Backed by Perry's band, The Upsetters, Marley, in collaboration Perry, penned songs such as 'Duppy Conqueror' and 'Trench Town Rock' which were issued by the band's own Tuff Gong label.

In 1972, Marley and The Wailers were signed by Island boss Chris Blackwell. Their debut, Catch A-Fire, was, as was the case with rock albums, conceived as an album, and the group was marketed to rock audiences as well. With its generous overlay of

Funk, Soul and blues, reggae had never sounded so polished and assured before. Burnin' followed in 1973. Featuring 'I Shot The Sheriff' and 'Slave Driver', Burnin' seemed more emblematic of Britain where society was riven by racial unrest. In 1974, Natty Dread came out. By now Rastafarianism, which hitherto had only been evident in the ghettoes of some inner cities, was commonplace, and the trademark dreadlocks seemed to be everywhere. Natty Dread included 'No Woman, No Cry', which became a massive hit when it was recorded live at London's Lyceum Theatre two years later.

While Marley and the group was now lodged into the rock band's cycle of touring annually in support of the yearly album release, Marley's espousal of Rastafarian beliefs was undiminished by his growing status. Even an assassination attempt seemed if anything to promote Marley's status. Very gradually, the rock influences seemed to decrease to be replaced by stronger African elements. Despite his political neutrality in Jamaica, Marley was closely allied with African liberation movements; in 1979, his song 'Zimbabwe' assumed anthemic proportions as it was taken up by African musicians. In 1980, he was diagnosed as having cancer. He died on May 11, 1981.

below: The young Bob Marley (second left) with an early line-up of the Wailers that included Bunny Livingstone (right) and Peter Tosh (second right).

SONGS OF FREEDOM
Island

1977, SEPTEMBER: BLACK CONSCIOUSNESS LEADER STEVE BIKO DIES IN POLICE CUSTODY AT THE AGE OF 30. A POST-MORTEM REVEALS EXTENSIVE BRAIN DAMAGE AND SEVERE BRUISING

MOR

MOR WAS COINED BY BROADCASTERS TO DESCRIBE A STYLE OF POPULAR MUSIC THAT IS HIGH ON MELODY, BUT SHORT ON SUBSTANCE. As with the equally pejoratively termed easy listening, MOR (Middle Of the Road) evolved through the American broadcasting system to facilitate the job of radio playlist compilers essentially. For during the 1960s, as radio continued to dominate as the prime medium for marketing music, so radio playlists increased in importance. However, as styles of music proliferated,

it was deemed necessary to come up with a soundbite that separated, say, the music of James Last and His Orchestra or the Ray Conniff Singers from that of Frank Sinatra, Neil Diamond, The Carpenters, Bread and so on. For although Frank Sinatra's popularity was unassailable, by the late 1960s he was no longer considered a Top 40 chart act. However artists such as Neil Diamond, The Carpenters and Bread were marketed towards not only Top 40 radio as pop acts, but also towards an older, album-oriented market.

NEWS

1978, JULY 26: THE WORLD'S FIRST TEST-TUBE BABY, LOUISE BROWN, IS BORN IN MANCHESTER, ENGLAND

left: After a song-plugging and later songwriting career that went back to the early 60s, million-selling albums and singles in the 1970s made Neil Diamond a household name.

right: Fleetwood Mac's multi-platinum album Rumours ensured the former blues band of MOR credibility forever.

Therefore this cross-pollination between two separate marketing strategies enabled artists to gain sales from audiences that might not have been influenced by the charts, but were still a target audience.

Such was the success of these twin strategies by the 1970s that crossover was occurring from Motown and Soul, through artists such as Diana Ross and Lionel Richie (formerly of The Commodores) and Kenny Gamble and Leon Huff's Philadelphia International label where The Three Degrees and Harold Melvin & The Blue Notes (featuring Teddy Pendergrass) held sway. However, while MOR audiences were deemed to be older and probably more affluent, they could not be fobbed with anything that didn't at the very least pay lip-service to passing trends. Consequently the disco era of the mid-1970s only served to augment the popularity of artists such as Diana Ross who were by no means unwilling to embrace fresh trends, no matter how derivative they may be.

Similarly, country music began to cross-fertilise nurturing and developing a parade of performers such as Glen Campbell, Anne Murray, Billy Jo Spears and count-less others too numerous to mention who found their biggest success with MOR audiences. Although the disco era thrust to the fore a plethora of one-hit wonders, the whole thrust of the business ethic in Nashville was to provide continuity. So Nashville and country music was ideally placed, with high-quality songwriters on tap, to milk the market for all it was worth. For the bottom-line when appealing to MOR audiences is quality.

Sinatra and other male vocalists of the genre such as Andy Williams, Johnny Mathis and Jack Jones always secured the services of the best and, perhaps, hippest producers, the finest orchestras and session men, and almost unlimited marketing budgets. Furthermore, it is as well to recall that writers such as Burt Bacharach, Hal David and Jim Webb, among others, who at their peak during the 1960s with artists like Dionne Warwick, The Walker Brothers and Glen Campbell, achieved an unprecedented crossover market.

During the 1980s and 1990s, divisions were eroded still further as vocalists with a background in Soul or R&B, such as Whitney Houston, Toni Braxton and Luther Vandross, attained formidable sales on the strength of the universality of their appeal. But the whole concept of what MOR actually represented was embodied by Canadian Celine Dion, Elton John and the modern musicals of Andrew Lloyd Webber and Tim Rice.

Furthermore the use of operatic arias in television commercials and the like enabled opera singers such as Luciano Pavarotti, Jose Carreras and Placido Domingo (popularly known as The Three Tenors) and Lesley Garrett and Kiri Te Kanawa to crossover and reach wider audiences. Although their willingness to crossover might have been perceived as a sell-out to crass commercialism, no compromise was really necessary, for shrewd repackaging gave record buyers the opportunity to hear the greatest tunes and arias by the best soloists without needing to acquaint themselves with the whole opera.

THE CARPENTERS
THEIR GREATEST HITS
A&M

right: The Bee Gees were thrust to the centre of the disco stage with their soundtrack contribution to the movie Saturday Night Fever.

DISCO

INITIALLY, A CONTRACTION OF THE TERM 'DISCOTHEQUE', discos sprung up as a movement in the mid-70s in response to a number of factors. And as discos, grew in popularity, so the DJs began to exert more influence in the shaping of popular taste.

In the early 1970s, record labels started to issue 12-inch singles in response to demands from DJs that the 7-inch single format was too restrictive. Ever since the escalation in popularity of the LP in the 1960s as the prime vehicle for recording purposes, musicians had moved beyond the conventional two- or three-minute standard, considered the optimum duration for a single: album (LP) tracks could sometimes last for up to 25 minutes. Jazz performers adapted to the LP format more-or-less overnight and increasingly rock bands had upped the ante to where the standard length for an album track was around four or five minutes. Similarly Soul and R&B artists such as James Brown, Curtis Mayfield and Isaac Hayes began to record tracks of greater duration. Consequently, when tracks were issued as standard 45

rpm singles, they required editing or splitting into a Part 1 and a Part 2 spread over the two sides of the disc. With the advent of 12-inch single, that all changed. Therefore, with more space available on the records, songs of three or four minutes duration could be re-recorded in longer versions.

The net result was that venues – nominally discos – proliferated, with each venue catering to its own specific audience. Accordingly, a multitude of hybrids evolved. While the most pervasive mainstream stimulus was the movie Saturday Night Fever, with a soundtrack largely composed by the pop group The Bee Gees, the Euro-disco of producers Frank Farian, with his band Boney M, and Giorgio Moroder, with Donna Summer, confirmed that disco was the pop music of the mid-1970s. If much of this stuff was instantly disposable and endlessly recyclable, as with all pop music, some of it possessed considerable appeal. Producers Kenny Gamble and Leon Huff did for Philadelphia what Berry Gordy had done for Detroit with Motown 15 years earlier. Groups such as

above: With hits like 'Brown Girl In The Ring' and 'The Rivers Of Babylon', (a double sided No1 in the UK) Boney M were disco-pop personified.

right: Out of New York's Studio 54 scene, Grace Jones made disco-posing into something of an art form.

GRACE JONES ISLAND LIFE

The O'Jays and Harold Melvin & The Blue Notes, featuring the soulful tones of Teddy Pendergrass, embodied the muscle of disco, while retaining a smooth and sexy warmth. Producer Howie Casey, with his group, KC & The Sunshine Band, orchestrated a series of hits for themselves and George Macrae for the Florida based TK label, owned by Henry Stone.

The bi-product of all this success was that discos catering to reggae audiences appeared, with others specialising in Funk at the jazzier end of the spectrum. As DJs gained more influence, so they were required to do something more than stand around all night, spinning records and cracking jokes. Gradually, some started to use instrumental tracks over which they would rap, others would pre-record samples from existing records and put them together, creating an entirely separate piece of work. As synthesisers basically became more affordable and computer technology more accessible, a new breed of musician began to emerge. Raised in the atmosphere of the dance-floor or disco, hip hop, Techno and House, later Acid Jazz, began to dominate. Initially it was perceived as little more than a new underground, but when rock bands such as Primal Scream and Happy Mondays began harnessing the strong, propulsive rhythm tracks, dance and rock seemed to have merged. As the barriers between genres became progressively more blurred, discos were superseded by clubs and an entire network of unofficial warehouse events known as raves came to be a regular feature in the late 1980s. Although raves were manifestations of a new underground, with – naturally – an attendant drug culture, within a broader context, its popularity caused bands such as The Prodigy and Massive Attack to break into the mainstream.

Although the reference to disco is now loaded with connotations of 70s retro style in both music and fashion, through the 1990s the drums'n'bass of Jungle, with Roni Size & Reprazent and Tricky leading the way, has proved that the dance-floor remains an accurate barometer of popular taste.

CHIC
EVERYBODY DANCE
Rhino

1979, DECEMBER 2: AYATOLLAH KHOMEINI'S REVOLUTIONARY GOVERNMENT IN IRAN ADOPTS A NEW ISLAMIC CONSTITUTION

POST PUNK, POST MODERN

The post-modern era of the 80s was marked in the UK early in the decade by a move back to a more theatrical approach in the guise of the New Romantics that included the likes of Duran Duran, Culture Club, Adam Ant and Spandau Ballet. Flamboyant in pirate gear and regency ruffs, and geared to the McLaren/Westwood fashion axis as much as to changes in musical trends, they were locked into the embryonic club scene that had gestated from disco and New York's Studio 54. While the New Romantics' frills and foppery – like many pop fashions – was short-lived, the emergence of a club counter-culture was confirmed with the spread of House music from its Chicago origins, and the associated street-oriented culture of rap and hip hop.

right: Leading faces and voices in the New Romantic movement of the early 80s, Britain's Duran Duran.

far right: The 'Magic Number' dance /swing outfit from the late 1980s De la Soul, and friends.

1980-1990

above, left: One of the major DJs in the world of British house music, Groove Rider.

above: American hip hop/ swing artists big on the house dance scene, Jodeci.

HOUSE MUSIC

JUST AS THE BIRTH OF ROCK'N'ROLL IS INEXTRICABLY LINKED WITH THE DEVELOPMENT OF THE ELECTRIC GUITAR, House music was born when electronic instruments became affordable. With cheap synthesisers, drum machines, sequencers and samplers, anyone could make a House track in their own bedroom. You did not even have to be a musician.

The first affordable synthesiser, the MiniMoog, went on the market in 1970. This opened the door to a flood of other machines. But it was the arrival of the Sequential Circus Prophet 5 that was the breakthrough. It was polyphonic – you could play five notes at once – and it had a memory. Although rhythm boxes were around in the 1970s, the first serious analogue drum machines did not become available until 1980, with the Roland tr-808. House act 808 State took their name from it. Next came the sequencer, which is a bit like a tape recorder without the tape. It memorised sequences of music – or rather the control signals that produced

them – and played them back through a synthesiser and drum machine. The Roland tr-909 allowed you to sample sounds – that is capture real recorded sounds – and mix them with synthesised sounds. Then, in 1984, the Ensoniq Mirage allowed you to manipulated sample sounds in any way you fancied. These electronic machines were used to create an entirely synthetic sound, with an alien atmosphere and an insistent 4/4 beat. This was House.

House was born in Chicago, though its roots can be found in New York's underground dance scene, which preceded the disco explosion of the 1970s. DJs were already experimenting with playing two different records at the same time, producing an hypnotic hybrid, punching a pause-button on cassette decks and hiring live drummers to create a bottom-heavy beat on the dance floor.

Frankie Knuckles took all these techniques – along with the trick of spiking the club's drinks with acid – to Chicago, where he took over as resident DJ in The

NEWS

1980, MAY 5: BRITISH SAS FORCES SUCCESSFULLY STORM THE IRANIAN EMBASSY IN LONDON TO RELEASE HOSTAGES BEING HELD BY A GROUP OF TERRORISTS

Warehouse from 1977 to 1983. He and another Chicago DJ Lil' Louis began mixing Soul and disco classics with more arcane tracks.

Nearby, in Detroit, Electro music was taking hold. The German band Kraftwerk were particularly influential. Two college students, Juan Atkins and Rick Davis, released their first single, 'Alleys Of Your Mind', under the name Cybotron on their own Deep Space label there in 1981, starting Techno. Other European electro-grooves from Depeche Mode and Human League were added to the mix. In New York, a gay club called The Paradise Garage opened which gave its name to its own oeuvre of the genre.

On the radio in Chicago, The Hot Mix Five were creating such blends that kids would cut school rather than miss their show. So many enquiries flooded in that they had to post lists of the tracks used in a local record store, called Imports Inc.

Another Chicago DJ, Jesse Saunders and Vince Lawrence, who had already independently released a synth track called 'I Like To Do It In Fast Cars', produced the first House record, 'Fantasy', with the singer Screamin' Rachael. They took it to Chicago's only pressing plant. The owner Larry Sherman liked what he heard and set up the first House record company, Trax.

He also inadvertently set up the rival DJ International when he pressed 10,000 for his Rocky Jones. The competition between Trax and DJ International was the foundation of House music, which soon spread across America and around the world.

THE CHEMICAL BROTHERS
DIG YOUR OWN HOLE
Heavenly

CD CHECKLIST

below: With hits like 'Rebel Without A Pause' and 'Welcome To The Terrordrome', US rap duo Public Enemy typified the seemingly racially aggresive stance of much of the genre.

right: The self-styled 'baddest man in rap' LL Cool J debuted chartwise with 'I'm Bad' in 1987, on the Columbia subsidiary label Def Jam.

far right: Erick, Scratch and Parrish of EPMD who hit big with their albums Strictly Business, Unfinished Business and Business As Usual.

RAP/HIP HOP

RAP BEGAN IN THE BLACK AND HISPANIC AREAS OF NEW YORK AND IN LESS THAN TWO DECADES IT HAS COME TO DOMINATE THE WORLD. Rap's roots can be traced back to the block parties and playgrounds of Harlem and the Bronx, where Afrika Bambaataa, Kook Herc, Grandmaster Flash and others pioneered the use of two decks and a mixer. While the disco revolution was in full swing, these DJs reverted to the harder, funkier black music that the disco sound was based on. They put two versions of the same record on the turntables and cut back and forth between them. Soon, chanted street poetry was overlaid and rap was born.

The name rap comes from a trendy 1960s word for talk. Hip hop was another designation after Lovebug Starsky used the lyric 'To the hip, hop, hippety hop'. But while rap only refers to the music, the term hip hop was also applied to the new culture of graffiti art, a looser way of dressing and breakdancing. Initially rap was confined to parties and dances. Tapes were made and circulated. Then, in 1979, the Sugerhill Gang released 'Rapper's Delight'. Afrika Bambaataa and his Soul Sonic force brought the authentic sound of rap to a wider audience in 1982 with 'Planet Rock'.

Grandmaster Flash began to montage records, adding sound effects and 'scratching' – producing rhythmic patterns by moving the groove of the record back and forth under the stylus. Run DMC took rap mainstream by adding elements of heavy metal in 1986, when their third album 'Raising Hell' went platinum. Then

MC Hammer introduced dance routines and made rap showbiz. At that time, there was also a slew of white rap artists – Vanilla Ice, The Beastie Boys, House Of Pain – who adopted the same dress and style.

However, the move into mainstream soon spawned a violent backlash – gangsta rap, which sprung up mainly on the West Coast. It was deliberately anti-social and sexually crude, filling its lyrics with words such as 'nigga', 'bitch' and 'ho' (whore). Despite this hardcore approach, sales were massive. Niggaz With Attitude's 'Niggaz 4 Life' sold over 900,000 copies in its first week. Dr Dre's 'The Chronic' sold over three million and Snoop Doggy Dogg's Doggy Style sold more than a million in its first month.

Unsuccessful prosecutions of gangsta rap artists for obscenity foundered on the First Amendment. There was even more outrage over the gangstas' glorification of violence. Ice-T was forced to remove the track 'Cop Killer' from his debut album 'Body Count' after the Texas Fraternal Order of Police threatened to boycott Times Warner – Warner Brothers were Ice-T's distributors. However, violence – particularly against the police – is still an essential part of gangsta rap. At the same time, there has been a plea from gangsta rappers themselves against gangland violence. Coolio's 'Gangsta's Paradise' was an international hit and has taken even a hardcore gangsta like Coolio mainstream. Likewise gangsta rapper Ice Cube has ended up in the movies, as has most famously the Hollywood star Willie Smith who started out in rap.

right: From their first hit 'Smells Like Teen Spirit', Nirvana caught the mood of the times with their honest evocation of the concerns of their youthful audience.

far right: The Smashing Pumpkins' represented a more mainstream-friendly version of grunge for the record buyer.

GRUNGE

left: The disaffected face of grunge was to be forever personified in Nirvan's lead vocalist Kurt Cobain, after his tempestuous relationship with Courtney Love, drug addiction and eventual suicide.

BY THE LATE 1980s IN THE US, THE MOOD OF DISAFFECTION THAT HAD BEEN GERMINATING FOR SOME TIME FINALLY REACHED A HEAD in the form of a plethora of bands such as Pearl Jam, Nirvana, Alice In Chains, Extreme and Smashing Pumpkins. Combining the visceral fury of Punk with a downbeat anti-style rhetoric, Grunge – as it was quickly dubbed – was the bi-product of an American music industry that had become ever more corporate in its ideology and ever more complacent in its musical endeavours. Despite the apparent benevolence of an industry that had taken Live Aid and other charitable concerns to its bosom, there was little altruism in its motives: Live Aid might have generated millions for the starving in Africa, but it also generated millions in record and CD sales.

With the advent of the CD and the attendant transferral of back catalogue to CD, the record industry rested back upon its laurels, raking in the cash without expending any discernible energy or creativity in the process. New signings were few, as A&R departments waited to see what would happen next. It was no surprise that new bands such as they were trod a careful line between rock and heavy metal, with the result that bands such as Guns n' Roses, Aerosmith and, to a lesser extent, Bon Jovi were able to pack stadiums on the strength of tried and tested formulae.

When the backlash came, it started in Seattle, Washington, as groups like Nirvana – through the independent Sub-Pop label and producer Steve Albini –

began to address global topics like child abuse with a chilling indifference to the accepted conventions of rock'n'roll. The music industry was ill-accustomed to its minions disseminating critiques on society's hypocrisy. With Nirvana's first two albums, Bleach (1989) and Nevermind (1991), they gave Grunge an agenda. Furthermore, with titles like 'Lithium', 'Smells Like Teen Spirit' and 'Come As You Are', they displayed a deceptively melodic quality that was seldom evident in Punk. Nirvana soon signed to a major label, and, as always, the record industry was quick to capitalise upon this disenchantment.

What started as a genuinely Indie-styled operation was absorbed into a broader context. Pearl Jam signed to Columbia – their second album, Vs. (1993), sold more units in its first week of issue than any other album – and Smashing Pumpkins (Siamese Dream, 1993) went to the Hut label, which Virgin bought and in turn sold to EMI. Other groups such as Mudhoney, Jane's Addiction, Soundgarden and Screaming Trees not only influenced their contemporaries on the grunge scene, but the rock'n'roll mainstream generally.

The most significant aspect of Grunge was that it fomented an Indie-style approach to recording in the US. Jazz, blues, country, Tex-Mex et al had always had more than their fair share of specialist labels, but Indie rock labels either went out of business or were absorbed. With labels such as Bloodshot in Chicago and Slow River in Boston, there are clear signs that the Indie culture is now established in the US.

1982, APRIL 2: ARGENTINEAN FORCES INVADE THE FALKLAND ISLANDS IN THE SOUTH ATLANTIC. WAR BETWEEN BRITAIN AND ARGENTINA ENSUES, CULMINATING IN A BRITISH VICTORY IN JUNE

THE ROLLING STONES

THE ROLLING STONES ARE THE SELF-STYLED 'GREATEST ROCK'N'ROLL BAND IN THE WORLD'. Few would challenge that claim.

Singer Mick Jagger and guitarist Keith Richards were at primary school together. As teenagers they met again on a train only to discover they were both fans of rhythm and blues. Together they travelled to the Ealing Blues Club, where they sat in with Alexis Korner's Blues, Inc.

The guitarist Brian Jones and drummer Charlie Watts also played with Korner, but Jones was keen to split and start a band of his own. By the time bassist Bill Wyman joined the line-up, the band was already calling itself The Rolling Stones, after a Muddy Waters song.

They became the house band at the Crawdaddy Club in Richmond and in June 1963 released their first single, a cover of Chuck Berry's 'Come On'. It reached number 21 in the British charts.

They toured with The Everly Brothers, Bo Diddley and Little Richard. Their next release, John Lennon's 'I Wanna Be Your Man', reached number 15 and in January 1964 their cover of Buddy Holly's 'Not Fade Away' reached number three in the UK and number 48 in America. Their first number one in the UK was Bobby Womack's 'It's All Over Now'.

After a successful US tour, they had another UK number one with 'Little Red Rooster'. But it was banned in America, where the lyrics were thought to be offensive. Such controversy only helped the Stones' bad boy image, however, which became firmly established when they were caught urinating in public.

The band quickly realised they could not sustain a career on covers alone, and Jagger and Richards began writing new material. They quickly clocked up a series of number one hits on both sides of the Atlantic. Their songs were always more caustic and direct than those of The Beatles.

'Get Off My Cloud', 'Mother's Little Helper', '19th Nervous Breakdown', 'Have You Seen Your Mother, Baby (Standing in the Shadows)' and 'Satisfaction' addressed real social issues. The Stones' songs were

far left: Released in 1978, the album Some Girls included The Rolling Stones' eighth American chart-topper 'Miss You'.

left: The 1996 CD collection Stripped also featured bonus CD Rom items showing the band in action.

below: The familiar 'tongue' logo adopted by Rolling Stones Records on their initial release, which was the LP Sticky Fingers in 1971.

left: Replacing Mick Taylor, ex-Faces guitarist Ron Wood (far left) made his first recording studio appearance with The Rolling Stones on the 1976 album Black And Blue.

also more sexually explicit. Mick Jagger was forced to mumble the title line of 'Let's Spend The Night Together' when they appeared on the Ed Sullivan Show in 1967, under threat of censorship. When The Beatles released Sergeant Pepper's Lonely Hearts' Club Band, the Stones released Their Satanic Majesties Request.

Upstaged by the Jagger-Richards writing team, Brian Jones left the band in June 1969. A month later, he was found dead in his swimming pool. A few days later, the Stones gave a free concert in Hyde Park. Jagger read from Shelley and released thousands of butterflies. Jones was replaced by Mick Taylor and the day after Jones was buried the Stones released 'Honky Tonk Women'.

The gold discs continued but the Stones' satanic image came home to haunt them. In 1969, during their 'Gimme Shelter' tour of America, a young black man, Meredith Hunter, was stabbed to death by the Hell's Angels the Stones had hired to marshal their free concert at California's Altamont Speedway. The incident was caught on film. There was an outcry that the Stones' song 'Sympathy For The Devil' was in some way to blame.

But the Stones went rolling on. They maintained an impressive output of singles and albums, and involved themselves in more than their fair share of sex and drug scandals. Ron Wood, already a star from his work with Rod Stewart and The Faces, took over from Mick Taylor in 1975. And, in 1993, bassist Bill Wyman quit. No permanent replacement has been announced.

In 1998, The Rolling Stones began another world tour – Bridges To Babylon. Despite being well into their fifties, The Rolling Stones show with no discernible waning of vigour. No other band comes close to them in longevity or achievement.

STICKY FINGERS
Rolling Stones Records

STRIPPED
Rolling Stones Records

CD CHECKLIST

1984: FAMINE RAVAGES ETHIOPIA. THE UNITED NATIONS ESTIMATE A DEATH TOLL OF BETWEEN 600,000 AND 1 MILLION IN THIS YEAR ALONE

EASY LISTENING

above: The ever-popular Nat King Cole, who died in 1965, has been a continuing best-seller as part of Capitol Records' easy listening catalogue.

above right: The manager of UK Philips Records presenting Ray Conniff with a copy of the album Hi Fi Companion which sold over a quarter of a million copies in the UK in 1960.

AS RADIO BEGAN TO EXERT AN INFLUENCE ON DOMESTIC LIVES BETWEEN THE TWO WORLD WARS, so radio programmers began to understand the need to provide a service of music that was low on rhythm, but high on melody: discord and dissonance discouraged the listening public. While most broadcast music was provided by dance bands and the great orchestras of Benny Goodman and Paul Whiteman, among others, so, very gradually, radio networks began to establish their own orchestras to provide a gentle and undemanding accompaniment for listeners as they went about their business. Consequently, a new breed of bandleader began to emerge – one who was able to provide music that drew from all facets of contemporary music whilst retaining an unchallenging cosmetic veneer. With orchestras led by Mantovani and Percy Faith, among others, vocalists such as Bing Crosby, Dick Haymes and Al Bowlly tended to croon their material, which was drawn from Hollywood musicals, light opera or popular songwriters such as George & Ira Gershwin, Cole Porter and Johnny Mercer.

More significantly – stylistically at least – was the gradual assimilation of Latin-American rhythms into the easy listening vocabulary in the early 1950s. For with dances such as the bossa-nova, the rumba and the tango, endless possibilities were presented for arrangers keen to add a slightly exotic flavour to their repertoire. The net result was that guitarists such as Laurindo Almeida or bandleaders like Sergio Mendes were soon gainfully occupied advising on the composition of film scores and the like.

Gradually, orchestras were augmented by choirs and arranger/producers such as Mitch Miller and Ray Conniff began to notch up record-breaking sales with albums covering the hits of the day. Despite the emergence of R&B during the 1940s and then rock'n'roll in the 1950s, the most consistently popular chart acts were vocalists such as Kay Starr, Jo Stafford, Al Martino and Tony Bennett.

NEWS

1985, JULY 10: THE GREENPEACE SHIP RAINBOW WARRIOR IS BLOWN UP IN AUCKLAND HARBOUR, NEW ZEALAND. FRENCH SECURITY SERVICES ARE INVOLVED IN THE INCIDENT

above: Kay Starr was an archetypal 50s singer who demonstrated the relaxed, accessible style that the term easy listening came to define.

above right: The occasional butt of jokes among the musician fraternity, German bandleader James Last; needless to say, Last laughed all the way to the bank.

With the advent of rock'n'roll, easy listening underwent a sea-change, as it began to appeal to and was directed at, specifically, a more mature audience. Throughout the 1960s, bands such as Herb Alpert & The Tijuana Brass, Bert Kaempfert, the indefatigable Arthur Fielder & The Boston Pops and James Last continued to sell albums in extraordinary quantities, but they were unable to fill the vacuum created by the rock era. Consequently, groups such as The Mamas & The Papas, Peter, Paul & Mary and The Carpenters began to fill the void.

Similarly, in the UK, ersatz rock and rollers like Cliff Richard and big-voiced balladeers such as Tom Jones, Englebert Humperdink and Shirley Bassey established themselves as real alternatives to The Beatles, The Rolling Stones and Led Zeppelin. However, it wasn't just the vocalists who flourished; French pianist Richard Clayderman had a field day and German bandleader James Last has sold in excess of 70 million albums worldwide since 1965.

In the end, easy listening – or, pejoratively, muzak – has become one of the key marketing devices of the 20th century, as it is now a ubiquitous ambient tool in shopping malls, airports, lifts and restaurants. Perhaps the most disquieting feature is that some of the more obviously tuneful pieces by classical composers, including Pachelbel (Le Canon), Vivaldi (The Four Seasons) and J.S. Bach (The Brandenburg Concertos), are being cast alongside the James Last Orchestra to inspire shoppers or calm apprehensive airline travellers. That may smack of a particularly venal brand of intellectual snobbery, but it is more illustrative of the insatiable appetites of a consumer society where everything has a purpose and can be tagged and marketed. So it goes.

JOHNNY MATHIS
GREATEST HITS
Columbia

CD CHECKLIST

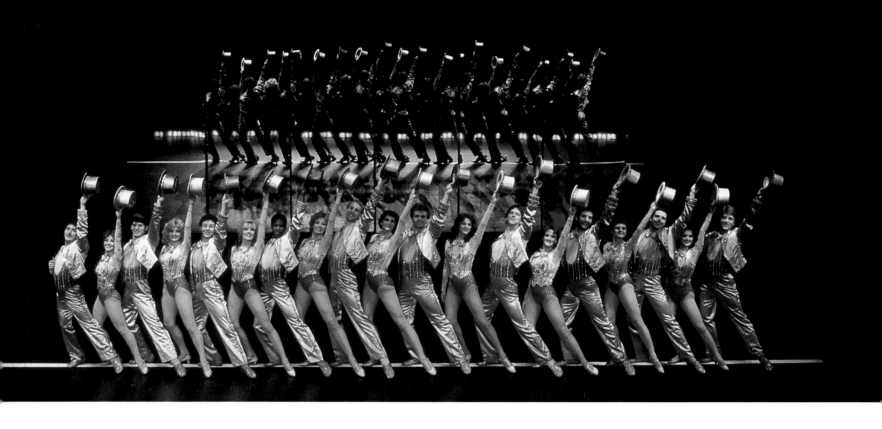

MODERN MUSICALS

below: The youthful Tim Rice (left) and Andrew Lloyd-Webber at the time of Joseph And His Amazing Technicolor Dreamcoat which was their debut musical, opening in 1972.

EVER SINCE ANDREW LLOYD WEBBER AND TIM RICE DABBLED THEIR TOES IN THE POOL that is the musical, with Joseph And His Amazing Techni-color Dreamcoat and then Jesus Christ Superstar, critics and the like have tended to look askance at their success and popularity. For their popular appeal has never been in accord with critical opinion. Many have suggested that their songs are derivative and hackneyed. All of this may or may not be true. Their achievement, though, has been to revitalise the musical as a viable, theatrical proposition. With producer Cameron Mackintosh, shows such as Cats (based on T.S. Eliot's Old Possum's Book Of Practical Cats), Evita, Starlight Express, Les Miserables, Martin Guerre and Five Guys Named Moe (based on the music of R&B bandleader Louis Jordan), among others, have managed to harness the immediacy of the theatre with the technological nous of the cinema: this is the suspension of disbelief. In a way, though, the stage musical, formerly constrained by the physical capacities

of a stage crew, has proven its adaptability. For despite the strictures of the critics – and those of a theatrical persuasion were always inclined to be more voluble and outspoken than their contemporaries in other areas of the performing arts – the musical has proved to be as pliable and adaptable as any other art form. Leonard Bernstein's West Side Story ushered in a new epoch in the evolution of the musical with its reliance upon movement and composition: the minimalist stage sets suggested that attempts to compete with the lavish spectacles that Hollywood could mount were worth bothering with. Similarly, Stephen Sondheim's A Chorus Line positively exulted in its minimalism. However, in addition to the starkness of the stage sets, what both West Side Story and A Chorus Line depended upon for their impact was a cohesive narrative allied with strong, memorable tunes. On both levels, they succeeded admirably well. When filmed, despite their success at the box-office, the electricity and magnetism that only a stage show can engender was notable for its absence.

above left: The spectacular chorus line in the finale of A Chorus Line in 1982.

above: On Broadway, New York City, with A Chorus Line playing at the Shubert Theatre.

above right: The Los Angeles 1989 stage production of Pete Townshend's Tommy with Elton John (left) and Townshend.

Movies confirmed conclusively that they were incapable of bridging that gulf.

Around the early 1970s, as the quality of sound improved at rock concerts, so performers such as David Bowie and Rick Wakeman and groups like Genesis and Pink Floyd started to harness the leaps forward in technology to create shows that were visually as extravagant as they were aurally impressive. As early as 1969, Pete Townsend of The Who had penned the rock-opera, Tommy, which was followed by Quadrophrenia (1973). Although Tommy was never produced until 1996 as a stage musical, it was filmed and performed in its entirety on several occasions. Bowie, with a cast of characters that included Ziggy Stardust and Aladdin Sane, demonstrated a keen sense of the theatre, while Peter Gabriel of Genesis, using costume and mime, made his first tentative steps towards creating an audio-visual extravaganza on stage. It was therefore only a matter of time before the technology of rock could be harnessed with the imagination of theatre. It was a

hesitant process, but with revivals of stage musicals such as Rodgers & Hart's Pal Joey at London's National Theatre and intriguing adaptations such as Flora Thompson's autobiographical memoire of rural life in England, Lark Rise To Candleford, with music by Folk Rock group The Albion Band, audiences started to queue round the block for tickets.

The beneficiaries may in the short term have been Webber, Mackintosh and Uncle Tom Cobbley, but with revivals of shows such as Chicago, featuring the incomparable Ute Lemper, the theatrical musical is no longer hampered by commercial considerations. Perhaps the most engaging irony of all occurred when Webber staged Sunset Boulevard, which is based upon Billy Wilder's film of the same name.

1986, APRIL 26: FIRE BREAKS OUT AT THE CHERNOBYL NUCLEAR POWER PLANT IN THE UKRAINE, SPREADING MASSIVE RADIOACTIVE CONTAMINATION ACROSS EUROPE

QUINCY JONES

THERE ARE PRODUCERS, AND THERE IS QUINCY JONES. It is difficult to imagine one individual who has had such an impact on all facets of American contemporary music. Born on March 14, 1933, in Chicago, Illinois, Jones grew up in Seattle where he met Ray Charles. After studying at Schillinger House (later Berklee School of Music) in Boston, his career started in 1949 when he was asked by the jazz bassist Oscar Pettiford to arrange a song. In 1950 he joined the Lionel Hampton Orchestra as a trumpeter; he remained there for three years, contributing arrangements as well as performing. By 1956 he was recording under his own name. His first album, This Is How I Feel About Jazz, was credited to Quincy Jones & The All Stars; among The All Stars were bassist Charlie Mingus and vibraphonist Milt Jackson. The following year saw the release of Go West Man, which featured, among others, Art Pepper and Shelley Manne.

Over the next ten years, he produced and wrote arrangements for a wide diversity of artists, including the Count Basie Orchestra, Ray Charles, Peggy Lee, Dinah Washington and Sarah Vaughan. In 1961 he was appointed musical director of Mercury records and, in 1963, he produced 'It's My Party' for Lesley Gore which went to number one in the US. As a reward for this he was appointed vice-president of Mercury in 1964.

In 1967 he composed and arranged the soundtrack for the film In The Heat Of The Night; other soundtracks for the films For Love Of Ivy (1968) and The Heist (1971) followed. In 1971 a collaboration with Ray Charles,

entitled Black Requiem, was performed by the Houston Symphony Orchestra with an 80-voice choir.

After signing with A&M, he recorded Smackwater Jack (1972). This album represented a change of direction inasmuch as it contained versions of material by contemporary writers like Carole King as well as self-composed material. The arrangements were less jazz-oriented than those in his previous work. As if to consolidate this change of emphasis, he produced Aretha Franklin's Hey Now Hey (The Other Side Of The Sky). In 1974, he released Body Heat, which was followed by Mellow Madness (1975). In 1977, he scored the soundtrack for the TV series Roots, which prompted Motown into securing his services to score and produce the soundtrack for their movie, The Wiz (1978), co-starring Michael Jackson. The same year saw the release of Sounds … And Stuff Like That, featuring vocals by Ashford & Simpson and Chaka Khan. While working with Jackson on the set of the The Wiz , it had been suggested that Jones should produce Jackson's first Epic solo album.

Off The Wall (1979) spawned a slew of international nine hit singles; in 1982, he produced the follow-up Thriller, which was to become the best-selling album of all time. 1981 saw the formation of his own record label, Qwest; signings to the label included Patti Austin, Siedah Garrett, James Ingram and Tevin Campbell, all of whom achieved a measure of success under his tutelage. The same year saw the release of The Dude (1981), which included 'Ai No Corrida' and 'Razzamatazz'.

NEWS

left: Producer and arranger supreme, the great Quincy Jones' career spans five decades of American music.

right: Commercially Quincy's most successful project ever, the 1982 Michael Jackson marathon seller Thriller.

In 1984 the Quincy Jones Orchestra recorded LA Is My Lady, featuring Frank Sinatra, and then scored Steven Spielberg's film The Colour Purple. In 1985 he produced 'We Are The World', the US contribution to Live Aid. Credited to US For Africa, the single featured a veritable who's who of the music business; that the song itself succeeded in plumbing new depths of mawkish sentimentality was no fault of Jones. It remained at the top of the US charts for four weeks and generated millions of dollars for the starving in Africa.

By 1987 Jones was back at work with Jackson, co-producing Bad, the follow-up to Thriller. In 1989 he released Back On The Block (1990), which featured Chaka Khan, Ray Charles, James Ingram and Barry White, among others. Indeed its guest list was almost as compendious and diverse as the cast of US For Africa had been and offered further proof – if any were necessary – that Quincy Jones remains one of the staunchest and most inventive upholders of the traditions of contemporary US music.

right: From the top clockwise, Benny, Bjorn, Anni-Frid (Frida) and Agnetha – Abba, the ultimate in production-pop, pure pop or Euro pop, call it what you might, it worked.

EURO POP

IT IS ONE OF THE ENIGMAS OF THE MUSIC WORLD THAT MAINLAND EUROPE HAS NEVER CRACKED THE US MARKET, WHILE SUCCESSFULLY PRODUCING POP MUSIC WITH OTHERWISE INTERNATIONAL APPEAL. Europe always had its fair share of icons: take Edith Piaf, for example, or what about Flamenco vocalist Camarron? Both extraordinarily popular in their own countries and to a cognoscenti beyond, but in terms of generating a mass-market, cross-cultural audience, neither of them had the faintest chance. One of the reasons for this, perhaps, is that in Europe the traditions of making music are so inextricably bound up with the cultural identity of each nation that the whole creative process is not something to be taken lightly. Popular music has closely reflected the artistic pulse of each country: the Neapolitan ballads that gained a brief moment of popularity through anglicised versions by Dean Martin are as potent in their sense of drama as Puccini's opera Tosca, for example. When violinist

Stephane Grappelli and guitarist Django Reinhardt teamed up in the 1930s for their ground-breaking performances at The Hot Club in France, their impact on jazz and the French cabaret network was immediate and their popularity was considerable. However, there was no way they were ever going to shift large numbers of records, even if a record label were prepared to manufacture them. For as much as they utilised the improvisation of jazz, they also drew from Reinhardt's gypsy heritage.

So, the European mainland, largely, has managed to avoid getting stigmatised by associations with groups like the appositely named Middle Of The Road or by performers with penchants for facial reconstruction and pigment transplants. Unfortunately, though, disco and the concomitant intrusion into the mainstream of synthesisers and, later, digital technology has meant that even businessmen can manufacture hits these days. The result is that from the mid-1970s, the German Hansa label, with producer Frank Farian, donated Boney

NEWS

1988, DECEMBER 22: A BOEING 747 FLYING FROM FRANKFURT TO NEW YORK EXPLODES OVER LOCKERBIE IN SCOTLAND, KILLING 270 PASSENGERS. EVIDENCE OF A BOMB IS FOUND

left: Abba enjoyed enormous success worldwide before they finally disbanded in the early 80s.

below: The latest in the Euro-pop stakes, Aqua have enjoyed huge international hits in the late 90s with 'Barbie Girl' and 'Turn Back Time'.

M as their contribution to the nation's cultural heritage. It wasn't all bad though, for Giorgio Moroder, another synth-king-cum-producer, launched the career of Soul singer Donna Summer on an unsuspecting public with 'Love To Love You Baby', a 12-minute extended disco mix that gave the 12-inch single its place in the market.

However, there are always exceptions. And, in 1974, at the least likely of events – The Eurovision Song Contest – a Swedish group called Abba claimed the nickel-plated door-stop with 'Waterloo'. Scandinavia had previously produced The Spotnicks – an instrumental combo of the early 1960s, who sounded like a cross between The Tornados and The Ventures. Abba's success was immediate. Over the next six years, Abba notched up eighteen Top Ten hits with titles like 'Mamma Mia', 'Fernando', 'Knowing Me, Knowing You' and 'The Name Of The Game'. These weren't disposable bits of tat either, but conformed to the highest standards, comparable to those at the Brill Building in the early 1960s: this was pop at its purest.

Furthermore, their singles' success did not adversely affect their album sales either. This was only just, as Arrival and Abba: The Album deserve inclusion on any list of great albums. During the 1980s, their popularity dipped and they quietly disbanded in 1982.

The Eurovison Song Contest continues to captivate audiences worldwide – except in the United States – and is a constant source of material for the singers and groups who embody the multi-national appeal, though never nearing their succes in terms of record sales, represented by Abba.

The dance culture of the late 1980s and 1990s has fomented an upswing in production values. Much of the time, though, the output has been based upon samples with augmented rhythm tracks,with vocal samples from Soul singers such as Jocelyn Brown or Loleatta Holloway. And groups like Aqua ('Barbie Girl') will always adumbrate the sheer perfection of Abba.

right: Despite criticism, on mainly political grounds, from a variety of sources, Paul Simon's use of South African musicians and styles on Graceland was undoubtedly the ingredient that made this well-crafted album a true classic.

far right: Participants on Graceland, Ladysmith Black Mambazo became stars in their own right with the release of Shaka Zulu in 1987.

PAUL · SIMON
GRACELAND

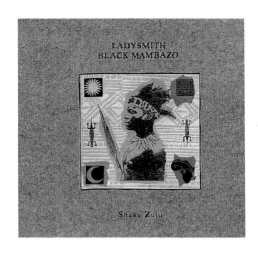

LADYSMITH
BLACK MAMBAZO

Shaka Zulu

AFRICAN POP

left: The music scene in the South African township of Soweto has produced some of the most vibrant pop sounds in the continent of Africa.

PAUL SIMON WAS CREDITED WITH INTRODUCING AFRICAN MUSIC TO A WORLD AUDIENCE with his 1986 album Graceland, which used artists from both South Africa and west Africa. However, the acappella group The Ladysmith Black Mambazo, trumpeter Hugh Masekela and singer Miriam Makeba already had a world-wide following and the Senegalese artist Youssou N'Dour was well known in the Francophone world.

Missionaries had first introduced church music to South Africa and the distinctive choral sounds there developed early on. The new South African national anthem, 'Nkosi Sikilel'i Africa', was written by Enoch Sontonga in 1912. In 1956, the acappella song 'Wimoweh' became an international hit. It was written by Solomon Linda and originally called 'Mbube', but was popularised as 'The Lion Sleeps Tonight' by Miriam Makeba.

The black American sounds of jazz and R&B were also an influence. Early recordings by Duke Ellington, Count Basie and Louis Armstrong had a huge impact and, by the early 1930s, groups such as The Jazz Maniacs and The Merry Blackbirds were widely acclaimed. But as apartheid forced black Africans off the land and into the townships a new music – Mbaqanga – emerged. This fused the traditional rhythms of the countryside with the American sounds popular in the cities. The political situation in South Africa also drove many people abroad, building a world-wide following for the likes of Miriam Makeba and Hugh

Masekela. Musicals such as Ipi Tombi and Kwa Zulu introduced traditional sounds to a wider audience too.

Inside the country, the major focal point of South African music was Dorkay House, a meeting point for artists that has launched numerous careers. Since the 1940s, it was managed by the remarkable Queeneth Ndaba and bandleader Ntemi Piliso, who organised benefits for the musicians.

Africa's best-known sound is Highlife, which emerged in Ghana and Sierra Leone in the 1920s. It fused traditional music with sea shanties, regimental brass band tunes, hymns and other western influences. Guitars, accordions and harmonicas were added to the sound of African drums. Highlife influenced all of contemporary African music, and Osibisa, formed in London in 1969, brought Highlife to a western audience.

The best-known exponent is Fela Kuti, who has fused Highlife with Modern Jazz. In 1958, already a singer in the Laos Highlife band Cool Cats, he went to London to study at the Trinity College of Music. He formed his first band in London in 1961 and returned to Nigeria in 1963, spending time in Ghana to hone his music. During a 10-month sojourn in America in 1969, he studied black history and developed what he called a new 'Afro-beat'. This took Lagos by storm. Like other west African musicians, Kuti based his musical career around his own club, The Shrine. His huge bands soon made it impossible for him to tour outside Nigeria. A critic of successive governments, Kuti also became well known as a politician.

LADYSMITH BLACK MAMBAZO
SHAKA ZULU
Warner Bros

ALI FARKE TOURE & RY COODER
TALKING TIMBUKTU
World Circuit

CD CHECKLIST

NEWS

1989, FEBRUARY 15: AFTER NINE YEARS OF WARFARE, SOVIET TROOPS WITHDRAW FROM AFGHANISTAN. THE GOVERNMENT, BEREFT OF SOVIET SUPPORT, IS BESIEGED BY MUJAHEDIN REBELS

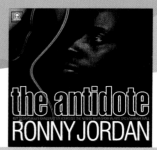

POP CENTENNIAL

The last decade of the century has seen pop music proliferate as never before, but with no central thrust as in more simple days of yore, when a dominant genre, be it Swing, rock'n'roll or British Beat, forced the pace and defined its time. Now a multitude of pigeon holes and styles co-exist, as disparate as strident vocalists like Sheryl Crow and Jungle-driven dance music, 60s-leaning British pop bands and Asian-disco Bhangra artists.

And the song lives on. Whatever the technological change, whether pop is consumed on the CD, mini-disc or straight down the line via the Internet, the good tune with the catchy lyric that can be captivating or downright annoying depending on your taste, and whether delivered by Tori Amos or The Spice Girls, The Back Street Boys or Björk, has remained a constant criteria of pop quality and success in an otherwise changing world.

1990-1999

▶

CONTEMPORARY ROCK

above: The Dublin band U2 were one the huge success stories of the 90s, taking their brand of contemporary rock from the clubs to the biggest stadia across the world.

BY THE 1990s, ROCK HAD ESTABLISHED ITSELF AS THE DOMINANT STRAIN OF CONTEMPORARY POPULAR MUSIC. With independent radio and MTV providing round-the-clock coverage, it was hardly surprising that the billions of dollars the record companies were grossing would necessitate higher and higher advances for the biggest bands. Despite the success of Indie bands, such as Oasis, there was a feeling in record companies that the profits they had been accustomed to reaping were in jeopardy. Some of this was due to the way tastes had altered: opera, jazz, blues, country and folk were no longer perceived as specialist niche markets. Furthermore, the growth in technology meant that independent record labels could, with the assistance of a web-site, be run on a shoe-string. Even established performers such as Prince started issuing his albums by mail-order through the Internet. David Bowie, who at the beginning of the 1980s was said to be down to his last fifty quid, retrieved the rights of his back catalogue in 1987, and proceeded to do limited licensing deals; by 1998, his personal fortune was estimated at around $500 million, and his back catalogue had been licensed to venture capitalists. The monopolies long held by the major labels were being threatened.

So it was the tried and tested performers that were able to negotiate the best deals. REM picked up a reputed $80-million advance from Warner Bros. for the rights to their existing back catalogue and the next three albums. REM's success came right out of the blue, first tasting success on the US college circuit, when guitar-led bands seemed slightly out of kilter. Eschewing the showbiz posturing endemic in global celebrity, and settling instead for the tranquil backwaters of Athens, Georgia, they concentrated upon honing individual skills. Drawing from America's rich musical heritage, REM use elements of country, R&B, jazz and so on, to come up with a style that is unique. Some of this is attributable to the world-weary wisdom – replete with abstract imagery – of Michael Stipe's lyrics, but it is Peter Buck's guitar work that has made REM the band of the 1990s, evoking a vision of America that is contemporary but romantic.

Similarly, U2 have shown other bands the best way to go about their business, presenting a united front, with each member of the band and the manager, Paul McGuinness, drawing the same amount of money. And it is this unity in U2 that has

rock

made them the band they are today, for the more successful they become the less individual contributions stand out, witness Zooropa (1993). The Edge is the antithesis of the popular guitar hero, seldom indulging in the flamboyant solo, preferring instead techniques such as drone ('I Will Follow'), feedback and anthemic but simplistic power chords ('Sunday Bloody Sunday'). That a group mentality determines the musical direction of the band rather individual writers has enabled the group to take chances by adapting dance rhythms and trip-hop beats.

While the climate surrounding Brit pop has yielded some genuine superstars such as Radiohead and Pulp and, in the US, country-influenced bands such as Wilco and Whiskeytown have the potential to be massive, it is debatable whether the major labels will ever have it quite so good again. Additionally, the American fondness for solid rock bands like Bon Jovi or Bush – the latter being an English outfit who were inspired by Grunge – suggests that a major shake-up such as happened with Punk in the mid-1970s or Grunge in the late 1980s might be the only thing to save the bacon of the major labels and restore some confidence to their bottom lines.

right: Georgia's REM traded in the traditional rock mix of country and R&B, coming up with a personal version of an American music for the 90s.

1990, FEBRUARY 11: IN SOUTH AFRICA, THE AFRICAN NATIONAL CONGRESS LEADER NELSON MANDELA IS RELEASED FROM VICTOR VERSHER PRISON AFTER 27 YEARS IN DETENTION

below: The daddies of Heavy
Metal, Jimmy Page and Robert
Plant in their Led Zeppelin
days; the duo still perform
together into the late 1990s.

HEAVY METAL

THE TERM 'HEAVY METAL' WOULD SEEM TO BE DERIVED FROM
WILLIAM BURROUGHS' THE NAKED LUNCH (1959), in which he used the
phrase 'heavy metal thunder'. Consequently, it was coined during the 1970s by an
English music newspaper to describe the loosely blues-based extravagances
developed by rock bands. Although it's easy to run it down, heavy metal was a
welcome antidote to the cerebral and bombastic musings of Progressive Rock.
While Led Zeppelin may, in many imaginations, have been the template for a squillion
imitators, it was groups such as Iron Butterfly, whose bass-heavy live album, In-A-
Gadda-Da-Vida, stayed on the US charts for several years, and Jimi Hendrix, with his
high-volume arpeggiated solos, who were at the root of it all.

Despite the death of Hendrix in 1970, heavy metal didn't capture the public
imagination until the emergence of Led Zeppelin. Formed by former Yardbird and
session guitarist Jimmy Page, with vocalist Robert Plant, bassist John Paul Jones and
drummer John Bonham, Led Zeppelin were the quintessential rock band, thriving on
the concert stage and only recording albums. While they borrowed heavily from the
blues, Page's instrumental virtuosity extended through all areas of the guitar. His
prowess on the acoustic guitar gave titles such as 'That's The Way' and 'Tangerine' a
pronounced folk influence, which caused him to be hired as a session musician by folk
artists such as Roy Harper, Sandy Denny and Michael Chapman. Similarly, the
anthemic 'Stairway To Heaven' and the Eastern influences of 'Kashmir' caused many
lesser players to attempt to imitate his style. Other groups such as Black Sabbath,
with their erstwhile eccentric lead vocalist Ozzy Osborne, illustrated the enduring
appeal of the genre, for titles such as 'Paranoid' were melodically strong, while lyrically
suggesting basic emotional insecurities: a not uncommon feature of adolescence.
As the genre became more popular, groups such as Kiss adopted the dress code of
Glam Rock: make-up, feathers, leather and spandex. While make-up was not
obligatory, the regulation apparel was emphatically more outré than the early
purveyors of heavy rock had managed.

While groups such as AC/DC were reaping plaudits through the latter half of the
1970s, heavy metal was desperately unfashionable in the UK until the new wave of

below, right: Van Halen with (l to r) Alex Van Halen, Mike Anthony, Dave Lee Roth and Edward Van Halen.

below: Alice Cooper took the stage performance of rock music to new limits, with an act that involved gallows, snakes and other sensational effects.

British heavy metal manifested itself with bands such as Iron Maiden, Motorhead, Whitesnake and Thunder, among others. If heavy metal had never lost its popularity in the United States, groups such as Van Halen, with 'Jump', a massive international hit, Def Leppard and Metallica revitalised the flagging stadium circuit and stimulated album sales: Def Leppard's Pyromania (1983) and Hysteria (1988) sold around 30 million units worldwide. By the late 1980s and early 1990s, heavy metal had spawned a variety of styles such as Thrash (Ministry), Death Metal (Slayer) and Gothic (Cult and The Sisters Of Mercy). Above all, though, Grunge was the most significant derivative.

Despite the fact that heavy metal would appear to be dated, US and European audiences, in particular, never seem to tire of it. Bands like Poison, Cinderella and Guns'n'Roses have guaranteed its continuing appeal with huge fan followings and marathon record sales statistics, while new variations such as the shock tactics of Marilyn Manson have ensured that the genre is nowhere near extinction, unlike the dinosaur it is often compared to.

BON JOVI
SLIPPERY WHEN WET
Mercury

MINISTRY
FILTH PIG
Warner Bros.

C D   C H E C K L I S T

1991, JANUARY 16: OPERATION DESERT STORM BEGINS AS WAR BREAKS OUT IN THE GULF. ALLIED CASUALTIES TOTAL 250 DEAD, IRAQ'S LOSSES ESTIMATED AT BETWEEN 35,000 AND 100,000

below: Morrissey, lead singer with The Smiths, brought a highly individual literary approach to bear in the lyrics of this archetypal indie band.

INDIE

WHEN PUNK POKED ITS TOUSLED HEAD OVER THE PARAPET, THE MAJOR LABELS WERE CONFUSED AS TO HOW BEST TO DEAL WITH THIS RENEGADE. Most pursued the time-honoured policy of ignoring it in the hope that it was just another bad dream and would eventually go away of its own accord. Also, at the heart of Punk, was the desire to get away from the exploitative commercialism endemic in major record labels. Therefore, a DIY mentality began to grow, bringing with it a bunch of independent labels such as Stiff, whose artists included Elvis Costello and Nick Lowe.

Independent record distributor Rough Trade was one of the first operations to evolve with a clear mandate to offer New Wave bands an alternative to the usual path of compromise and incipient insolvency that seemed to be the main bargaining tools of the major labels. In 1980, after three years with another Indie outfit Step Forward, Rough Trade signed up the wildly eclectic The Fall. Led by Mark E. Smith, The Fall underwent a series of line-up changes, but still the uncompromising nature of Smith enabled them to make music that was both discordant and challenging. Smith's literacy and dogmatic attitude towards the rhetoric enabled albums such as Perverted By Language and This Nation's Saving Grace to offer a particularly savage indictment of the zeitgeist of Margaret Thatcher's years in office.

Other labels such as 4AD, formed as a subsidiary of another independent label, Beggar's Banquet, offered a home to groups such as The Cocteau Twins and The Birthday Party, the latter featuring the extraordinarily louche Nick Cave, who would later emerge as one of the great iconoclasts of the late 1980s and 1990s. Tony Wilson's Factory label would become the backbone of the Manchester scene with New Wave groups like Joy Division and then New Order. In the meantime, as technology had wrought its indescribable magic, more bands were adapting or forming to harness synthesisers and drum machines, in place of guitars and drums, as primary tools. This caused an upswing in the number of record labels that were being formed: for technology was low maintenance apart from anything else. Groups such as Depeche Mode on the Mute label and The Cure on Fiction both started their careers amid this upheaval. Still, though, some persevered with the traditional guitar, bass and

above: With a fan following that rivals that of more mainstream supergroups, The Manic Street Preachers have been pillars of the UK indie establishment.

drums. The Smiths, featuring the idiosyncratic writing of Morrissey and the guitar work of Johnny Marr, signed with Rough Trade and seemed to revive traditional skills like songwriting. For Johnny Marr possessed a coherent grasp of melody and structure, and those cardinal requirements enabled Morrissey to put together some of the most strikingly visual songs since Ray Davies' (of The Kinks) heyday in the mid-1960s: 'Hand In Glove', 'This Charming Man', 'What Difference Does It Make?', 'Heaven Knows I'm Miserable Now' and 'Panic'.

In Manchester, The Stone Roses, with Ian Brown and guitarist John Squire, were squaring up for the issue of their eponymous debut in 1989, while the funkier Happy Mondays, with the redoubtable Shaun Ryder, combined dance rhythms with a fiery brand of urban folk. By the beginning of the 1990s, through groups such as Primal Scream and Massive Attack, rock had assimilated the beats instinct of the dance culture, and labels such as Creation had emerged, under Alan McGee, one of the most perceptive and assiduous collectors of talent, signing bands like Primal Scream, My Bloody Valentine, The Curve and Oasis. Elsewhere One Little Indian signed The Sugarcubes, featuring Björk, and Nude were kept afloat by Suede. US indie labels who steered a similarly pioneering path included Sub Pop, Matador and Drag City.

By 1996, when the world was agog at the spectacle of Oasis and Brit pop, McGee had sold off a chunk of Creation to Sony. While an Indie culture survived, most of the successful small labels were picked off and absorbed by the majors in this way.

PORTISHEAD
DUMMY
Go! Beat

THE STONE ROSES
THE STONE ROSES
Silvertone

1991, FEBRUARY 7: THE IRA LAUNCH A SERIES OF ATTACKS IN LONDON, A VAN EXPLODING JUST 200 YARDS FROM THE PRIME MINISTER'S RESIDENCE IN DOWNING STREET

below and right: From their debut album Freak Out! the Mothers Of Invention and their leader Frank Zappa were at the forefront of rock's avant garde.

AVANT-GARDE

WHILE THE INFLUENCES OF EXPERIMENTALIST COMPOSERS JOHN CAGE AND KARLHEINZ STOCKHAUSEN OSTENSIBLY LOOMED LARGE, INFORMING THE AGENDAS OF COUNTLESS YOUNG MUSICIANS DURING THE 1960s, the reality was perhaps slightly more prosaic, in that anyone who dabbled with electronics or expressed interest in the free-form jazz of Ornette Coleman was considered weird. For some, though, like Francis Zappa, weird was good. Zappa, though, wasn't so weird that he didn't understand the theories he espoused. For Zappa could reasonably lay claim to being one of the most articulate and experimental composers of his generation; others such as John Cale of The Velvet Underground, Robert Wyatt of the Soft Machine and Zappa's protégé, Captain Beefheart, were up there too.

It was, with hindsight, not inappropriate that Zappa's debut with his band The Mothers Of Invention was called Freak Out! (1967). For the very term wormed its way into the vernacular, meaning 'a temporary loss of control of one's mental faculties'. The musical definition implied extended improvisation, and both meanings were variously applied to Zappa and his output. For his approach to music was uncompromisingly cerebral, while his guitar work (Hot Rats ,1968) was melodic, lyrical and fluent, demonstrating an economy of phrasing that was in stark contrast to his propensity for verbose, indulgent lyrics that oscillated between the unpalatable and the anachronistic. Impervious to the machinations of the record industry and the thoughts of press or critics, Zappa picked his way through 20th-century musical styles, adapting them to his own view of the world. Captain Beefheart's view of the world was summed up in Trout Mask Replica (1969), where his harsh, rasping vocals contrasted sharply with the discordant, atonal riffing and abrasive soloing of his band. Another erstwhile Zappa protégé, singer-songwriter Tim Buckley, used his voice to evoke moods instead of following the usual route and adapting large chunks of autobiography.

Meanwhile in the UK in 1970, The Soft Machine augmented their line-up by bringing in a horn section that featured saxophonist Elton Dean, among others. Against this backdrop, other groups such as Henry Cow began to emerge. With an emergent Indie culture developing among record labels in the late 1970s, the avant-garde

became less attenuated. In a sense, because labels such as Virgin, initially, and Rough Trade, with The Fall, were committed to espousing an 'alternative philosophy', the avant-garde became assimilated for a spell. Formed in 1980, 4AD, especially, championed groups such as The Cocteau Twins, who contributed to the creation of a climate in which the Indie culture of the 1980s could thrive.

These days, accessibility is still a popular barometer, but with the plethora of independent labels, irrespective of how avant-garde or arcane a group or performer may appear to be, there is always a level which will find a response. Both Brian Eno and David Byrne of Talking Heads have been the fervent admirers of fresh ideas. For without a vibrant 'avant-garde', there is no progress. It's that simple.

below: From a late 1970s record company press release celebrating 'ten years on the road with Frank Zappa and The Mothers Of Invention'.

CD CHECKLIST

CAPTAIN BEEFHEART
TROUT MASK REPLICA
Straight

FRANK ZAPPA
UNCLE MEAT
Rykodisc

NEWS

220/1   A Century of **Pop**

1992, NOVEMBER 3: BILL CLINTON, THE 46 YEAR-OLD GOVERNOR OF ARKANSAS, WINS DECISIVELY IN THE AMERICAN PRESIDENTIAL ELECTION

EAT/KISS MUSIC FOR THE FILMS OF ANDY WARHOL JOHN CALE

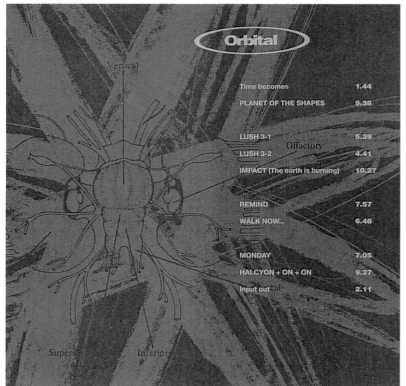

Orbital

Time becomes	1.44
PLANET OF THE SHAPES	9.38
LUSH 3-1	5.39
LUSH 3-2	4.41
IMPACT (The earth is burning)	10.27
REMIND	7.57
WALK NOW...	6.48
MONDAY	7.05
HALCYON + ON + ON	9.27
Input out	2.11

Vertical

Olfactory

Super   Inferior

(Artificial Intelligence)

far left: German techno pioneers Kraftwerk made a trio of influential albums between 1977 and 1981, Computer World being the final one, and certainly the most danceable.

far left, below: The Hartnoll brothers – Paul and Phil – as Orbital, made their most complete work, though not their biggest commercially, in the untitled 'brown album'.

left: One-time member of the seminal Velvet Underground, John Cale has long occupied a respected place in the musical avant garde, be it techno-oriented or instrument-driven.

left, below: A radical idea in 1992, the album Artificial Intellegence was a collection of techno doodlings from various producers which meshed to make an electronic whole.

TECHNO

THE USUAL IMAGES CONJURED UP BY THE TERM TECHNO ARE THE FRANTIC BEATS PER MINUTE ISSUED THROUGH MEGA-WATT STACKS TO HOARDS OF SWEATY DANCERS IN SOME INIQUITOUS DEN ON THE EDGE OF NOWHERE. Certainly that may well be a piece of the story, but it is a very small piece. For the roots of Techno can be traced back to the early 1970s when German Progressive Rock bands such as Can and Tangerine Dream began to substitute traditional instrumentation – guitar, bass and drums – with synthesisers and drum machines. At first, these items of new technology were considered too sophisticated for anyone other than an electronics engineer, but gradually, through groups like Yes and Motown star Stevie Wonder, they acquired a wider currency. The advent of the 12-inch single, 'Love To Love You Baby', by disco queen Donna Summer in 1975, with its hypnotic, rhythmic pulse, showed the potential of the synthesiser and the drum machine.

Producer Brian Eno, formerly of Roxy Music, oversaw a trilogy of albums, Low (1977), Heroes and The Lodger (1978), by David Bowie that evoked a bleak, post-industrial landscape. For if Brian Eno with his own solo albums such as Music For Airports and Another Green World had invoked the minimalism of avant-garde composer John Cage, Bowie's fragile vocals and gift for a strong melody, overlaying a hypnotic pulse, combined to create an effect that was desolate and unsettling in the extreme. The notion of a post-apocalyptic society germinated and took root through later performers such

as Gary Numan, Orchestral Manoeuvres In The Dark and Human League.

By the 1980s, groups such as Kraftwerk and Japan assuaged the post-industrial gloom with extant images that were inherently more user friendly. Ironically, Japan endeavoured to invoke a quasi-romanticism that was as lifeless as it was lush. Through groups such as Depeche Mode – and later Erasure – and Heaven 17, the synthesiser and the drum machine reigned supreme.

While rock remained the dominant form, aided in no small way by events such as Live Aid, House was acquiring currency in the clubs and warehouses of Detroit and Chicago. Groups like Kevin Saunderson and Inner City began grafting House onto samples from groups like Tangerine Dream and Kraftwerk, sparking a rash of groups such as Beats International and Technotronik. Although raps were often introduced, it was the propulsive rhythmic interface that was the central motif of Techno. As the dance culture took hold, Techno flourished through the raves of the late 1980s, which, with its attendant drug culture, invoked memories of the Psychedelic era of the late 1960s.

By the late 1990s, Techno had become fully integrated into the mainstream as artist such as Ultra Naté and Sash dominated the charts throughout Europe. Although groups such as The Prodigy have continued to promote themselves as an underground band, the dance and club culture is ubiquitous, penetrating even the remotest corners. The result is The Prodigy sell as many albums in the US as rock bands like Bush.

1993, JULY: WAR BREAKS OUT IN THE FORMER YUGOSLAVIA AS THE BOSNIAN CAPITAL SARAJEVO COMES UNDER INTENSE ATTACK

JUNGLE

JUNGLE WAS ENGLAND'S ANSWER TO
HOUSE. It sprang out of the warehouse, acid-house
and rave scenes of the late 1980s, and the melting pot
of ecstasy-fuelled parties on Ibiza. In Jungle, a rhythmic
pattern or breakbeat is created by stretching two short
musical passages, or breaks, by playing the same record
on two decks and switching back and forth between
them to create an infinitely extendible passage. The
same effect can be produced by digitally encoding the
break with a sampler and repeating it continually in a
loop. A combination of time-stretched breakbeats are
played at around 160 beats per minute over a reggae
baseline, with the 4/4 bass drum removed, at 80 beats
per minute. The result, since co-opted by mainstream
figures such as Everything But The Girl, David Bowie
and Rickie Lee Jones, is hypnotic.

The first Jungle record was released by Ibiza. It was
a white label attributed to 'Johnny Jungle', also known
as Pascal of High Wycombe's Ganja Kru. However, the
term 'Jungle Techno' had already been coined. Some
trace it back to Jamaica, where the Tivoli Gardens in
Kingston are known locally as the Jungle. In 1991,
Rebel MC sampled a Jamaican 'yard-tape' – a tape of a
Kingston sound-system – which featured the chant 'alla
the junglists', calling out for the posse from Tivoli.

The term Jungle was quickly denounced as racist.
Although the music had a strong black flavour, it was
generally conceded that 'jungle' referred to 'the urban
jungle' where disaffected youth, both black and white,
found themselves. Some people embraced the name

Jungle; others shun it, saying that Jungle is simply an English version of House. Like their Chicago precursors, English Jungle artists use down time in recording studios to create simple dance tracks without vocals.

In 1994, Jungle split in two. Ragga Jungle added a vocal lick, 'chatted' by an MC in Jamaican patois or inner-city London slang. Meanwhile the purist strain began to call itself drum'n'bass. This has always been a basic element of Jungle but now the technology could develop it further. Sadly, this split had racial overtones, as Jungle raves were dominated by black youths, while drum'n'bass seemed to be aimed at a white audience.

Some argued that drum'n'bass was simply preserving the original ethos of Jungle, but it soon became increasingly more sophisticated. This gave birth to ambient drum'n'bass or Artcore, a smooth style where a wash of dreamy string sounds are combined with time-stretched breakbeats. The key here was that modern technology allows you to alter the tempo of a sample without changing its pitch.

Jazzy Jungle added jazz refrains, sampled from 1980s' Jazz Funk records. This was too much of a sell-out for some Jungle fans and Jazz Step was invented. This took Hardstep, a stripped-down version of Jungle with a cleaned-up treble, and added crisp jazz lines from Miles Davis, say. Hardstep also gave birth to Techstep, adding metallic sounds and an undercurrent of menacing noises over a distorted bassline. Then there's Darkcore, which employs horror film samples over a disorienting ambience. And all a musical jungle to the uninitiated.

REPRAZENT/RONI SIZE
NEW FORMS
Talkin' Loud/Mercury

1993, SEPTEMBER 13: ISRAEL AND THE PALESTINE LIBERATION ORGANISATION (PLO) SIGN A HISTORIC PEACE ACCORD ON THE LAWNS OF THE WHITE HOUSE IN WASHINGTON

POP MUSIC IN THE 1990s

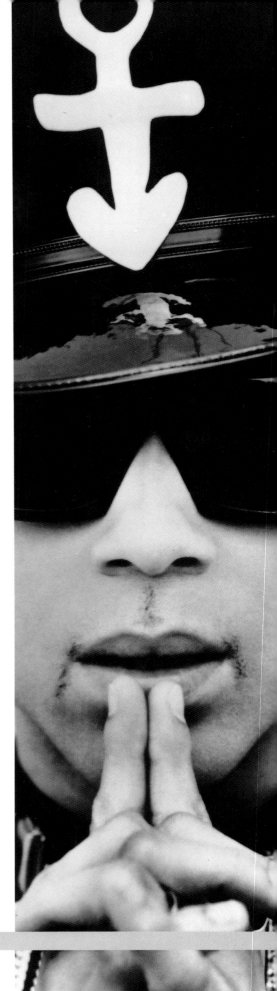

AS THE NEW MILLENNIUM APPROACHES, pop music in the 1990s shows little inclination to grow old gracefully. Its capacity for reinvention is peerless. That groups such as The Spice Girls and All Saints vie with one another for supremacy merely recalls bygone battles when all-girl groups at Motown like Martha & The Vandellas considered that The Supremes received preferential treatment by getting the best material. They probably did. The growth in popularity of boy bands like Boyzown and 911 suggest just one thing and that is that the consumers of the 1990s are getting younger all the time. For singles, long held to be little more than promotional devices for forthcoming albums, have revived their fortunes significantly over the last ten years.

However, it is the emergence of clubbing as the great popular pastime of younger audiences that has caused the revived interest in the single. For the dance culture, with its desire for fresh mixes by different DJs, has stimulated demand, ensuring that 12-inch club mixes have more than a passing value. For with the ascendancy of the dance culture, DJs such as Danny Rampling, Judge Jules and Boy George command massive followings. It is difficult to imagine any other epoch when a club culture has penetrated the mainstream as comprehensively.

While the dance culture may have impinged upon most facets of contemporary pop music, rock has continued to exert a magnetism upon audiences. For festivals such as Glastonbury and Phoenix routinely sell out, and the supposed rivalry between Oasis and Blur had positive advantages in sparking interest in other bands like Supergrass, Shed Seven and The Cast. Paul Weller has been elevated to the

status of a demi-god, and the realisation that in Pulp and Radiohead Britain had two bands that would actually endure and probably get even better at long last occurred. Perhaps the greatest indication of the physical health of rock is best gauged by the continuing popularity of Bon Jovi and the extraordinary – but not unwelcome – emergence of Robbie Williams, formerly of Take That, as a thoroughly credible performer. It is debatable whether the same will be true of other boy band incumbents.

Through the 1990s, the most enduring feature has been the continuing proactive relationship between the music and film industries. Although there are many precedents, with musicals such as Saturday Night Fever and Grease selling zillions of units, the humble soundtrack has picked up formidable mileage. Movies such as The Bodyguard ('I Will Always Love You' by Whitney Houston), Trainspotting ('Perfect Day' by Lou Reed and 'The Passenger' by Iggy Pop), Four Weddings And A Funeral ('Love Is All Around' by Wet Wet Wet), The Full Monty ('You Sexy Thing' by Errol Brown and Hot Chocolate) and Titanic ('My Heart Will Go On' by Celine Dion) have all had lasting effects on the record-buying trends.

The success of Celine Dion remains an enigma, but elsewhere Toni Braxton, Gabrielle and Shola Ama, among others, displayed some of the qualities of the classic R&B/Soul singers of the 1960s. Meanwhile Louise, formerly of Eternal, dispensed a good-natured, unmannered style of pop, where professionalism out-distanced attitude by quite a margin. As for The Spice Girls and All Saints, well, All Saints had the advantage by hitting the top with a great single, 'Never Ever', which will be a worthy addition to any juke-box.

Pure pop in the 90s was, for the first half of the decade, dominated by mega-stars like (l to r) Prince (formerly known as...), Madonna and the then ubiquitous Michael Jackson.

AY JAY JOHNSON   JACKIE McLEAN   ART BLAKEY   KENNY CLARKE   VOLUME 1   BLUE NOTE

MILES DAVIS

right: Acclaimed by many as the greatest jazz album ever made – though an impossible distinction to make – Miles Davis' Kind of Blue achieves a perfection as the classical music of the 20th century.

opposite: In his early be-bop days in the early 50s, in the company of players like Charlie Parker and Thelonious Monk, Miles was already forging a reputation as a total original which he would maintain for another four decades.

MILES DAVIS Kind of Blue

with Julian "Cannonball" Adderly
Paul Chambers
James Cobb
John Coltrane
Bill Evans
Wynton Kelly

MILES DAVIS

IN THE FEW SHORT YEARS SINCE THE DEATH OF MILES DAVIS (September 28, 1991), his recording output has been subject to almost as intense scrutiny as any other figure in contemporary music. That in the course of this examination the archives have failed to yield any true stinkers speaks volumes for the consistency of his work. Born Miles Dewey Davis on May 25, 1926, in Alton, Illinois, into a middle-class family, he took up the trumpet as war broke out in Europe at the age of 13. By 1944, he had graduated to playing alongside Charlie Parker in Billy Eckstine's band. This was followed by a spell at the Juillard School of Music – courtesy of a scholarship – but it was shortlived, as he dropped out to help Parker spear the Bebop revolution. More stints followed with Eckstine and Charlie Mingus, as well as Parker, until, in 1949, he recorded Birth Of The Cool. Featuring a nine-piece band with arrangements by Gil Evans and Gerry Mulligan, Birth Of The Cool intimated Davis's talents as a leader and innovator. This led to a series of albums with various small groups, including 'Bag's Groove' with pianist Thelonius Monk in 1954.

In 1955, a reputation-building performance at the Newport Jazz Festival won him a contract with the Columbia label. He remained with Columbia until 1986. In the course of those 30 years, Davis demonstrated his capacity for ringing the changes. This was especially evident in his choice of musicians, which at this stage included John Coltrane, Philly Joe Jones and Paul Chambers. But the real crunch came when he teamed up with Gil Evans for a series of orchestral albums that sent ripples through Modern Jazz. For with Miles Ahead (1957), George Gershwin's Porgy And Bess (1959) and Sketches Of Spain (1959), Miles's trumpet took on a spare elliptical character, allowing the orchestral arrangements the room to establish the landscape. Two more key albums followed, Milestones (1958) and Kind Of Blue (1959); the latter featured 'So What', which has become a defining moment for Miles.

In the early 1960s, while Ornette Coleman and Coltrane dabbled in the avant-garde, Davis continued to expand, establishing his next quintet, a combination of youth and accomplishment in Herbie Hancock (keyboards), Ron Carter (bass), Tony Williams (drums) and Wayne Carter (saxophones), on Miles Smiles (1966). With this phase, Miles opened the door for his next manoeuvres, which, with a new band featuring guitarist John McLaughlin, was the catalyst for Jazz Rock. Despite the criticisms levelled at Jazz Rock bands, Miles's In A Silent Way (1969) and Bitches Brew (1970) remain key works in the breaking down of the purist mentality implicit in the public perception of what jazz was all about. During the remainder of the 1970s and 1980s, Miles seemed to court rock audiences; in 1986, he moved to Warner Brothers for Tutu (1986) and Amandla (1988), while contributing to albums by singer-songwriters such as Joni Mitchell. These days, especially with the current interest in Funk, Jazz Rock and other derivatives, Miles is right up there in the pantheon of iconic influences upon 20th-century music.

KIND OF BLUE
Columbia

SKETCHES OF SPAIN
Columbia

IN A SILENT WAY
Columbia

1993, DECEMBER 2: THE US SPACE SHUTTLE ENDEAVOUR IS LAUNCHED ON A MISSION TO REPAIR THE HUBBLE SPACE TELESCOPE

right: With a string of UK hits through the 80s and early 90s, Sade was a forerunner of the independent-minded female chanteuse who would emerge later in the decade.

below: With hits like 'I'll Be There', Mariah Carey was one of the top-selling female vocalists of the early 90s.

bottom: Whitney Houston, daughter of Cissy Houston and cousin of Dionne Warwick, broke the Beatles' record with seven consecutive No 1s in the Billboard Hot Hundred chart.

CONTEMPORARY FEMALE

TIME FOR ANOTHER SWEEPING STATEMENT. In the 1990s there has been a tendency for singer/songwriters on the flaxen-haired side of the distaff to come up with the goods more frequently than their male counterparts. Call it genetic, if you like. Whatever, the late 1980s and 1990s have been more suited to those of a confessional disposition and, in that respect, women are less inclined to beat about the bush. What is especially interesting about this development is that it is organic and the lineage is distinct. Draw a line from principally interpretative singers such as Joan Baez and Judy Collins in the 1960s and you end up with Emmylou Harris and Mary Black in the 1990s. As far as interpretative singers are concerned, it is all a question of taste. And those four have taste in bucket-loads. Through their taste, they have brought on the careers of countless songwriters: Joan Baez and Judy Collins did it for Bob Dylan, among others; and Emmylou Harris and Mary Black have done it for Kate and Anna McGarrigle and Richard Thompson, respectively.

Similarly, for those who pen their own compositions, perhaps the differences between Joni Mitchell and Mary Chapin Carpenter are too stark to bear comparison. But Joni Mitchell's 'When Furry Sings The Blues' seems to come from the same palette of inspiration as Carpenter's 'John Doe'. This is not a question of two songs bearing striking melodic or lyrical similarities, it's a matter of perception transcending generic differences. It is not surprising, therefore, that when Madonna embraced dance rhythms at the start of her career, she was able to bring a confessional directness to a style that had been notably bereft of a confrontational lyrical input. By the same token, when Madonna signed up Alanis Morissette to her Maverick label, few could have been surprised at the confrontational directness of Morissette's debut, Jagged Little Pill (1995), but with its rock-based arrangements it seemed to be the direct antithesis of everything Madonna had ever stood for. What must have been galling for all those critics was the staggering success of Jagged Little Pill (20 million

NEWS

1993, DECEMBER 21: THE SOVIET UNION CEASES TO EXIST AS THE COMMUNIST PARTY IS DISBANDED AND MOST OF THE FORMER REPUBLICS DECLARE THEIR INDEPENDENCE

above: With her debut album Jagged Little Pill the Canadian Alanis Morissette set the standard for a whole school of late-90s girl singers.

above right: After some early support spots with Bob Dylan and others, Sheryl Crow really took off with Tuesday Night Music Club and the eponymous follow-up Sheryl Crow.

units, and counting). Initially Morrisette's success was perceived as a fluke: so many sad, angst-ridden girls moping in their bedrooms. Naturally, it was part of a much broader agenda and when rock-based performers like Sheryl Crow proved that being angst-ridden was not prerequisite with Tuesday Night Music Club, others such as Aimee Mann – despite unfortunate record deals and critical acclaim – failed to generate comparable sales.

In the country markets, performers such as Carpenter, Harris and Nanci Griffith have consistently straddled the fine line between country and folk, while others such as Shawn Colvin or Michelle Shocked have resolutely resisted any attempt to penetrate country markets. K.D. Lang, like Emmylou Harris, has proved to be impervious to all attempts at pigeon-holing, despite cutting albums in Nashville with veteran producer Owen Bradley. Others like the teenage Leann Rimes, with a vocal style redolent of Patsy Cline, remain firmly entrenched in the traditions of country music, while

possessing a mass appeal that is transcendent. Country vocalist Wynonna (Judd) has such a daunting vocal range that she can embrace gospel and Soul material with as much conviction as she can ordinary MOR stuff from Nashville's songwriting production line. Irish vocalists like Dolores Keane and Maura O'Connell have built their reputations upon their ability to draw from the richness of their Irish traditions, while recording material by writers from all generic milieus. Beth Orton, with Trailer Park (1997), brought elements of trip-hop to folk-based material such as 'She Cries Your Name'.

In the final analysis, it probably is genetic: do women arrange their CD collections alphabetically or by category? The answer is probably alphabetically, so why should female recording artists record their music by category? No reason, at all. It's just that men have always tended to do it that way. The result is that in the late 1980s and 1990s, female singer-songwriters have predicated Robert Palmer's assertion, 'Man Smart, Woman Smarter'.

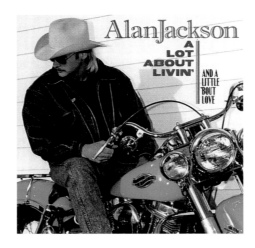

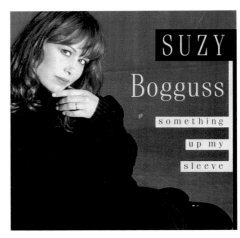

right: The nearest rival in the US to Garth Brooks and Clint Black in the New Country stakes, Alan Jackson, with his blend of honky-tonk and bar-room ballads, was first discovered by Glen Campbell.

far right: With well-received albums produced by Jimmy Bowen, Suzy Bogguss is a name of the 90s who combines her own songs with those of other writers like John Hiatt and Nanci Griffith.

NEW COUNTRY

INITIALLY, THE RADIO SHOW THAT WAS THE GRAND OLE OPRY – LIKE ITS NEAR NEIGHBOUR IN SHREVEPORT, LOUISIANA, THE LOUISIANA HAYRIDE – WAS A SHOWCASE PROMOTING ALL THAT WAS BEST IN HILLBILLY MUSIC, a parochial exercise aimed at bringing rural communities together through the power of radio. Throughout the 1950s, country music edged further and further towards MOR. Not much changed really with the emergence of rock'n'roll and Rockabilly. By the 1960s, while great country music was being made that was due more to the talents of individual writers, producers and performers, Nashville provided the environment and The Grand Ole Opry had become Nashville's equivalent of Hollywood.

In 1967 Bob Dylan went to Nashville to record John Wesley Harding, followed by Nashville Skyline. Shortly after Dylan's stint in Nashville, Kris Kristofferson, Willie Nelson and Waylon Jennings, among others, started to distance themselves from Nashville and The Grand Ole Opry, basing themselves in Austin. In a sense they deinstitutionalised themselves. This was the first step towards New Country. Still Nashville and The Grand Ole Opry remained arbiters of taste, but as Willie Nelson and Waylon Jennings' collaborative concept album The Outlaws started to sell by the truckload, Nashville became slightly more liberal in what could be described as country.

Throughout the 1970s a crop of stuff by artists such as Glen Campbell, Olivia Newton-John, John Denver,

Anne Murray and The Bellamy Brothers gave country a broader appeal, much to the horror of established country artists such as Loretta Lynn, Tammy Wynette and George Jones. With the release of Urban Cowboy in 1980, anything with a twang became cool, and so Nashville radio playlists nurtured the proliferation of country-pop acts. Despite all this, a backlash kicked in as a new, younger generation began to look beyond Nashville and draw inspiration from regional styles and older forms of country music such as Western Swing, Cajun, Bluegrass, Tex-Mex and honky-tonk and adapt them to contemporary requirements. Simultaneously many highly individual instrumentalists such as guitarist Peter Rowan, fiddler Mark O'Connor, banjo man J.D. Crowe and mandolinist David Grisman began to find that demand for their talents was increasing not only as session musicians, but also on the acoustically oriented folk club and festival circuit. In addition to this, as independent labels started to gain wider distribution, it became feasible for artists to conduct their careers independently of the supposedly influential Nashville radio playlists and video.

Nashville – noticing this trend – started to sign up young musicians such as Garth Brooks, Steve Earle, Vince Gill and George Strait. While Brooks hit paydirt spectacularly, by adapting his stageshow to incorporate the dynamics of the stadium rockshow, the others adhered to the ethos of country music. Steve Earle, in particular, after many dust-ups with the law, including a spell in prison for drug possession, embodies the

NEWS

1994, APRIL 26-29: ELECTIONS ARE HELD IN SOUTH AFRICA, WITH AN OVERWHELMING VICTORY FOR THE AFRICAN NATIONAL CONGRESS PARTY

above: Garth Brooks is without doubt the biggest country name ever in commercial terms, with record sales and concert attendances rivalling those of the top superstars.

maverick spirit of the true country star: driven and possessed by a demon spirit that threatens to send him spiralling into the abyss at any moment.

Now into the 1990s, the influence of female artists such as Nanci Griffith and, of course, Emmylou Harris remains at an all-time high, despite their exclusion from radio playlists; traditionalists such as Bluegrass fiddler Alison Krauss and vocalist Patti Loveless continue to espouse the old-time virtues of country music and young performers such as the teenage LeAnn Rimes continues

where Patsy Cline left off. In a sense New Country made Nashville less parochial, but more than that, it spawned a style of singer-songwriter, such as Matraca Berg and Gretchen Peters, who was as influenced by Bob Dylan as by The Eagles and George Jones. With interpretative performers such as Joan Baez recording in Nashville, Nashville is the centre of the universe if you're a writer. As for New Country as a genre, it doesn't really exist any longer – perhaps it never did and was just the product of an ad-man's wet-dream.

right : The UK DJ/producer Bally Sagoo mixed Indian film music in his 1994 album Bollywood Flashback.

below: The West London DJ and producer who did much to introduce Bhangra to the UK club scene, Apache Indian.

BHANGRA

BHANGRA IS THE TRADITIONAL MUSIC OF THE RURAL PUNJAB AND TAKES ITS NAME FROM THE BHANG OR HEMP THAT IS GROWN THERE. In Britain in the 1980s and early 1990s, when it was mixed with reggae, rock, Jungle and House, it was briefly considered 'the next big thing'. However, it never really succeeded making it out of the dance halls and into the mainstream. Its distinguishing feature is the trance-inducing beat of the dhol, a large, wooden, barrel-type drum found everywhere from Nepal to Albania. However, even in traditional styles, this has largely been replaced by the dholak, a double-headed drum widespread in northern India.

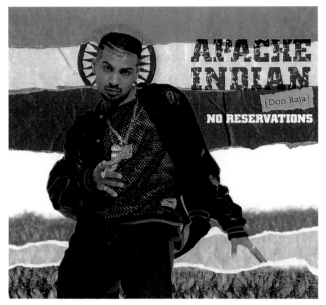

Asian immigration brought Bhangra music to Britain and it soon gained popularity in the wider Asian community outside the Punjabi clique. Bhangra bands, employing a range of traditional instruments, played at Asian house parties. The more progressive bands added guitars and saxophones, and the 'Southall sound' – named after the predominantly Asian west London suburb – was born.

In the 1980s, a younger generation of Asians sought new excitement. Banned by their parents from attending discos and night-clubs, they started playing truant from school to attend 'all-dayers' or 'day timers' – day-time dances initially in the back rooms of pubs, then in dance halls. At first, disco music, reggae and Soul were played. But the audience craved something that expressed their own identity. Bhangra bands were booked. These bands quickly reinvented the music for their younger, more westernised audience. They added western-style drum kits and synthesisers. Soon they were producing Punjabi and Hindi versions of hits by Abba and Boney M. The British media 'discovered' Bhangra in late 1986, when artists such as Holle Holle and Heera were attracting audiences of up to 3,000 to venues like the Hammersmith Palais. Clubs, such as London's Wag, began putting on Asian nights.

However, none of these bands were fully professional. Although they had large followings, there

NEWS

1995, JANUARY 17: SOME 5000 PEOPLE DIE AND MORE THAN 250,000 ARE MADE HOMELESS AS AN EATHQUAKE MEASURING 7.2 ON THE RICHTER SCALE DEVASTATES THE JAPANESE CITY OF KOBE

BALLY SAGOO

Rising From The East

left: Bally Sagoo's Rising From The East, in which he mixed old songs from India and Pakistan, featured the track 'Dil Cheez' which made the UK Top Ten singles chart in 1997.

was not enough work around for them to give up their day jobs. Another thing holding back the growth of Asian music was the tradition of pirating. A young Asian businessman called Morgan Khan tried to tackle this. He had been an A&R man at Pye, handling such artists as Donna Summer, Gladys Knight and Barry White. He had quit to launch his own record label called Street Sounds and began signing Bhangra acts.

Khan had a success with Culture Shock, two Asian boys who had enough style to cross over. And the chic, westernised female duo, Romi and Jazz, were signed to Arista. But the biggest Bhangra act is not Bhangra at all. Apache Indian, though Asian, is a West Indian-style ragamuffin DJ. His genre is largely reggae and R&B, though he adds elements of Jungle, hip-hop, Rock Steady, rock and, occasionally, Bhangra. However, after a couple of hits in the mid-1990s, his career began to wane. And, apparently, the odd dash of the Bhangra beat that he had added to his tracks was enough to convince the world at large that it had done Bhangra.

ASIAN DUB FOUNDATION
RAFI'S REVENGE
London

CD CHECKLIST

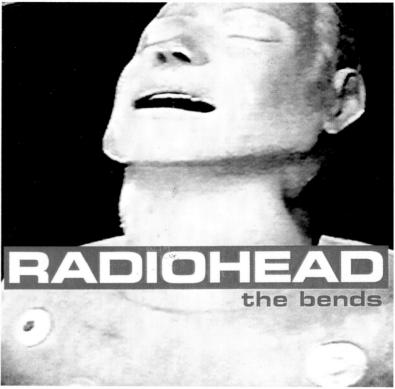

BRIT POP

above: Jarvis Cocker and Pulp won critical acclaim with his quirky stage presence and songs to go with it; the CD Different Class gave the listener a choice of a number of different cover pictures.

above right: All from the same public school, the members of Radiohead succeeded with two well-received albums, The Bends and OK Computer.

WHEN GROUPS SUCH AS THE SMITHS CAME TO PROMINENCE THEY BROUGHT WITH THEM NOT ONLY AN INDIE CULTURE AMONG RECORD LABELS, but also a backlash against the dominance of the synth'n'drum machine that exerted such a grip during the 1980s. For The Smiths were the traditional guitar, bass and drums type of line-up, so beloved of the 1960s Beat group explosion. This reversion to the more orthodox characteristics of rock'n'roll caused many to speculate that guitar-led bands were due for a revival. By the late 1980s and early 1990s, groups such as Blur, Radiohead, Pulp, Manic Street Preachers and The Verve were beginning to show their colours.

With the upsurge of interest in guitar-led bands, A&R men from the major labels started checking out small gigs in out of the way areas in the hope that they might sign up the putative next Beatles. For the melodic lyricism of The Beatles, the quirky observation of The Kinks' Ray Davies, the provocative attitude of Paul

Weller, formerly of The Jam, and the anthemic Folk Rock of XTC were the desirable traits everyone was looking for. Soon groups like Ocean Colour Scene and Pulp, who had languished in semi-obscurity, were plucked from the gloom and thrust into the limelight.

The attention took each somewhat differently. The Manic Street Preachers, who had made a string of albums, including Generation Terrorists (1992), that were gloomy and despondent but characterised by superb songs with excellent guitar work, came close to splitting up when Richey Edwards walked out one day, never to be seen or heard of again.

His disappearance remains a mystery, but the group went from strength to strength with Everything Must Go (1996). Similarly, Pulp, who had been threatening to breakthrough on a major level ever since the release of their 1994 offering His 'N' Hers, issued Different Class (1995). Lead vocalist and songwriter Jarvis Cocker came up with a bunch of songs such as 'Disco 2000', 'Common People' and 'Deborah' that were pithy pop

NEWS

1995, JANUARY-FEBRUARY: TORRENTIAL RAIN BRINGS FLOODING TO NORTHERN EUROPE, A QUARTER OF A MILLION PEOPLE BEING EVACUATED FROM THEIR HOMES IN THE NETHERLANDS

songs with neat, ironic twists that will stand up in years to come alongside the best this century has to offer. Radiohead, too, first with Pablo Honey (1993) and then The Bends (1995), showed guitarist Thom Yorke to be an unyielding writer capable of attacking any issue with unflinching integrity. When they returned with OK Computer in 1997, much of the attendant hype of Brit Pop seemed justified.

In the end, though, the hype was based upon the alleged rivalry between Blur and Oasis. Through much of 1995 and 1996, the rivalry was played out on the front pages of the tabloids, but it was only Oasis who seemed to care or participate in the slanging match. It was very one-sided.

But they did succeed in selling records by the truckload and songs 'Wonderwall' and 'Look Back In Anger' may well survive the test of time. As for Blur, albums like Parklife (1994) and The Great Escape (1995) showed comprehensively that, like their more celebrated peers, The Beatles, they had the knack of

cutting albums rather than stringing a few singles together that ended up on the same album; and their guitarist Graham Coxon is similarly under-rated.

At the end of 1997, another Indie band had come back from the dead, by all accounts. The Verve had not recorded for several years until they released Urban Hymns. Featuring songs like 'The Drugs Don't Work' and 'Bittersweet Symphony', Urban Hymns was lush, with expansive string arrangements, while vocalist Richard Ashcroft remained agreeably dismissive of the wave of approbation that was suddenly showered upon the group.

And then, of course, there were the all-conquering Spice Girls. Cast in the classic production-pop mould of the manufactured act, they nevertheless produced a string of instantly accessible hits for the 90s. Was it all hype? Who knows? Who cares. For in 1998, Pulp followed up Different Class with This Is Hardcore, which was as accomplished as its predecessor, confirming that some of it certainly wasn't hype.

DANCE

DANCE MUSIC IS JUNGLE GONE MAINSTREAM. When Jungle split into Ragga Jungle and drum'n'bass and returned to the underground scene, there were some who wanted to take it to a wider audience. And that meant going live. In 1994, Goldie produced the single 'Angel' using samples lifted from David Byrne and Brian Eno, taking Jungle away from hardcore, back more in the direction of Soul. Until that time, Jungle and drum'n'bass had largely been promoted on compilation albums. Goldie produced his own album, Timeless, in 1995. That same year, A Guy Called Gerald released 'Black Secret Technology', with a second version in 1997 reaping even more acclaim.

Orbital, Underworld, Leftfield and The Chemical Brothers had all shown that a dance act could reach a wider audience by live gigs. So in 1995 Goldie teamed up with Metalheadz in America. However, when he brought 'Goldie Presents Metalheadz' to London the following year, it attracted huge crowds to the Forum in Kentish Town but was generally poorly received. Goldie then toured America with Björk. By the time he returned to England, he had added Motown Funk to the mix. Soon even BBC Radio One had a Jungle show. The Goldie-Björk tie-up was condemned by Keith Flint of The Prodigy. They had been 'corrupted by TV', he said – but Prodigy videos soon featured on Top Of The Pops.

Everything But The Girl dropped their previous commitment to guitar-strumming jazz-pop with lush orchestration, and launched into dance music with 'Walking Wound'. Although condemned by purists, it immediately catapulted dance music into the mainstream. They had a top 20 hit with the title track. Dedicated drum'n'bassers Omni Trio got their own back by reworking 'Walking Wound', while Adam F. remixed 'Before Today' from the album to startling effect.

By the end of 1996, David Bowie had released 'Telling Lies', which appeared to be a collaboration with A Guy Called Gerald. In fact, the mix had simply borrowed from Gerald and Adam F. However, in February, Bowie released the Jungle single 'Little Wonder', combining time-stretched breakbeats with Glam Rock, to the grudging acclaim of purists. Here, Bowie had absorbed the influence rather than simply adding dance ideas in afterwards.

Dance music was quickly spreading around the world. France took dance to heart, and clubs opened in Switzerland, Germany, Spain and Holland. And there were breakbeat feasts in Australia, New Zealand, Singapore and Malaysia. Advertisers used dance mixes to promote soft drinks and soap. As the legendary MC Moose once said: 'Jungle is like malaria. It's contagious.' However, under the surface, the new music is still evolving. Jungle has been recombined with hip hop to produce Jump-up Jungle, just as hip hop recombined with House to make Hip House. Because the equipment used to make the new dance music is cheap and ubiquitous, the evolution of the new sound does not depend on big studios in London, New York or LA. You are just as likely to find that the latest hot dance tune came from St Albans or Ipswich.

GOLDIE
TIMELESS
ffrr/Z London

PRODIGY
THE FAT OF THE LAND
Warner Bros.

CD CHECKLIST

1995, FEBRUARY: RUSSIAN PRESIDENT YELTSIN'S CREDIBILITY PLUMMETS AS GUERRILA FIGHTERS IN THE FORMER SOVIET REPUBLIC OF CHECHNYA STEP UP THE FIGHTING AROUND THE SHATTERED CAPITAL GROZNY

BOY BANDS

IN THE 1990s, THE PHENOMENON OF THE BOY BAND HAS BEEN THE POPTASTIC SOUND OF THE DECADE as groups such as Take That, Boyzown, 911, East 17 and 3T have slugged it out on the bedroom walls of teenagers across the globe. It might seem novel, but anyone who has seen a church choir will recognise that young boys singing together is a fundamental adjunct of worship in the Christian church. Now to fast-forward to the rock'n'roll era, it was producer George Goldner who was the first to recognise the enormous commercial potential of juvenile vocal groups.

Spotted on a Harlem street corner vocalising by Richard Barrett, a talent scout for Goldner, in 1955, The Premiers comprised Frankie Lymon, Jimmy Merchant, Sherman Garnes, Herman Santiago and Joe Negroni. Barrett, though, wasn't happy with the name, suggesting they change their name to that of The Teenagers. Making their debut with 'Why Do Fools Fall In Love?' – written by a 14-year-old Frankie Lymon – it

established a precedent of turning children into pop stars. With the success of 'Why Do Fools Fall In Love?', Frankie Lymon and The Teenagers became stars of stage and screen overnight – TV that is – earning around a thousand dollars each for appearances at the Brooklyn Paramount and on The Ed Sullivan Show. Later records such as 'I Want You To Be My Girl', 'I Promise To Remember' and 'I'm Not A Juvenile Delinquent' possessed a hectic urgency, and the breaking of Lymon's voice signified the downward spiral. After a brief flirtation with fame, including an even briefer solo career, Lymon, having acquired a heroin problem, died on February 28, 1968, at the grand old age of 25.

While Frankie Lymon and The Teenagers scaled the rickety ladder of fame and fortune, Goldner and Barrett had come upon another young hopeful. Anthony Gourdine was another New Yorker, who engaged the public for a spell with 'Tears On My Pillow' while a member of Little Anthony and The Imperials. Despite later hits such as 'I'm On The Outside (Looking In)' and

1997, AUGUST 31: DIANA, PRINCESS OF WALES, DIES IN HOSPITAL JUST HOURS AFTER A CAR ACCIDENT IN CENTRAL PARIS

left: In the UK boy band stakes, Boyzone have occupied the throne left vacant by the disbandment of Take That.

above: Take That, certainly the most successful of British boy groups through the 1990s.

right: After the Spice Girls were launched as direct competition to boy bands, and succeeded massively, groups like East 17 found it harder to attract the teeny following they thought was naturally theirs.

'Hurt So Bad', Little Anthony & The Imperials took to the cabaret and oldies circuits.

Of all the boy bands the greatest tussle occurred at the end of the 1960s when The Osmonds were formulated in opposition to Motown's Jackson 5. Starting in 1963 in Gary, Indiana, The Jackson Family featured Jackie, Tito and Jermaine Jackson with two of their cousins. By 1964 the two cousins had been replaced by two younger brothers, Marlon and Michael, and the group was renamed The Jackson 5. After winning a local talent contest, they came to the attention of Motown boss, Berry Gordy. After being signed they made their debut with 'I Want You Back', featuring Michael as lead vocalist. Over the next six years the group notched up a series of hits including 'ABC', 'The Love You Save', 'I'll Be There', 'Mama's Pearl', and 'I Am Love, Parts 1 & 2'. In 1971 Motown launched Michael Jackson's solo career, which – despite a move to Epic – has made him one of the most popular performers in the world.

During the 1980s, New Edition, comprising Bobby Brown, Ralph Tresvant, Ronald DeVoe, Michael Bivins and Ricky Bell, nourished ambitions that they might emulate the success of The Jackson 5 after the popularity of 'Candy Girl' and 'Mr Telephone Man'. They didn't. But each used his start in the group to develop careers as singers or producers, with Bobby Brown achieving some sort of professional and personal pinnacle by marrying Whitney Houston.

So, while UK bands like Take That, Boyzown, 911, East 17, and in America The Backstreet Boys, have enjoyed immense success in the 1990s, it is a sobering thought to bear in mind that only one former incumbent of a famous boy band has gone on to international glory in recent years. And his name is Michael Jackson.

Although various members of Take That – Mark Owen, Gary Barlow and Robbie Williams – are having some solo success, they should, perhaps, remember Michael Jackson and ask themselves the very serious question, 'Do I really want to be that famous?'

VIRTUAL POP

THE ADVENT OF COMPUTER TECHNOLOGY TO THE RECORDING PROCESS HAS UNDOUBTEDLY ENABLED A GREATER FIDELITY OF SOUND QUALITY, although some would contend that analogue recordings possess a greater warmth than their digital counterparts. However, computer technology has created more opportunities in that making music no longer requires any talent or aptitude. That is a pretty damning indictment, but there is an up-side. For it could be argued that those with talent and aptitude are so immersed in the formal disciplines that their freedom is impaired. On the other hand, there are those whose technological skills are such that their musical talents attain dizzying heights.

Producer Brian Eno displayed those qualities during his brief tenure with Roxy Music in the early 1970s. Since leaving Roxy Music, his clear-headed abilities as a producer have enabled artists like David Bowie, Tallking Heads, U2 and James to flourish. In the case of James the task might have appeared more difficult in that

expectations were high; they had after all been associated with bands like Happy Mondays and their anthemic qualities had been taken as far as they could probably go, so when Eno produced Laid (1993), the band reverted to a stripped-down, experimental approach. While it may not have achieved the sales of its predecessors, it had the effect of revitalising the band's creative juices. Eno's own musical career, often in the company of avant-garde musicians such as Robert Fripp and Harold Budd, reflected the ways in which the new technology impinged upon the creative process.

Singer-songwriter Ani DiFranco has used computer technology to fashion a body of work where the sophistication is integral to its creation. One of the best examples is her collaboration on The Past Didn't Go Anywhere (1997), with the great singer-songwriter Utah Phillips. Using fragments of his songs and stories from Phillips's concert appearances, DiFranco assembled backing tracks that provided a framework for what becomes an introduction to the thoughts and

LAURIE ANDERSON
BIG SCIENCE
Warner Bros.

CD CHECKLIST

NEWS

left: The most progressive
voice in the retro-inclined Roxy
Music, Brian Eno has gone on
to be a leading figure in the
world of computer-based pop.

aspirations of one of America's most original and
acerbic storytellers.

If DiFranco has applied technology as a catalyst for
her songwriting skills, Laurie Anderson has used her
songwriting skills as a facet of her role as a multi-media
performance artist. Songwriting has equal importance to
other disciplines such as dance, mime, film and lighting
effects. While these performers have used the
sophistication of the technology to maximise the effect
of their work, others such as Todd Rundgren and Peter
Gabriel have used the advances in technology to
facilitate a greater awareness of their work: the creative
processes have not altered, just expanded to
incorporate a wider range of possibilities.

While computer technology has affected the way in
which artists present themselves, with most now setting
up websites on the Internet as a matter of course, the
full benefits – if benefits they are – are yet to be
realised. Sampling may now be easier through digital
technology, but that must seriously threaten safety nets
like copyright protection. Furthermore, that Prince has
chosen to dispense with a record company in favour of
merchandising his work through the Internet is only
likely to restrict the potential audience. Although these
advances represent real breakthroughs, the notion of
all-in-home entertainment being governed by the use of
computer terminals has far-reaching implications where
personal privacy is seriously jeopardised. But then that
has been under attack for more years than most would
care to acknowledge.

FESTIVALS

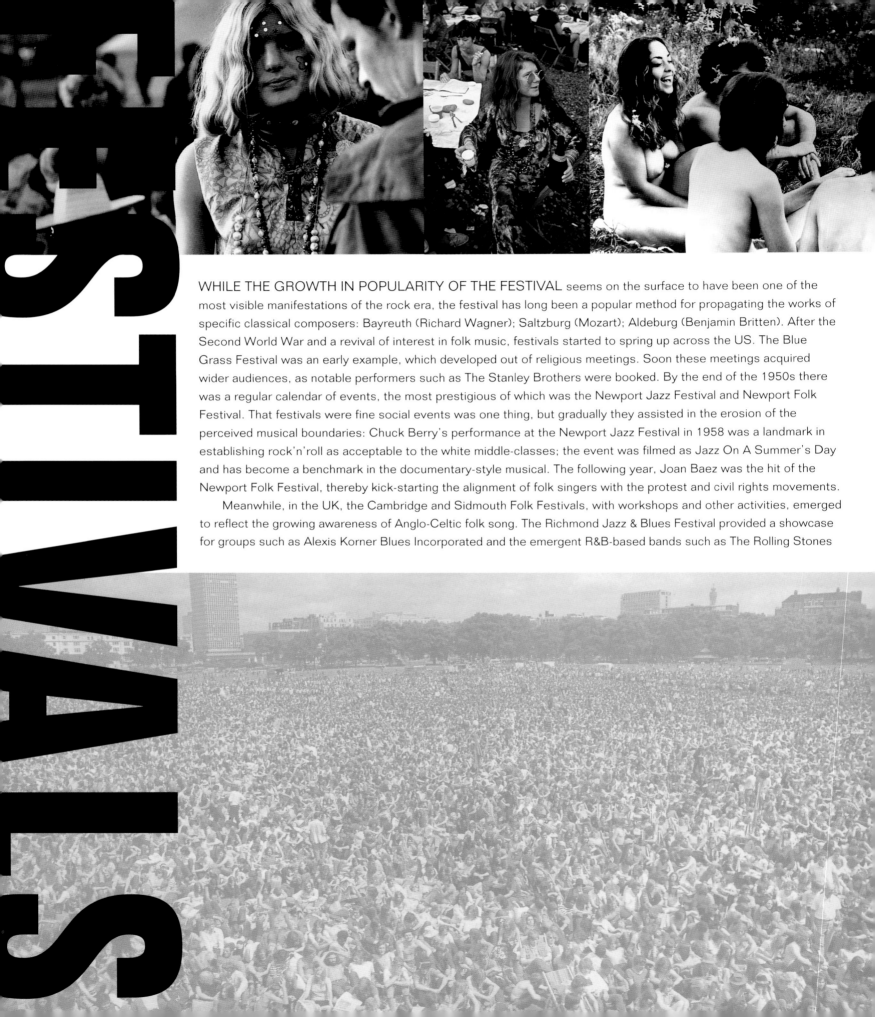

WHILE THE GROWTH IN POPULARITY OF THE FESTIVAL seems on the surface to have been one of the most visible manifestations of the rock era, the festival has long been a popular method for propagating the works of specific classical composers: Bayreuth (Richard Wagner); Saltzburg (Mozart); Aldeburg (Benjamin Britten). After the Second World War and a revival of interest in folk music, festivals started to spring up across the US. The Blue Grass Festival was an early example, which developed out of religious meetings. Soon these meetings acquired wider audiences, as notable performers such as The Stanley Brothers were booked. By the end of the 1950s there was a regular calendar of events, the most prestigious of which was the Newport Jazz Festival and Newport Folk Festival. That festivals were fine social events was one thing, but gradually they assisted in the erosion of the perceived musical boundaries: Chuck Berry's performance at the Newport Jazz Festival in 1958 was a landmark in establishing rock'n'roll as acceptable to the white middle-classes; the event was filmed as Jazz On A Summer's Day and has become a benchmark in the documentary-style musical. The following year, Joan Baez was the hit of the Newport Folk Festival, thereby kick-starting the alignment of folk singers with the protest and civil rights movements.

Meanwhile, in the UK, the Cambridge and Sidmouth Folk Festivals, with workshops and other activities, emerged to reflect the growing awareness of Anglo-Celtic folk song. The Richmond Jazz & Blues Festival provided a showcase for groups such as Alexis Korner Blues Incorporated and the emergent R&B-based bands such as The Rolling Stones

and Manfred Mann. While these events served to give a focus for contemporary music in the UK, it wasn't until the end of the 1960s when the rock festival emerged that these events began to enjoy widespread coverage.

In the US, Woodstock was the most widely celebrated, as the advertisements trumpeted 'Three days of Love and Peace', causing some 450,000 fans to descend upon Max Yasgur's farm in upstate New York. Although few people paid for the privilege of attending, Woodstock came to symbolise the mood of optimism in the youth culture of the late 1960s. Later the same year, The Rolling Stones gave a free concert at Altamont, where a fan was murdered: this effectively killed off any notion that youth culture was inherently different from any other microcosm.

Despite the hype, festivals continued to flourish through the 1970s and into the 1990s. Most areas of contemporary music are reflected now, with Glastonbury the major UK event. Vince Power, the owner of various London music venues, has established himself as the undoubted King of the Festival: The Fleadh in Finsbury Park and New York has become the official opener to the festival season. The Phoenix Festival, with a bias towards Indie bands, offers an array of contemporary styles, while the Reading Festival tends to concentrate on heavy metal bands. Womad provides a showcase for the folk-based styles of other cultures. Although the ostensible altruism of events like Woodstock has long since evaporated and been replaced by a solid commercial base, it is debatable as to whether there was much there in the first place: perhaps altruism was just a euphemism for bad management.

Clockwise from top left: Memorable festivals have included the Windsor Jazz and Blues in 1967, Woodstock (Janis Joplin and naked fans), Bob Dylan at Blackbushe, Ray Charles at Newport, the annual UK events at Glastonbury and Reading, and a 1970 gathering in London's Hyde Park.

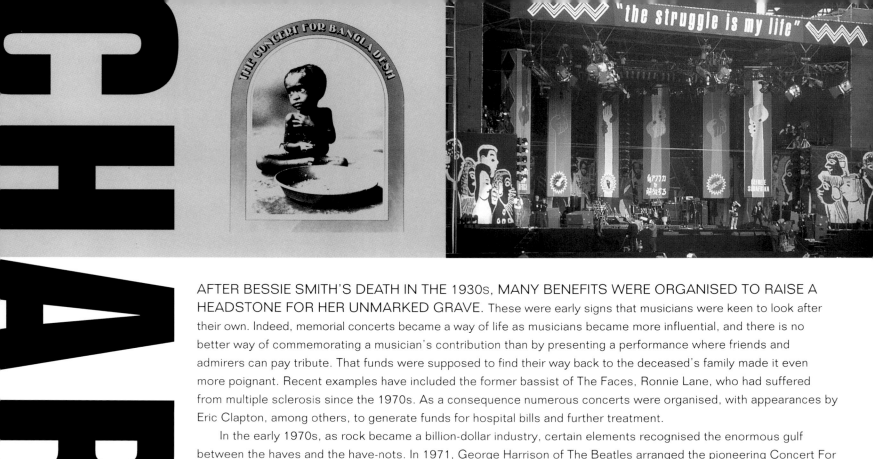

CHARITY

AFTER BESSIE SMITH'S DEATH IN THE 1930s, MANY BENEFITS WERE ORGANISED TO RAISE A HEADSTONE FOR HER UNMARKED GRAVE. These were early signs that musicians were keen to look after their own. Indeed, memorial concerts became a way of life as musicians became more influential, and there is no better way of commemorating a musician's contribution than by presenting a performance where friends and admirers can pay tribute. That funds were supposed to find their way back to the deceased's family made it even more poignant. Recent examples have included the former bassist of The Faces, Ronnie Lane, who had suffered from multiple sclerosis since the 1970s. As a consequence numerous concerts were organised, with appearances by Eric Clapton, among others, to generate funds for hospital bills and further treatment.

In the early 1970s, as rock became a billion-dollar industry, certain elements recognised the enormous gulf between the haves and the have-nots. In 1971, George Harrison of The Beatles arranged the pioneering Concert For Bangladesh to provide funds for famine relief in the beleaguered country. Featuring Harrison, Clapton, Bob Dylan, Ravi Shankar, Leon Russell and Ringo Starr, it generated income of around ten million dollars. This opened the door for a number of charitable operations. No Nukes, organised by singer-songwriter Jackson Browne under the banner of MUSE (Musicians United for Safe Energy) in 1979, endeavoured to harness the rock industry on behalf of the campaign to abolish nuclear power. Most must have been sanguine about the real likelihood of a bunch of rock stars

being able to check the power of the pro-nuclear lobby, but still, it demonstrated concern about ecological issues. Amnesty International was to become a frequent benefactor of similar ventures: Rock Against Racism was instituted to help eradicate racism in British society, and the Prince of Wales launched The Prince's Trust to help provide a wider choice of initiatives for the young. All these programmes benefited from concerts of one sort or another.

In 1984, as reports unfolded on a nightly basis from Africa concerning widespread famine, Bob Geldof of The Boomtown Rats stepped in and launched Live Aid. That year at Christmas, under the collective name of Band Aid, some of rock's most vaunted names gathered together in a recording studio to cut 'Do They Know It's Christmas'. It sold millions the world over. By July 1985, plans for a concert in London, linked by satellite with a similar bash in Philadelphia, had come to fruition. Live Aid generated in excess of a hundred million dollars. After Live Aid, Dylan observed that American farmers were suffering and helped set up Farm Aid with the help of country singer Willie Nelson. Since Live Aid, charity concerts and albums have proliferated with War Child, a benefit for the victims of the Bosnian conflict, being one of the more recent, high-profile events. Opera singer Luciano Pavarotti also raised funds for a special school devoted to greater musical appreciation in Bosnia, believing this might have a positive effect on the victims of the bloodshed. Whether rock can ever make a long-term political difference remains to be seen, charity events certainly appear to achieve one of their aims, that of drawing the attention of a wider audience.

Clockwise from top left: The Concert For Bangladesh, the Nelson Mandela concert, Freeddie Mercury at Live Aid, the Live Aid finale with Bob Dylan, the Wembley (London) Live Aid stage, and some of the massive audience.

FEED THE WORLD
JULY 13th 1985 at WEMBLEY STADIUM

right: A spectacular stage set in the movie Gold Diggers of 1933 which starred Ginger Rogers, Dick Powell, Ruby Keeler and Joan Blondell.

below: Liza Minnelli in her memorable role as Sally Bowles in the musical Cabaret, adapted from Christopher Isherwood's biographical book Goodbye To Berlin.

MOVIE MUSICALS

WHEN AL JOLSON PROCLAIMED IN THE JAZZ SINGER, 'YOU AIN'T SEEN NOTHING YET', FEW COULD HAVE IMAGINED JUST HOW PROPHETIC THOSE WORDS WOULD TURN OUT TO BE. For during the 1930s, after the coming of sound to the movie business, the Hollywood musical went through a golden age that would only be challenged by the coming of television. What made the musical such a staggering success was the combination of technological advances, facilitating not just a greater degree of realism, but also a use of illusion and trickery that would make Houdini look like a performing seal. Furthermore, if the theatre had nurtured a generation of songwriters and musicians who had learnt their craft on Broadway, the movies enabled these same writers to pen tunes that would eventually reach audiences globally. At first, the tendency was to use the format of the revue – song and dance with very loose storylines. Films such as The Gold Diggers Of 1933 by Busby Berkeley were brash, vulgar and visually stunning, and a series of musicals, starring the dancing talents of Fred Astaire and Ginger Rogers, proved huge box-office attractions, allowing airings for songs such as 'The Way You Look Tonight'.

Gradually, though, storylines were elaborated, where the limitations of the sound-stage could be dispensed with and replaced by extensive location shooting or elaborate sets. Inevitably, shows that had already proved their worth as stage musicals, such as Irving Berlin's Annie Get Your Gun (1949) starring Betty Hutton, and featuring songs like 'There's No Business Like Showbusiness' and 'Anything You Can Do', became almost unrecognisable from the original stage show. Jerome Kern and Oscar Hammerstein's Showboat underwent several different treatments – 1929, 1936 and 1951 – before its full potential was realised. Interestingly, the three separate versions of Showboat present a fairly accurate reflection of how attitudes towards the construction of the musical evolved, culminating in the light and frothy, glorious technicolour of the 1951 version, where any sense of the original script's examination of black culture – albeit very superficial – was totally subordinated to the lavish spectacle. Similarly Rodgers & Hammerstein's Oklahoma (1955), with Gordon Macrae, endeavours to celebrate the pleasures of agricultural life: for that read, the glories of America's silent majority in the Mid-west. Although the stage musical was a popular source, movies such as The Philadelphia Story, starring Katharine Hepburn, Cary Grant and James Stewart, became the Hollywood musical High Society. Starring Grace Kelly, Bing Crosby and Frank Sinatra, what the film lacked in dramatic brio was more than compensated for by Cole Porter's score.

During the late 1950s and 1960s, despite the threat posed by the popularity of television, musicals such as My Fair Lady (1964), The Sound Of Music (1965) and Oliver! (1968) endeavoured to keep the fine traditions alive. Increasingly, though, fewer writers were emerging capable of providing enough songs of substance. Admittedly some, like Leonard Bernstein's West Side Story (1957), Marvin Hamlish's A Chorus Line and Cabaret, brought a hint of expressionist naturalism to the genre. But by the 1970s and 1980s, the genre seemed dead and buried, and Andrew Lloyd Webber and Tim Rice, with film versions of shows such as Jesus Christ Superstar, and Pete Townsend with Tommy, were the only writers to make significant inroads. In 1996, Evita was brought to the screen. Instead of a nail in the coffin, Evita might well have stimulated sufficient interest to spark some sort of revival in the genre.

below left: The first-ever sound film or 'talkie' with the hugely popular Al Jolson in the lead, The Jazz Singer, 1927.

below: Audrey Hepburn in the movie version of the stage hit My Fair Lady, which in turn was based on the play Pygmalion by George Bernard Shaw.

„Ich hätt' getanzt heut' nacht…"

(I COULD HAVE DANCED ALL NIGHT)

AUDREY HEPBURN · REX HARRISON
my FAIR LADY
VON WARNER BROS.
TECHNICOLOR®
SUPER PANAVISION 70

CABARET
MCA

WEST SIDE STORY
Columbia

International
Twisters and
World-famed
Swingers
crash head-on
in musical,
dancing
BATTLE
ROYAL!

TWIST VS. SWING!!!

Play it COOL!

BILLY FURY · HELEN SHAPIRO · BOBBY VEE

HEAR THESE HITS!
"PLAY IT COOL"
"YOU'RE SWELL"
"ONCE UPON A DREAM"
"WHO CAN SAY"
"CRY MY HEART OUT"
"AT A TIME LIKE THIS"
"BUT I DON'T CARE"
...and more!

Directed by MICHAEL WINNER · Screenplay by JACK HENRY · A Julian Wintle - Leslie Parkyn Production · An ALLIED ARTISTS Release

COPYRIGHT © 1962 ALLIED ARTISTS   PRINTED IN U.S.A.

63/111

ROCK'N'ROLL MOVIES

THE COMING OF ROCK'N'ROLL IN THE MID-1950s MUST HAVE
CAUSED DOLLAR SIGNS TO FLASH BEFORE THE EYES OF MANY FILM
PRODUCERS. Exploitation was the name of the game and no-one was more eager
for a taste of the Hollywood bucks than Elvis Presley. While Hollywood had
demonstrated its ability at handling musical trends before, especially during the Swing
era, there was a sense of novelty that seemed appropriate somehow. Vocal groups
such as The Ink Spots and Mills Brothers were regularly included and vocalists such as
Fats Waller had appeared in the film Stormy Weather (1943) with Lena Horne, Cab
Calloway and Dooley Wilson. There was no suggestion in these films that they were
anything other than musical revues. Plot lines were skinny in the extreme. Only films

AMERICAN GRAFITTI
MCA

CD CHECKLIST

like Pete Kelly's Blues, with vocalists such as Ella Fitzgerald and Peggy Lee, where the jazz milieu was used as the backdrop to the dramatic action, had worked properly. So when Elvis came along and started churning out one film after another, it was scarcely surprising that plot lines were quickly subordinated by the handful of songs that Elvis would sing. As it turned out the number of reasonable films Elvis made, such as Jailhouse Rock (1957) and King Creole (1958) probably exceeded most expectations.

Still, the mood of disaffection associated with rock'n'roll was caught admirably in movies like The Blackboard Jungle and Rebel Without A Cause (1955), though the former only featured one musical number ('Rock Around The Clock' over the credits), and the latter none at all. In the 1970s films like American Graffiti (1973) and American Hot Wax (1977) – the latter based upon the recollections of DJ Alan Freed – endeavoured to harness the music of the rock'n'roll era to narrative themes that explored adolescence. That both films relied for their thrust upon nostalgia merely served to emphasise the inherent difficulties in trying to encapsulate the enthusiasm and energy of a trend or movement while it's still mutating. Consequently, rock'n'roll threw up few memorable films and those that overcame the stigma of exploitation, such as The Girl Can't Help It (1957) with Jayne Mansfield and Edmond O'Brien, used rock'n'roll performers such as Little Richard, Gene Vincent, Eddie Cochrane and Fats Domino as little more than window-dressing.

During the 1960s, The Beatles in A Hard Day's Night (1964) and Help! (1965) exposed the limitations of the genre by poking fun at it. Other Beat groups such as The Dave Clark Five and Herman's Hermits endeavoured to follow the same route, but the outcomes were hardly memorable. In the 1990s, The Spice Girls starred in Spiceworld (1997), which seemed to take The Beatles' A Hard Day's Night as its template. Of all the movies about rock'n'roll, only This Is Spinal Tap (1983) – the account of a fictional heavy metal band – has come close to capturing the essence of a musical style in all its absurd glory, while The Great Rock & Roll Swindle (1979), starring The Sex Pistols, displays the exploitative potential of rock'n'roll with ill-disguised glee.

Otherwise it is the filmed records of events that have been most effective. Documentary movies based around festivals such as Woodstock or Jazz On A Summer's Day (The Newport Jazz Festival in 1958) tell as much about the mood of the era as they do about the music that was performed. Quite why films about pop music should be so crass is an enigma, especially when recent films based around jazz, such as Bird (1988) or Round Midnight (1986), have as much to say about the music as they do about the way the characters are developed. Strange but true.

below left: One of the better attempts by Hollywood at a rock biopic, The Buddy Holly Story starring Gary Busey.

below: One of the less-successful biographical films about a rock legend was the sensationalised vision of the life of Jim Morrison in Oliver Stone's 1991 film The Doors.

ORIGINAL MOTION PICTURE SOUNDTRACK—MUSIC BY RY COODER

PARIS, TEXAS

SOUNDTRACKS

BEFORE SOUND CAME TO THE FILM INDUSTRY, SILENT MOVIES WERE ACCOMPANIED BY EITHER A PIANIST, ORGANIST OR ORCHESTRA. With the arrival of sound, composers such as Eric Wolfgang Korngold wrote lush orchestral scores to accompany the swashbuckling derring-do of Errol Flynn in films like Captain Blood and The Sea Wolf. While Korngold belonged to the Viennese traditions of Strauss, his scores were arranged to accentuate interest and stimulate the pulse. This was not a case of a bit of music being tacked onto the soundtrack: the music was integral to the film's drama. Korngold was not alone. Others included Alfred Newman, who was recruited by Sam Goldwyn after heading for Hollywood in 1930. While

Newman scored many musicals, such as Alexander's Ragtime Band (1938) and Tin
Pan Alley (1940), he also scored dramas such as John Ford's epic, The Grapes of
Wrath (1940), based on John Steinbeck's novel.

By the 1940s and 1950s, the die was cast as composers such as Elmer Bernstein
and Bernard Herrmann were drafted into Hollywood to add their touches with scores.
Herrmann, scoring films such as Citizen Kane and The Magnificent Ambersons for
Orson Welles, built an enduring relationship with Alfred Hitchcock, scoring eight films,
including Psycho, Vertigo and Marnie. With Psycho, in particular, Herrmann's score
contributed sharply to the shock value of the film, making producers recognise the true
value of a proactive score. Other film directors such as Federico Fellini began
developing comparable relationships with composers and it is difficult to imagine films
such as Eight And A Half or Juliet Of The Spirits without Nino Rota's lush, evocative
scores. Indeed, as the importance of the score and soundtrack increased, so styles of
film could be adumbrated by the composer as much as by a film's director: the success
of the 'spaghetti westerns' of Sergio Leone was due as much to the atmospheric
scores of Ennio Morricone as to the clinical violence of Clint Eastwood.

As early as the 1960s, the film industry recognised that using pop singers for a
movie's theme basically provided constant advertising. No series of films adopted this
principle more successfully than the James Bond films; over a 35-year timespan
singers as diverse as Shirley Bassey, Paul McCartney, Carly Simon, Sheena Easton
and Sheryl Crow have fulfilled that role. Once it was recognised that films could be
powerful allies for the music industry, the 1970s yielded a series of trends such as the
Blaxploitation movies with scores by Soul men such as Marvin Gaye (Trouble Man,
1973), Isaac Hayes (Shaft, 1971) and Curtis Mayfield (Superfly, 1972). The disco
explosion of the mid-1970s was ignited by the John Travolta vehicle, Saturday Night
Fever (1977). However, Saturday Night Fever brought home another reality: movies
could successfully reactivate the careers of pop stars. The Bee Gees were enlisted to
write a bunch of songs that were germane to the film's script. At that juncture, The
Bee Gees' career had stalled, but songs like 'Night Fever' and 'How Deep Is Your
Love' not only revitalised their career, but also made them bigger than ever.

Since the 1970s, the music industry routinely parcels off songs for inclusion on
soundtrack albums. Sometimes, as in the case of Bob Dylan, with Pat Garrett And
Billy The Kid (1973), and Whitney Houston, with The Bodyguard (1993), not only does
the performer contribute songs to the soundtrack, they also have co-starring or even
starring roles. The results can be wildly different though – Dylan's career continued in
pretty much the same direction as before, Houston's went through the stratosphere.
Indeed, such was the success of The Bodyguard that Houston looks as if future career
opportunities will be more as an actress than as a singer.

If pop music has benefited from the movies, composers such as Michael Nyman
have also been beneficiaries, because even 'art-house' films like The Draughtsman's
Contract or The Piano – both featuring Nyman scores – have accrued as many plaudits
for the scores as for the visual appeal of the film itself. While for many years, the
movie looked as if it might capitulate in the face of television, the cinema is big box
office again, and the entertainment conglomerates that own the record labels as well
as the film studios can make sure the soundtrack music is up there as an essential part
of the commercial package.

MICHAEL NYMAN
GATTACA
Virgin

GATO BARBIERI
LAST TANGO IN PARIS
United Artists

Publishing Director: Laura Bamford
Executive Editor: Mike Evans
Editor: Michelle Pickering
Art Director: Keith Martin
Senior Designer: Geoff Borin
Design: Birgit Eggers
Production Controller: Julie Hadingham, Clare Smedley
Picture Research: Liz Fowler, Roy Carr

First published in 1998 by Hamlyn,
a division of Octopus Publishing Group Ltd

This edition published in 2006 by Bounty Books,
an imprint of Octopus Publishing Group Ltd
2-4 Heron Quays. London E14 4JP
Reprinted 2008
Copyright © Octopus Publishing Group Ltd 1998, 2006

A Catalogue record for this book is
available from the British Library

ISBN 978-0-753714-75-1

Printed and bound in China

ACKNOWLEDGEMENTS

The Author and Publishers would like to acknowledge the many music publishers, music archives and published works of reference too numerous to mention without which this book would not have been possible.

And special thanks to Roy Carr for his vast and vital visuals, Nigel Cawthorne for additional text contributions, Tarda Davidson-Aitkins for some hip (hop) info, and Humaira and Michelle for their news flashes over the years.

This book is dedicated to the ordinary people who make music popular, and John Hammond Jnr, Ahmet and Nesuhi Ertegun, Alan Freed, Phil Spector and the other visionaries who made it happen.

PHOTOGRAPHIC ACKNOWLEDGEMENTS

The pictures reproduced in this book have been provided by the **ROY CARR COLLECTION** with the exception of those listed below:

AKG, LONDON 3 Top, 28 Insert, 46/Paul Almasy 27/Baron Raimund Von Stillfried 2 Top/Erich Lessing 14 Bottom/Morton Roberts/The Historic New Orleans Collection 21 Top/Warner Bros 249 Right

CHRISTIE'S/Davron (Theatrical Managers) Ltd. 121 Left

CORBIS UK LTD 104 Top Left/David Lees 2 Bottom/Denis O'Regan 5, 247 Top Left/UPI 30 Right/Everett 251 Left, 251 Right/Bettmann 23 Right, 41 Bottom/Frank Driggs 40 Right

CULVER PICTURES 30 Left, 59 Bottom

ELVIS PRESLEY ENTERPRISES/Gil Michael 128 Left

DENIS GIFFORD COLLECTION 41 Top, 94 Bottom Left

REED CONSUMER BOOKS LTD. Front Cover Top Centre Right, Front Flap, Back Cover Top Right, Front Cover Centre Left, 8, 20, 24-25, 26 Bottom, 56 Background, 124 Top, 129 Top, 142-143, 159 left, 168 Top Right, 168 Top Left, 179, 245 Top Left/Allied Artists 250/Art Rock 150 Bottom Right/Bibliotheque Nationale, Paris 17/James Bland/IBC Sound Recording Studios, Decca Spine/Boosey & Hawkes 26 Top/"Courtesy of The Country Music Foundation Library & Media Center" 71 Top/Courtesy of The Country Music Foundation Library & Media Center 70-71/Decca Record Company Ltd 125 Right/Deran Records (Decca Record Company Ltd) 121 Top Right/EMI Electronics Ltd. Front Cover Bottom Centre Right/John Goldman Collection 125 Left/Grassroots Records 94 Top Right/Harbinson Back Flap/Heidelberg University Library 16 Left/Kunst Museum, Vienna/photography by K.G. Meyer 24 Bottom/MCA Records 134 Top/Microdot/ Brian Cannon/M. Spencer Jones 237 Left/courtesy, Museum of Fine Arts, Boston/Spaulding Collection 16 Right/Norlin 25 Right/Polydor Back Cover Centre Left, 150 Top/The Country Music Foundation Library and Media Centre 94 Bottom Right/Isaac Tigrett Collection/photo: James Bland 112 Left, 146 Right/Universal Pictorial Press 202 Left/The Voice Front Cover Bottom Centre/WEA Records 137 Left

HULTON GETTY PICTURE COLLECTION Front Endpaper, Back Endpaper, 10-11 Background, 23, 28, 48, 57 Background, 72, 244 Bottom, 246 Bottom/Mark Ellidge 244 Top Left

IMAGE BANK/Eric S. Cohn 76 Top/B. Hickey 205 Left/John Leifert 34/John Liefert Collection 83 Right

KOBAL COLLECTION 32 Left, 106/ABC/Allied Artists 248 Left/Warner Bros 248 Right

LEBRECHT COLLECTION 14 Top, 15, 21 Centre, 22 Right, 36 Right, 37 Right, 60, 61 left, 62 Top/ Private Collection 87 Right

MANDER & MITCHENSON 29, 32 Right, 33 Left, 33 Centre, 33 Right, 37 Left, 45, 49 Left

THOMAS L. MORGAN COLLECTION Back Cover Centre Right, 55 Left, 55 Right

PERFORMING ARTS LIBRARY/Clive Barda 36 Left/Michael Le Poer Trench 61 Right/Ron Scherl 204 Top

PHILLIPS, THE FINE ART AUCTIONEERS Back Cover Bottom Centre

JOHN PLATT COLLECTION 149 Left/Osiris Visions 149 Right/Bill Graham/Victor Moscoso/artist: Rick Griffin 150 Bottom Left

REDFERNS 114, 132, 240-241, 247 Bottom/A. Putler 167/Richie Aaron 240 Left, 247 Top Right/Nigel M. Adams 225/Glen A. Baker Archives 40 Left, 44, 122, 246 Top Left/Kieran Doherty Front Cover Bottom Left/Ebet Roberts 186 Bottom/Patrick Ford 238 Top Right, 241 Right/GEMS 91/William Gottlieb/DRP 86-87/Sue Hamilton 238 Bottom Left/Tim Hall 246 Top Right/Mick Hutson 195, 218 Bottom, 219, 238 Bottom Right, 245 Bottom, 245 Top Right/Max Jones Files 53, 54/Elliot Landy 151 Right, 244 Top Centre/Michael Linssen 198, 209 Bottom/MJF 4, 50 Left/Michael Ochs Archives 23 Centre, 68, 69 Left,69 Right, 77, 84, 85, 86 Left, 187/Outline 22 Left/David Redfern 151 Left, 206, 209 Top/Simon Ritter 194 left/Ebet Roberts 205 Right, 242 left/Des Willie 238 Top Left

RETNA/Armando Gallo 242 Right/Martin Goodacre 243/Frank Micelotta Front Cover Bottom Left

SOTHEBY'S LONDON Back Cover Top Left, 129 Bottom/Sid Bernstein 142/Music City 154 Right

TONY STONE IMAGES/Nigel Dickinson 3 BottomVictoria & Albert Museum 62 Bottom

THE VINTAGE MAGAZINE CO. ARCHIVE 49 Right/Hawkes & Son, London 21 Bottom

VAL WILMER 97 Left

M. WITMARK & SONS Front Cover Top Left

and the following Record Companies and Labels:

Ace, A&M, Arista, Arhoolie, Asylum, Atco, Atlantic, Blue Note, BMG, Capitol, Charly, Chrysalis, Circa, Columbia, Creation, Decca, Def Jam, Document, Elektra, EMI, Epic, Food, Geffen, Hannibal, HMV, Internal, Island, Kling Klang, Liberty, London, Maverick, MCA, Motown, One Little Indian, Parlophone, Pathe Marconi, Ploydor, Polygram, RCA , Red Star, Reprise, Rolling Stones Records, Rough Trade, Sire, Sony, Stax, Stiff, VC, Verve, Virgin, Warp, Warner Bros, WEA, World Circuit

The Publisher has made every effort to credit the artists, photographers and organizations whose work has been reproduced in this book. We apologize for any unintentional omissions which will be corrected in future editions.